Susan Imel

Elizabeth J. Tisdell

Exploring Spirituality and Culture in Adult and Higher Education

JOSSEY-BASS
A Wiley Imprint
www.josseybass.com

Published by Jossey-Bass
A Wiley Imprint
989 Market Street, San Francisco, CA 94103-1741   www.josseybass.com

Jossey-Bass books and products are available through most bookstores.
To contact Jossey-Bass directly call our Customer Care Department within
the U.S. at 800-956-7739, outside the U.S. at 317-572-3986 or fax 317-572-4002.

Jossey-Bass also publishes its books in a variety of electronic formats. Some content
that appears in print may not be available in electronic books.

Quote from bell hooks on page 1 from *All About Love* by bell hooks. Copyright © 2000
by Gloria Watson. Reprinted by permission of HarperCollins Publishers Inc.

Quote from Parker Palmer on page 89 from *Let Your Life Speak* by Parker Palmer.
Copyright © 1999 by John Wiley & Sons, Inc. Reprinted by permission.

Quote from Steven Glazer on p. 183 from "Conclusion: The Heart of Learning" in
The Heart of Learning by Steven Glazer. Copyright © 1999 by Steven Glazer. Used by
permission of Jeremy P. Tarcher, an imprint of Penguin Putnam Inc.

Library of Congress Cataloging-in-Publication Data
Tisdell, Elizabeth J., 1955-
   Exploring spirituality and culture in adult and higher education /
Elizabeth J. Tisdell.
      p. cm. — (The Jossey-Bass higher and adult education series)
Includes bibliographical references and index.
   ISBN 0-7879-5723-2 (alk. paper)
   1. Teaching—Religious aspects. 2. Spiritual life. 3. Educational
anthropology. 4. Adult education—Philosophy. 5. Education,
Higher—Philosophy. I. Title. II. Series.
   LB1027.2 .T57 2005
   78.1'2—dc13   2002152871

Printed in the United States of America
FIRST EDITION
HB Printing   10 9 8 7 6 5 4 3 2 1

The Jossey-Bass
Higher and Adult Education Series

*This book is dedicated to the memory
of my mother,
Mary Donohue Tisdell
(April 29, 1921–March 24, 1999),
an educator herself,
whose memory and spirit continue
teaching me about the connection
of spirituality to culture.*

Contents

Preface

Spirituality is an important part of human experience. So is culture. In the last decade, there has been much discussion of the cultural dimension of human experience, and the importance of attending to it in higher and adult education. More recently, there has been some consideration of the role of spirituality in teaching and learning as well. For the most part, however, there has been little discussion of the connection between culture and spirituality—the cultural dimension of spirituality and the spiritual dimension of culture—and the importance of their connection to adult and higher education. Thus, the purpose of this book is to explicitly connect spirituality and culture and to focus specifically on the potential role of spirituality in teaching for cultural relevance with multicultural populations in higher and adult education.

If one wants to understand the processes of teaching and learning, it is important to pay attention to how people understand new knowledge, and ultimately, to how they construct knowledge. Indeed, learning takes place in many contexts. Typically higher education has focused on knowing through rationality. But learning and constructing knowledge is also embedded in people's growth, development, and new experiences. Further, learning and constructing knowledge are rooted in, but not limited to, people's culture of origin. Knowledge construction takes place in the workplace, in relationships, in therapeutic contexts, and in somatic learning contexts such as Tai Chi, exercise programs, or yoga. Knowledge construction is present in creative work in music, visual art, storytelling, dance, writing, and it is present in people's spiritual lives as well. All of these and other indicators of learning are manifested through cultural expression—in language, in symbol, in art, in gesture, in all forms of communication. A part of teaching for cultural relevance is to understand this—that knowledge will ultimately be expressed through culture. Therefore, learning will be better anchored if teaching is approached in a way that is culturally relevant to learners' lives.

What is the role of spirituality in this process? Faith development theorist James Fowler (1981), in discussing how people construct knowledge, noted that Piaget and Kohlberg contributed greatly to our understanding of how people come to know and learn. However, Fowler also noted "their restrictive understanding of the role of imagination in knowing, their neglect of symbolic processes generally and the related lack of attention to unconscious structuring processes other than those constituting reasoning" (p. 103). While Fowler brought spiritual knowing to the fore, he didn't pay attention to "symbolic processes" that are often deeply cultural.

Why is it beneficial for higher and adult educators to pay attention to spirituality in teaching for cultural relevance? After all, higher education has been primarily about "intellectual" knowledge—the rational world of theory and ideas. Furthermore, in North America, we have argued for and founded our education system based on "the separation of Church and State," except of course in the case of religiously affiliated institutions. Perhaps it's appropriate to deal with spirituality in some adult education contexts, but how could it possibly be appropriate in higher education? The answer to this is grounded in how *spirituality* is defined in this book and what my underlying assumptions of it are.

Assumptions About Spirituality and Culture

Spirituality is an elusive topic; it seems to defy definition, or at the very least, all definitions of it seem to be inadequate. Although Chapter Two will discuss what is meant by the terms *spirituality* and *culture* and the way that they are used for the purposes of this book, a brief definition of each is useful here. First, *spirituality is not about pushing a religious agenda*. Drawing on spirituality in higher education does not suggest in any way that one should abandon the analytical and critical reading and writing work that is part of higher education. But if one wants to educate, it is incumbent upon educators to examine the variety of ways in which people construct knowledge. With that said, there are seven assumptions that I am making about the nature of spirituality: (1) spirituality and religion are not the same, but for many people they are interrelated; (2) spirituality is an awareness and honoring of wholeness and the interconnectedness of all things through the mystery of what many refer to as the Life-force, God, higher power, higher self, cosmic energy, Buddha nature, or Great Spirit; (3) spirituality is fundamentally about meaning making; (4) spirituality is always present (though often unacknowledged) in the learning environment; (5) spiritual development constitutes moving toward greater authenticity or to a more authentic self; (6) spirituality is about how people construct knowledge through largely unconscious and symbolic processes, often made more concrete in art forms such as music, image, symbol, and ritual, all of which are manifested culturally; (7) spiritual experiences most often happen by surprise.

There are probably as many definitions of culture as there are of spirituality, a point that is also taken up in Chapter Two. But as it is meant here, *culture* is the shared beliefs, values, behaviors, language, and ways of communicating and making meaning among a particular social group. In order to develop culturally relevant approaches to education, it is important to have some understanding of what the beliefs, values, language, and behaviors are of that cultural group. It is also important to become more conscious of one's *own* culture and what the assumptions are of making meaning in that culture. Often times white people, for example, have little sense of their culture. But it is important for all educators to have a sense of their culture if they are attempting to conduct culturally relevant education.

How This Book Came to Be

This book has emerged in a context. It is, in essence, a response to the complexity of education in a multicultural society and arises from a deep concern for spirituality as a way of making sense of one's life experience. For more than ten years, I have been attempting to teach in a way that is culturally relevant to adult students from a variety of cultural backgrounds. Part of my motivation to do so is my concern for cultural and social justice issues that is rooted in some of my own spiritual commitments, though I rarely discuss spirituality in my classes.

Teaching classes that are culturally relevant and that attempt to work for greater equity in adult and higher education in regard to race, culture, national origin, gender, sexual orientation, and dis/ability can at times be controversial and emotional. But over the years, I found that occasionally conducting activities that draw on image, symbol, music, or an art form, which to me are grounded in spirituality, seems to help groups to move beyond conflict to some degree. While the term *spirituality* is rarely used, learners are better able to focus on what is connecting and similar in our human experience, as well as what is quite different based on our culture, gender, or national origin. Such activities are often led by students in presentations or teaching demonstrations based on the books and readings that are a required part of their work in higher education. Further, students are able to see the multiple ways in which people construct knowledge: through the rational or cognitive in analytical reading and discussion; through the affective and relational in connecting ideas with their emotions, life experience, and relationships with others; and through the symbolic and artistic, or the spiritual.

This book has also emerged out of discussions and a concern that education be not only culturally relevant but also transformative. There have been a number of discussions about transformative learning, though few focus on the significance of spirituality in the process. But if education is going to be culturally relevant and transformative on the individual or social level, it must engage learners on a variety of levels: the cognitive or rational, the affective, the sociocultural, and the symbolic or spiritual level. While there is greater freedom to do this in some adult education settings, the issue for me at the beginning of this journey was how to educate by engaging learners on all these levels, particularly in adult higher education settings where I work.

Because of my own strong interest in understanding more about the connection between spirituality and culture, I began by conducting a qualitative study of a multicultural group of women adult educators who were teaching or working with cultural issues in higher education or as community activists. In addition all were motivated to teach partly because of their spiritual commitments. The study was so fascinating to me that I continued the study to include men as well as women. Interviews focused on how participants' spirituality changed over time, how it related to their childhood religious traditions, their culture, and their gender, and how it informed their teaching. Participants also discussed their definition of spirituality and three of their most significant spiritual experiences. In the appendix, I explain the details of the methodology.

This book emerged out of this study and is primarily intended for those in higher and adult education settings, as well as those who work with adult learners in any setting in which issues of spirituality and culture intersect, including in one-on-one settings in counseling or advising and in group settings such as classrooms and community groups. Given that my own teaching is in the context of higher education, the suggestions for practice are especially related to higher education settings. Since the ideas in this book were based on a sample of adult and higher educators of different cultural backgrounds who directly challenge systems of power and privilege in their classes and community work, social activists may find this work useful. But the book is especially intended for those attempting to teach for cultural relevance grounded in a sense of spirituality, and attempts to develop a theory-in-progress of a spiritually grounded and culturally relevant pedagogy for transformation.

Chapter Overview

This book is divided into three parts, each of which is made up of four chapters. All parts of this book feature the stories and experiences of real people, especially those I interviewed for this study. Stories touch our hearts and put a human face on the world of ideas. Further, they provide examples and a way to illustrate a concept or idea. Throughout the book I have tried to keep the focus partially on what the themes of each chapter suggest for educational practice. Thus, even though practice is dealt with in depth in Part Three, throughout the text I have offered brief implications for practice.

Part One provides a framework for breaking the silence about spirituality in adult and higher education, and more particularly the connection of spirituality to culture. Chapter One serves as an introduction and draws on the stories of four educators who work in adult and higher education settings to illustrate how spirituality connects to culture and informs educational work. I also share some of my own story to provide background context as an educator doing cultural work and as a human being on a journey with others in the world. Chapter Two provides an overview of the way spirituality has been dealt with in academia and then defines what I mean by the terms *spirituality* and *culture* as I use them throughout the book, particularly in developing culturally relevant approaches to higher and adult education. Chapter Three emphasizes that spirituality and religion are not the same and considers the convergences and divergences among spirituality, religion, and culture. It also examines how spiritual and cultural knowledge is constructed through image, symbol, ritual, art form, and music. Chapter Four deals with the themes and variations of spiritual experience itself through the use of story and example.

Part Two focuses on identity issues related to spiritual development as *change over time*. Chapter Five focuses on overall spiritual development as a spiral process of moving forward and spiraling back, rather than as a linear process, and examines the way educators can further their spiritual development and stay spiritually grounded through a balance process of inner reflection and outer action. Chapter Six takes a more narrative perspective on development and deals with the intersection of gender and culture in relationship to spiritual development, particularly as manifested during midlife integration. The focus of Chapter Seven is on the process of "claiming a sacred face" and the role of spirituality in claiming a positive cultural identity in light of some of the cultural and race and ethnic identity models of development. Chapter Eight deals with the experience of crossing culture in spiritual development, with the role of spirituality in dealing with the complexity of intersecting identities, and with White identity.

Part Three deals with issues related to the practice and further development of a theory-in-progress of a spiritually grounded and culturally relevant pedagogy. Chapter Nine focuses on ways of approaching transformative teaching that are spiritually grounded and culturally relevant in the different contexts of adult and community education and in higher education. Chapter Ten presents the multiple theoretical influences on and then the theory-in-progress of a spiritually grounded and culturally relevant pedagogy particularly related to adult higher education settings. Chapter Eleven provides stories and examples of how this theory-in-progress has been applied in practice. Chapter Twelve discusses the possibilities and challenges of spiritually grounded and culturally relevant teaching. Finally, the epilogue is a final reflection about the role of spirituality in education for individual and social transformation as we move into the future. I hope you enjoy the journey as we forge that future together.

Acknowledgments

The construction of knowledge is always a collaborative process. Even though I have been the scribe that has put these ideas to paper, these ideas have been constructed in dialogue with many people over the years. Here I would like to acknowledge and thank several of them. Certainly my parents and family provided a foundation for me to understand spirituality and culture. My colleagues and students over the years have taught me a lot, often inadvertently, about the importance of the connection of spirituality and culture; many have also been important cultural mentors for me, but there are several that have been especially important.

This book came to be somewhat by accident. I had been doing research related to spirituality and culture, though I didn't intend to write a book. Then I received notification that the then Dean of the College of Arts and Sciences at National-Louis University, Dr. Richard Roughton, had given me course release time to "write my book." I found this surprising since I hadn't requested course release time to write a book but rather to do research. I took it as a sign that perhaps I should write a book. Thus, I would like to thank the late Dr. Richard Roughton, who passed away in August 2002, not only for his generosity but also for reading and commenting on several chapters of the manuscript along the way. May you rest in peace, Richard!

I would also like to thank Dr. Scipio A. J. Colin, III, the chair of the Department of Adult and Continuing Education at National-Louis University, who not only agreed to release time but also provided much support and thoughtful dialogue on the topic of this work—in hallway conversations or over dinner at Bennigans. My other colleagues on the faculty at National-Louis University where I wrote most of this book, Gabriele Strohschen, Randee Lawrence, and Stephen Brookfield, also provided either thoughtful conversation or comments on the manuscript. I would especially like to thank Tom Heaney for his careful read and comments on much of this manuscript and for the quick feedback that he has always been known for.

I thank my colleagues across the country who have read some or all of this manuscript, particularly Tal Guy, Ed Taylor, Sharan Merriam, Larry Daloz, Juanita Johnson-Bailey, Carolyn Clark, Marvin Garcia, Pam Hays, Tito Rodriguez, Silvia Villa, and Alvaro Alcazar—all have been equally supportive. In addition, I would also like to thank those who have been important cultural mentors and teaching partners with me. In addition to those mentioned above are Viviana Aguilar, Nadira Charaniya, Clarice Perry Ford, Ming-Yeh Lee, Robert Guerrero, Mary Stone Hanley, and Jane West Walsh to name a few. The participants in this study have also taught me the most about spirituality and cultural relevance, and while most are known only through a pseudonym, their participation and insight have made this book possible. A special thanks goes to my good friend, colleague, cultural mentor, co-teacher and presenter, Dr. Derise Tolliver, whom I initially met as a participant in this study. Our endless conversations on this topic and our projects together since the time of our initial meeting have strongly informed aspects of this work, as noted throughout the text. Another special thanks goes to my editor and friend at Jossey-Bass, David Brightman, for his excellent suggestions, very important feedback, and unfailing moral support, and to Melissa Kirk for attending to the details of the editorial process.

Books only come to be with the support of important friends who nurture you, cook with you, take care of you in a variety of ways, and have fun with you. Special thanks go to Teri Bernstein,

Laura Etchen, Debra Daspit, Ruth Largay, David Tisdell, Betsy Rich, Ellen McMahon, and Carol Melnick. Finally, important thanks go to Terry Miles, my partner and friend, who provided many meals, fun conversation about his world travels flying airplanes, and continued personal and spiritual support to help see this project through to completion.

October, 2002   *Elizabeth J. Tisdell*
Harrisburg, Pennsylvania

About the Author

ELIZABETH J. TISDELL joined the faculty at Pennsylvania State University-Harrisburg as associate professor of adult education in August of 2002. She received an Ed.D. degree in adult education from the University of Georgia in 1992, an M.A. degree in religion and religious education from Fordham University in 1979, and a B.A. degree in mathematics from the University of Maine in 1977.

Prior to joining the faculty at Pennsylvania State University, Dr. Tisdell was associate professor of adult and continuing education at National-Louis University in Chicago and was on the faculty at Antioch University, Seattle. She worked as a campus minister for the Catholic Church from 1979–1989 at Central Michigan University and Loyola University, New Orleans.

Her research interests include spirituality and culture in adult development and adult learning, critical and feminist pedagogy, and multicultural issues in adult education. Her work has appeared in the *Adult Education Quarterly*, the *Journal of Adult Development*, many edited books on adult education, including the 2000 edition of the *Handbook of Adult and Continuing Education*. She is also author of the monograph *Creating Inclusive Adult Learning Environments* (1995) and the coeditor with Dr. Mary Jane Eisen and contributing author to *Team Teaching and Learning*. She considers this book *Exploring Spirituality and Culture in Adult and Higher Education* the work of her soul and part of an ongoing life work.

Part I

Breaking the Silence

Spirituality and Culture in Adult Meaning-Making and Education

The spiritual awakening that is slowly taking place countercultur-ally will become more of a daily norm as we all willingly break mainstream cultural taboos that silence or erase our passion for spiritual practice.

bell hooks (2000, p. 82)

1

Introduction

Culture, Spirituality, and Adult Learning

W e live in a culturally pluralistic society and a culturally complex world. Trying to teach adult learners in a way that is culturally relevant to their own lives in a culturally pluralistic teaching context is a challenge. Many who do this work do so precisely because they are absolutely passionate about it. It is their vocation, the work of their very souls, often grounded in their spiritual commitment, as well as in their own cultural background and concern for cultural issues. At least, this was the case for the many adult and higher educators that I interviewed in the past two years who are doing this work. Most of them rarely speak publicly about the role of their spirituality relative to this work, however; as hooks (2000) suggests in the opening quote to Part One, there have been mainstream cultural taboos that have kept them silent about their spirituality, especially if they are teaching in higher education. Still, spirituality is a major organizing principle in their lives, and perhaps in the lives of many who are trying to attend to cultural issues in learners' lives in adult and higher education. The following are a few examples.

Four Stories

Julia Gutierrez is forty-eight years old, a Chicana, who was raised Catholic in the barrio of Southern California in a Mexican-American family. Spanish was the primary language spoken at home as a child, and Catholicism, with an especially strong devotion to La Virgen de Guadalupe, was very important in her family. Although Julia no longer practices her Catholicism with any regularity, her spirituality is very important to her work in adult education with teachers focusing on the creation of culturally relevant curricula for schools and community groups both in the United States and in the Pacific Islands. In reflecting on the place of her spirituality in the educational consulting group with whom she works, she notes:

> I find there is a dimension of spirituality in the way we relate to each other and in the way we collectively approach the work of social change. Because we are each from a different cultural background, we express our spirituality in different ways—Hawaiian chants, prayers to the four directions, Christian prayer. The interesting thing though, as I think more about it, I suspect that there are also atheists among the group, yet we somehow seem to delve into spirit. It might be striving to be human, I don't know. But we all believe in the goodness of people and the possibility of change, while trying to live a life of community.

Marcus Washington is an African American education professor in his early fifties who grew up in the African Methodist Episcopal (AME) church. Aside from a period in his twenties when he pursued other interests, he has spent his life involved in African American churches as an activist and adult educator, in addition to his work as a professor. His current spirituality, with its emphasis on working for social justice, is informed by the church of his youth, the work of African American liberation theologians (Cone, 1990), and to some extent the economic class analysis of Marxism (but not its antireligious aspects). In reflecting back to his spiritual foundation nurtured through his church, juxtaposed with the Marxist idea that religion is the opiate of the people, Marcus notes:

Growing up, in terms of equal rights, civil rights, and justice for black folks, religion was not an opiate! It was something that animated us!

He adds, in speaking about the role of spirituality, justice, and community,

I always saw the church as being, in the black community at any rate, sort of a vanguard.

It was a vanguard that provided inspiration to continue to do civil rights and other social justice work. It is for this reason that he continues to be involved with church: it feeds his spirituality, is rooted in his own cultural tradition, and nurtures his willingness to teach for social change, both in higher education and in community-based settings.

Lisa Riddle is a forty-two-year-old white woman, a singer-songwriter and community educator who was raised in Alaska. She describes her spiritual formation and spirituality as mostly related to the wilderness surrounding her as she grew up.

I was raised in the temple of the great outdoors. . . . It wasn't like my parents were engaging in some kind of spiritual instruction; we just lived in the lap of God! Let's face it, it's hard to miss the spirit when you are surrounded by wilderness! Wilderness is a spiritual source for me, which usually links to indigenous nature and indigenous cultures, not because that was my training, but that was my exposure. My folks did get us out to some major hikes where we are out there with whatever bear might happen to come your way, and to me that's a spiritual experience!

It is this wilderness spirituality that connects her to the environment, the indigenous people of Alaska, and larger concerns about culture overall that inspires her work as a singer-songwriter and educator in dealing with environmental, antiracist, and cross-cultural education programs.

Aiysha Ali is a thirty-five-year-old professor of education, a Muslim woman of East Indian descent, born in Africa, who immigrated to North America from Africa and England as an adolescent. She notes that her commitment as an educator is rooted in her belief that the purpose of education is "the improvement of the human condition through both individual and social change." Further, she notes, "It is my interpretation of the Qur'anic and prophetic injunctions regarding human responsibility that lead me to hold this belief." Her commitment as an educator around individual achievement, multicultural and language issues, and educational policy studies is rooted in her understanding of the Qur'an and Islam in general, which require the nurturing of one's intellect, as well as working for social responsibility. Her educational work is strongly informed by her spirituality and religious identity, and more recently she has chosen to be a bit more overt in claiming her Muslim identity. She resonates strongly with the literature on education as transformation; however, in explaining how she recently wrote her philosophy of education, she noted:

> It is not that I do not find resonant voices in this arena, but rather I chose to highlight the voice from within. I can no longer continue to separate my American and professional self from my religious self; I can no longer see myself as an educator first and a Muslim second. I am a Muslim who has chosen to become an educator and to use education as my contribution to the improvement of life for all in society— regardless of race, religion, creed, and nationality.

Four stories—four educators, with vastly different cultural backgrounds, are teaching adults in higher education or community-based settings and are trying to do so by attending to cultural issues in a culturally pluralistic society. Spirituality is an important underpinning to the work they do, although it is manifested in different ways for each of them. Like many people in North America, the spirituality of Marcus Washington and Aiysha Ali is very much rooted in their respective religious traditions, which also connects with their cultural and ethnic identity. But like many others in North America, Julia Gutierrez and Lisa Riddle prefer to describe themselves as "spiritual but not religious." Julia has moved away from the Catholicism of her upbringing. She has no affiliation with any organized religion and has developed a more eclectic spirituality, but one related to Chicana culture with elements of Catholicism that she still finds life-affirming and relevant to her cultural background. Lisa, however, was raised in no particular religious tradition, but her spirituality, rooted in the wilderness, is very much a part of the culture of Alaska where she grew up. While spirituality as a concept is more thoroughly explored in Chapter Two, it is already clear that the spirituality of all four of these educators is connected to their own cultural backgrounds and histories. Their view of spirituality also has to do with making meaning and with a sense of interconnectedness and wholeness.

Julia Gutierrez, Marcus Washington, Lisa Riddle, Aiysha Ali (all pseudonyms), and many of the people whom I have interviewed, rarely speak about their spirituality in any kind of public forum unless explicitly asked about it. However, they do recognize the importance of the spiritual dimension in their own lives and in the lives of those they teach. They also recognize that in trying to teach to honor the cultures and multiple dimensions of learners' lives, they must find ways to acknowledge the important ways people construct knowledge and find meaning in their own spirituality and traditions. Although they rarely use the term *spirituality* in their educational work unless learners bring it up, they are gradually beginning to take more risks in some places in talking about its importance. They are perhaps like many in higher and adult education whose spirituality is important but who may be tentative about discussing it; yet slowly they are beginning to give voice to that which is such a central motivating force in their lives. So there seems to be a place for attending to a sense of spirituality that focuses on wholeness and the interconnectedness of all things in dealing with the complexity of communicating across cultural differences.

In this book I look at how spirituality relates to teaching for cultural relevance in adult and higher education in a culturally pluralistic context in an increasingly complex world and explore the place of spirituality in the lives of educators and learners. Because I always want to know how an author came to be interested in a subject, most of the remainder of this chapter gives some background to how I became interested in the topic personally and professionally, and uses some of my own story to explore how culture and spirituality intersect. After providing a general discussion on why it is important in this new millennium to consider the connection between spirituality and culture in higher and adult education, I will provide a brief overview on the organization and content of the book.

Background Context

My own thinking about spirituality and its connection to culturally relevant education has emerged over time. It has a lot to do with my commitments and what I see as part of my life's purpose. But it emerged in dilemmas I have faced in trying to live out what I understand as part of that life's purpose, in particular, to create greater access and equity to education for adults who have been marginalized because of their race, ethnicity, gender, sexual orientation, or ableness. This does not mean simply opening up access to a canon of knowledge created and dominated by white people. It is also about hearing the voices of members of different cultural, class, and gender communities, recognizing the knowledge that is present in those communities, and including it in the curriculum. It means attending to what is culturally relevant to those community members and honoring what is sacred for them in terms of academic

knowledge, narrative writing, art, poetry, symbols, and ways of interacting. It also means, as Guy (1999) suggests, that as an instructor,
I need to try to increase my awareness and understanding of my own
cultural background. There are often occasions in our day-to-day life
experience that invite reflection on our own cultural backgrounds.
I begin with one experience that caused me to revisit my own cultural history and consider what it has to do with who I am now.

Revisiting My Own Cultural Background: A Time Warp

It was in the spring of 2000 that I first saw the interactive play *Late
Nite Catechism*, created by Vicki Quade and Maripat Donovan in
1993. My eighty-year-old father had come to visit me in Chicago,
and I always look for something that we can do together that I think
he can relate to and enjoy, something that builds on our common
father-daughter history but adds to our shared experiences. So during this visit on a spring Sunday afternoon, we opted to see *Late Nite
Catechism*, the off-Broadway comedy that is extremely reminiscent
of the version of Catholicism in which my parents raised me, back
in my predominantly Jewish and ethnic-Catholic hometown in the
northern suburbs of Boston where I grew up. I was sure my father
and I would find this entertaining.

The setting as described in the playbill was "an adult catechism
class, Chicago, 2000." The participatory audience was the "class,"
and instantly it seemed as though we had entered a time machine
that brought us back to 1963, as "Sister" (she had no "last name"),
dressed in full habit, retaught us "the facts" of the Catholicism of
our youth. There were some minor differences between this and the
setting of our childhood, of course: this was 2000, not 1963; we were
adults, not children; and this was Chicago, not suburban Boston.
But here I was. Here we were. All adults looking backward with a
lot of laughter, and looking inward with a little longing. Such is the
power of cultural memory.

There is a note from the director in the playbill that says:
"Catholics (and yes, that includes you lapsed ones) do *share a strong*

cultural bond and we hope that most of the memories we stir up tonight will give you a warm tingle inside that will make you want to sit up straight and pay attention!" (p. 2, emphasis added).

Indeed, *Late Nite Catechism* is a cultural experience. Given that it is (as the playbills says) "an adult catechism class," it is also an adult education experience, but of a particular cultural ilk. Approximately 98 percent of the participatory audience were white adults who were raised Catholic, most of whom were of Irish, Italian, or Polish descent. Being in Sister's "adult education class" had us spiral back through time to familiar cultural territory. Perhaps it was some of the symbols around the room that brought us back: the black-and-whiteness of Sister's habit; the statue of the Blessed Mother, bedecked with her May-crown of blossoms; the words to the song "Hail Mary, We Crown Thee" on the chalkboard; the carefully written small and capital letters side by side in the Palmer Method of Handwriting sprawled horizontally from A to Z along the wall right underneath the crucifix. But I think it was also the way Sister ran the class. She not only retaught us the shaky "facts" about the verities of Catholic traditional beliefs, such as the perils of missing Sunday Mass or eating meat on Friday, the state of the Blessed Mother's perpetual virginity, and the four stages of the afterlife: Heaven; "Limbo" where unbaptized infants go; Purgatory, if you only need to do some time; and Hell. She also reminded us of how we were to behave: to be disciplined, to *always* answer in complete sentences that include a subject and verb, to respect our elders, never to answer yes or no, but to *stand up* and respond with "Yes, *Sister*" or "No, *Sister*," to sit up straight and fold our hands. In short, we were reminded not only the content of what we were taught but also the culture of the way she taught, in all its goodness and badness. It made us laugh at what at times seemed to move from the sublime to the ridiculous and at other times seemed oddly poignant and revealing of who we still are and of what is still very much a part of us. In short, Sister reminded us of from whence we came: spiritually, culturally, and for many of us, educationally as well. The director was successful: these memories did indeed give many of us a "warm tingle inside" that made us "sit up straight and pay attention!"

Cultural Connections, Spirituality, and Adult Learning

I use these initial reflections on my experience of *Late Nite Catechism* primarily because they make apparent some of my own cultural background rooted in the norms of the American Irish-Catholic family in which I grew up. It is one relatively recent event that has invited me to increase my own cultural self-awareness and take a closer look at my own roots. I agree with the director of the play: Catholics, especially those of northern and middle European descent who attended Catholic school, do share *a common cultural bond,* whether we are one of those "lapsed ones" or not. The common cultural history that weaves together our early religious training with our ethnicity has been formative to who we are, both spiritually and culturally. Perhaps this is why we hear people refer to their cultural background in terms captured better in hyphenation, such as Irish-Catholic, Black–Baptist, East Indian–Muslim. For many of us, it is difficult to distinguish where one side of the hyphen ends and the other begins in thinking about the ongoing development of our cultural and spiritual identities. Our cultural background exists somewhere in the juncture of the hyphen.

The cultural bond that I shared with many in the *Late Nite Catechism* audience had some particular manifestations. One was a common understanding of many of the symbols around the room—in the statue of the Virgin Mary in her May crown, for example, and in the words to the song on the wall. Another was the meaning that we projected onto those symbols. Some of these meanings are likely to be common for those of us who grew up with this or similar cultural heritage—the meaning attached to cultural memory. When Sister made a woman in the audience sit and face the Blessed Mother and reflect on how she might help her change her misbehavior for being caught whispering to her friend, many of us smiled, remembering how this had happened to us back in the fourth grade.

It brought back common memories. But projected onto such symbols and events was individual meaning as well. For example, the statue of the Blessed Mother reminded me of a similar likeness that stood in our bay window when I was growing up, sort of the guardian of the plants that surrounded her and of the house that we made our home. This same statue, years later, stayed at my mother's bedside and was somewhat a guardian to her as she was dying—a powerful image in my mind's eye, this image of Mary, the Blessed Mother, with outstretched arms providing comfort and safe passage for my mother (who was also named Mary) as she transitioned from this life to something beyond.

Although I was only barely conscious of these collective and individual projections onto this one symbol that is part of my Irish-Catholic cultural heritage during the play itself, all of this was somehow going on within me as I looked backward, as I looked inward. I am sure there were similar collective and individual projections going on for others in the audience around this and other symbols.

It's not just the symbols, however, that were part of the cultural bond that I shared with other members of the audience. It was the odd familiarity of ways of interrelating between Sister and her "class" and the ways that we related with each other in this setting. After all, culture is not just about symbols; it includes mannerisms, nonverbal interaction, speech patterns, music. Sister's behavior, in her demands for discipline, for respect, that we speak in complete sentences with a subject and a verb, and her severity somehow softened with her sense of humor were also a way of teaching culture. It was a way of teaching "standard English," as well as how to behave in the world that felt all too familiar, and is still very much a part of who many of us in that audience were and still are to some extent. So, too, are some of the meanings that are still attached to some old but familiar symbols that we may have thought we found no meaning in as adults at all. It is these projections and the meanings that were stirred up within us that we attach to the symbols and ways of interrelating that probably gave us the "warm tingle inside" and that made us pay attention.

One could easily say that the play *Late Nite Catechism* is about how American Catholics (primarily of European descent) were socialized culturally and religiously and has little to do with spirituality. On one level this is true; *Late Nite Catechism* is not reflective of my own current spirituality. However, as a child, I believed a lot of what Sister said as spiritual "truth." Although I no longer believe or worry about Limbo, Purgatory, or eating meat on Friday, those days in Catholic grammar school with many sisters so much like Sister were foundational to who I am culturally and spiritually today. This was probably also the case for a large percentage of the participatory audience in *Late Nite Catechism*. Yet on that Sunday afternoon, many members of that participatory audience, who grew up Irish- or Italian- or Polish-Catholic, probably spiraled back to reconsider what this foundation stage of spiritual development meant to them now, no matter whether they still identified as Catholic or not.

Adult learning and development take place in many contexts, sometimes in individual settings and sometimes in group settings. Individually, we may construct new knowledge in self-directed learning efforts or when we make new meaning out of significant life experiences or through our interactions in significant relationships. And of course, we construct new knowledge in group settings, such as formal higher education classes. But we also do it through other group-learning situations, such as through pop culture events such as movies and plays or when we analyze and find new meaning in the text and subtext of a story in discussion groups around a particular book, theme, or subject. *Late Nite Catechism* is one such example—it is a play about an adult education class. It is a pop culture event that is a satire on the subculture and educational experience in which I grew up. My experience of watching that play was different than if I had simply read the script or had rented a video

of the production of the play and had seen it on my own. Although
my individual reactions may have been similar, I was affected by the
facts that I saw it with others of a similar cultural ilk and that I saw
it with my father. The comedy or the poignant moments were more
intense because of the affect of others in the experience with me. I
could feel the emotions, the "warm tingle" of their reactions as we
projected our collective meaning onto those symbols and events
while also projecting our own individual meanings. This is partly
what makes group learning different from individual learning: we
are affected by the collective experience of projection onto symbol,
or collective meaning. And indeed, I was affected by my dad's reactions, as I knew he was reflecting on the kind of schooling that he
and my mother provided for me and my four brothers and sisters—
the joy of laughter in personal and cultural memory and perhaps the
bittersweet recognition that time marches on. But through the march
of time we continue to make meaning of our lives and our earlier
experiences. We often spiral back.

Adult Education for Cultural Consciousness

I use the experience of seeing Late Nite Catechism not only because
it is reflective of my own cultural background but also because it was
a group-learning experience that helped me increase my own cultural consciousness and cultural self-awareness. I have been teaching classes that deal with race, culture, or gender in the context of
higher education since completing my doctorate in 1992. I come to
this work as a middle-class white woman, a perspective with its own
strengths and limitations. I have had to examine my own cultural
and gender story in doing this work and what it means to have
white skin privilege in American society, as well as how my Irish-
Catholic, middle-class-with-educated-parents background affected
my own access to education and beliefs about teaching and learning. The educational system that I was trained in from grade school
to graduate school primarily emphasized what white people have
done from white people's perspectives. But the whiteness of the pro-

tagonists was rarely pointed out, for as McIntosh (1988), Johnson-Bailey and Cervero (2000), and Shore (2001) suggest, whiteness and the invisible norms of white culture are the standards of the educational system. Given that these norms are rarely made visible, white people, myself included, often have little consciousness either of what it means to be white or of their own particular cultural background. The experience of seeing *Late Nite Catechism* helped me become more conscious of my own cultural background; in trying to teach for cultural relevance, I always look for opportunities to increase my understanding of my own culture as well as that of the students with whom I work.

In trying to teach classes that deal with aspects of culture, I not only have had to become more culturally conscious of my own background and my own whiteness, I have also had to become familiar with other cultural paradigms of teaching and learning and to specifically seek out the works of people of color to include in the curriculum. Simply knowing the literature, however, does not make one able to teach in a culturally relevant way. It's a step of an ongoing journey and process. Other important aspects include getting to know some of what is happening in local cultural communities and nurturing authentic relationships with people of different cultural groups. Friends, colleagues, and students from various cultural backgrounds have been important mentors to me and have helped facilitate my *moving toward* being able to teach in a more culturally relevant way. Yet I can never totally get inside another's cultural experience, anymore than someone outside the experience of growing up Irish-, Polish-, or Italian-Catholic will totally relate to or understand all the cultural nuances of *Late Nite Catechism*. But I'm learning. Furthermore, in my classes, and in this book, I try never to speak *for* people who are from cultural or class backgrounds different from my own. What I hope to do here, as in my classes, is to make vivid different cultural and spiritual perspectives by either explaining such work as I understand it or, where possible, by relying on the words of people from these communities to do the explaining.

Teaching classes that focus on multicultural issues and that examine power relations and systems of privilege and oppression based on race, ethnicity, gender, class, sexuality, and ableness is sometimes controversial, sometimes emotional, and sometimes conflictual. Over the years, I always tried to find ways that would help us move through rather than avoid conflict but that would also focus on what is common among us. I thought that it was important for courses that deal with these issues to end on at least a relatively positive note. While I had a number of strengths that I brought with me into the teaching environment, I also had the limitations of my own cultural background, my own blind spots, my own knowledge base. I developed some strategies to deal with these. One was to team-teach classes with someone who was a member of a different cultural group than I, who could offer a different perspective and lived experience. In this way we could be allies for each other in the classroom; we could also play off each other's strengths and counter the other's weaknesses. Another strategy that my various teaching partners and I developed was to very occasionally make use of activities that seemed to access other ways of knowing—activities that sometimes involved music, art, poetry, movement, or nonverbal experiences. To me, fundamentally, such activities were related to both spirituality and culture in that they seemed to touch people's souls and they generally arose out of a particular cultural context. They were also helpful in moving beyond conflict, in creating closure to the course, and to moving forward with a sense not only of what is culturally different about each of us but also of what is common among us. Such experiences seemed to educate the heart and spirit, while the various readings and critical analysis assignments educated the head. Both were important in these classes in higher education contexts. But the very occasional use of activities that made use of other ways of knowing led to the larger question of what is the place of spirituality in working with adult learners, especially in the higher education classroom. Furthermore, in developing some of these experiences, I found myself relying on and reframing some activities that I had done when working with groups in my earlier professional life. I spiraled back.

Spiraling Back: Spiritual Roots

After completing a master's degree in religion in 1979, I worked as a campus minister for the Catholic Church on two college campuses as a self-described feminist from 1979 to 1989. In this growing and changing role over those years, I directed many liturgical music groups, worked with community-action projects, and did retreats and programs related to spirituality and social justice issues, including gender and race relations. I did a lot of counseling and work with groups. In addition, after having gone through a certification and training program in massage therapy in 1985 and 1986, which concentrated not only on muscles and bones but also on how to work with energy, how to be present in nonverbal ways, and how to create a meditative presence, I worked one day per week in the campus recreation center doing therapeutic massage. It was impossible to say where my pastoral work in ministry ended and my therapeutic massage work began in those days. I used many of the activities that I had learned in my massage training that focused more on how to work with energy and be present in particular ways in some of my retreat and other work with groups. In short, the two approaches were blended into one, as both were related to spirituality and healing of communities, on the one hand, and individuals, on the other.

Although my drive to be involved in this kind of work during those years had a lot to do with spirituality and my concern for justice issues, it had little to do with religion. Technically, of course, I was working for the Catholic Church on a Catholic university campus, which is a religious institution. And to some extent, there was no getting around having to deal with the politics of both the Catholic Church and the university. I had had an ambivalent relationship with the Catholic Church from the time I was an adolescent. On the one hand, I loved and appreciated many of the rituals of Catholicism and had some important spiritual experiences, both personally and in relationship to social justice work within the context of those rituals celebrated in a community I cared deeply about. On the other hand, I was at odds with the Catholic Church's official position on many issues, especially those related to women and sexuality. Because I had also been teaching classes related to religion and education in the academic curriculum as an adjunct instructor during those years to nontraditional-aged adults, I also saw myself as an adult educator. I was familiar with liberation theologians and grassroots educators such as Paulo Freire and was using some of their work in my classes. As a result, after ten years of work in campus ministry, I decided to pursue a doctorate in adult education, which I completed in 1992, and emphasized multicultural and women's educational issues, and have been teaching in higher education ever since. Although I did not leave my spirituality behind and it continued to be important to me personally, I did not draw on it in any direct way in doing my academic work, as a doctoral student or as a professor—that is, until I started trying to create environments in my classes dealing with culture and gender that didn't get overly caught up in controversy. If one wants to teach to challenge power relations based on race, gender, or class, it is simply not possible to teach only by using the tools of rationality and critical thinking. These are emotional subjects for people. To teach for personal and social change also requires a way of engaging people's hearts and spirits. I began once again to think about the role of spirituality, specifically in trying to deal with multicultural issues in the classroom.

Moving Forward: Connecting Spirituality, Culture, and Education

I began pursuing the work of connecting spirituality and culture initially by conducting a qualitative research study of how spirituality informed the work of a multicultural group of women adult educators for social change primarily in 1998 and 1999. As I've discussed elsewhere (Tisdell, 2000a) some of these women were teaching classes in higher education settings like those that I teach; the others were community activists who were doing educational work related to culture, gender, and class in local communities. I was interested in not only how spirituality informed their work but also how they might draw on it in the learning environment itself. As one might expect, those who worked in higher education were much more reticent about drawing on spirituality or discussing it very overtly in their classes. Higher education, after all, has been primarily about rationality. The community educators, however, noted that spirituality often came up, not because they brought it up, but because community members brought it up. All of these women did believe that spirituality has a place in culturally relevant approaches to social justice education. After all, many who have initiated social change movements, such as Gandhi and Martin Luther King, have been important spiritual leaders as well. But the question for those working in higher and adult education is how to draw on it and acknowledge its presence in the learning environment without being impositional.

Since completing that initial study, I have interviewed many other adult educators of different cultural backgrounds, both male and female, who are working in higher education or community-based settings and say that spirituality is a strong influence in their teaching about cultural issues. Julia Gutierrez, Marcus Washington, Lisa Riddle, and Aiysha Ali, featured at this chapter's opening, are among them. As noted in the Appendix (which includes a thorough discussion of the methodology), the choice of participants for this study was purposeful, as it is in all qualitative research (Merriam, 1998). I was specifically interested in talking to adult educators in higher education and community settings who say that spirituality is important in their own lives and is connected to their work dealing with cultural issues. I wanted to hear about their spiritual journeys and how they draw on spirituality in doing cultural work. Their stories, along with some of my own, are featured in this book; it is their insights that have influenced my own thinking about how spirituality might affect teaching for cultural relevance.

Bringing Spirituality to Culturally Relevant Adult and Higher Education

As hooks (2000) suggests in the opening quote of Part One, educators and cultural workers are beginning to break the silence about the connection between spirituality and education. This stems perhaps from the changing cultural fabric of North America. There is a greater emphasis on creating culturally relevant programs for specific population groups, and when spirituality is integral to the fabric of a community, it makes sense that educators might attend to it. But there are also greater numbers of people of color represented both in higher education classrooms and in the ranks of adult educators working in community settings and as professors in higher education. Their greater numbers are perhaps beginning to displace the strict focus on rationality, particularly from a Eurocentric perspective, as the only valid form of knowledge, even in higher education. As Dillard, Abdur-Rashid, and Tyson (2000), in their recent discussion on what it means to be African American women in the academy, note:

> Many scholars and activists involved in the reformation of the academy have worldviews deeply embedded in the spiritual. The heretofore silencing of the spiritual voice through privileging the academic voice is increasingly being drowned out by the emphatic chorus of those whose underlying versions of truth cry out "We are a spiritual people!" (p. 448).

Indeed, spirituality is one of the ways people construct knowledge and meaning. It works in consort with the affective, the rational or cognitive, and the unconscious and symbolic domains. To ignore it, particularly in how it relates to teaching for personal and social transformation, is to ignore an important aspect of human experience and an avenue of learning and meaning-making.

This book is explicitly about the connection between spirituality, *culture*, and adult and higher education. In particular my focus here is on what this connection suggests for the ongoing development of multicultural education and culturally relevant educational opportunities that attempt to teach for greater equity among cultural groups. Indeed, trying to discuss the interplay between spirituality and culture and its significance in developing culturally relevant approaches to working with adult learners is a complex task. Trying to do so is really only a beginning—a commencement, or a moving forward, just as college commencements are so named because they commence something new at the same time that they are both a closure and a continuation of the past. I hope that the discussion of the connection between spirituality and culture in this book will further open the discussion that has already begun on the role of spirituality in adult and higher education.

Spirituality and culture in adult and higher education are always about people's stories and experiences. The stories featured in this book are primarily based on those I heard from the many educators who generously shared their lives with me about how spirituality informs their cultural work in education.

With three exceptions, all the names used for those I interviewed are pseudonyms, including Julia Gutierrez, Marcus Washington, Lisa Riddle, and Aiysha Ali. I indicate the three participants who specifically requested that I use their real names throughout the text with an asterisk.

For the most part and where possible, I tried to use participants' own words to describe their experiences. Out of respect to them, I almost always used the language they used to describe their cultural identities. This accounts for why participants of a similar cultural group are described differently; for example, some are "black," whereas others are "African American" or "of African descent," and some interchange the terms; similarly some are "Latino" while others might define themselves more specifically or politically as "Chicano" or "Chicana" or as Puerto Rican.

As noted in the Preface, the book is in three main parts. Part One lays the groundwork for considering the connection between spirituality and culture and how it relates to developing culturally relevant approaches to adult and higher education. Part One defines as clearly as possible *spirituality* and *culture*, considers the convergences and divergences between spirituality and religion, and discusses themes and variations of spiritual experience. Part Two focuses on spiritual development as *change over time* and as a spiral process of moving forward and spiraling back. This part of the book explores the role of spirituality in developing identity based on gender, claiming a positive cultural identity, and dealing with the complexity of intersecting identities. At various points in both Part One and Part Two, I discuss some brief implications for higher and adult education practice in relationship to the topic in order to make clear the connection to educational practice throughout. The entire focus of Part Three, however, is the detailed consideration of what a spiritually grounded and culturally relevant approach to education might look like in practice. Part Three also considers what spirituality brings to the ongoing theory development of a spiritually grounded, culturally relevant pedagogy in higher and adult education.

The spiritual dimension of our lives is an important source of our adult learning and is most often represented through art form, music, or storytelling. It is connected to how we create meaning in our relationships with others. It is in our living and loving, in our attempts to move beyond power struggles in personal relationships. It is in the stories we tell to stay connected—in the interconnecting web of mothers and fathers, grandmothers and grandfathers, and adult daughters and sons. It is in how we struggle for justice, on behalf of ourselves and others, and in the spirituality of our ancestors that inspires us to work against racism and move forward in the world. For many adults, the spiritual dimension is connected with understanding a higher power or a transcendent being. It is in how we represent that meaning in our culture that spirituality and culture are interconnected.

I have interviewed many people about the interplay of spirituality and culture in their lives and have been honored to hear their stories. Stories touch our hearts; they put a human face on the world of ideas. In the pages that follow, I will pass on a lot of the stories that participants told me about the interplay of culture and spirituality. Some stories may tell you something about your own spiritual and cultural story. Other stories will be about people who have very different cultural and spiritual perspectives. But I hope that at least a few of them will have a similar effect as the stories that Sister told in *Late Nite Catechism* had on me. I hope at least a few of them may give you a "warm tingle inside" that make you want to "sit up straight, and pay attention." And of course I hope they are culturally relevant for your own work with adult learners.

2

Breaking the Silence

Defining Spirituality in a Culturally Relevant Educational Context

S pirituality is a hot topic. Bookstores are replete with many popular titles on the subject. This growing interest among the wider
population is also beginning to be reflected by authors in academic
areas of study and professional practice, such as in health care, education, and psychology, who have heretofore ignored, downplayed,
or kept silent about spirituality relative to their discipline.

Examining Spirituality in Academia

Of course, religiously affiliated higher education institutions have
historically dealt with issues related to their specific religion and the
educational process. Indeed, there is some overlap between religion
and spirituality; yet the two are *not* the same. Other than in religiously affiliated institutions, which are partially invested in a specific religion as opposed to *spirituality* more broadly, institutions of
higher education have historically avoided spirituality. Perhaps the
prior silence on the topic of spirituality in areas of academic and
professional practice is due not only to the difficulty of defining *spirituality*, but also to the ambivalence of many who work in an academic world that has emphasized rationality and the scientific
method for most of the twentieth century. On the one hand, many
of us resonate with educator bell hooks (2000) when she observes
that it is time to break the silence about spirituality, as it plays an

important role in fueling our passion for our work, love, and meaning-making. On the other hand, we may also wonder, as Robert Wuthnow (1998) observes, "whether 'spiritual' has become synonymous with 'flaky'" (p. 1).

In spite of ambivalence, many in academia and in health care have indeed begun to explore the role of spirituality related to their areas of study and professional practice. In the area of health care, Sloan, Bagiella, and Powell (1999) note that in a recent study of family practice physicians, 99 percent reported they believed in the importance of spirituality in the healing process, and 79 percent of a thousand nonphysician adults surveyed believed spirituality could help people recover from disease. Koenig, McCullough, and Larson and their contributors (2001) review the many research studies that have been conducted on spirituality and religion in relationship to specific health issues, including mental health issues and specific physical conditions from hypertension to cancer. These studies suggest strong supporting evidence for the role of spirituality in health and healing. Such studies, along with the substantial interest in spirituality and its role in healing, have also begun to affect medical education, and more than thirty medical schools across the country now offer courses exploring the connection between spirituality and health (Sloan et al., 1999; Ziegler, 1998).

Just as there is growing interest and acceptance of the role of spirituality in health care among health care workers, researchers, and medical educators, there is a similar growing interest among educators in adult and higher education. But this recent development of focusing on the role of spirituality in the educational process is a continuation of the examination of the multiple ways in which people construct knowledge. For example, Howard Gardner's (1993) groundbreaking work on "multiple intelligences" brought attention to the ways people manifest different types of intelligence. Belenky, Clinchy, Goldberger, and Tarule's (1986) work on the role of connection or relationship in women's knowing and learning brought attention to, and much subsequent research and publication on, the role of the affective domain in learning. The many authors in adult education who have focused on ways adults construct knowledge beyond the rational, including Clark's (2001) discussion on creativity and somatic knowing and Dirkx's (1997, 2001) consideration of the role of imagination in learning, call attention to other ways adults learn and create meaning. In addition, the direct discussion of the role of spirituality in learning in adult and higher education, as indicated by book-length discussions that deal directly with these issues (English & Gillen, 2000; Glazer, 1999; Kazanjian & Laurence, 2000; Jablonski, 2001; Palmer, 2000), indicates that academics and educators are beginning to break the silence about the role of spirituality in education. Furthermore, there is a growing recognition of the importance of spirituality to many who are trying to educate for social justice. For example, the Brazilian activist and educator Paulo Freire was a deeply spiritual man, heavily influenced by the liberation theology movement of Latin America (Freire, 1996; Horton & Freire, 1990). Mechthild Hart and Deborah Holton (1993) have noted the role of spirituality in emancipatory adult education efforts, and hooks (1994, 2000) has discussed the significance of spirituality in her own work as a writer and educator around culture, class, and gender issues.

Although there has been some discussion on the role of spirituality in education, book-length discussions thus far on spirituality and education have given little attention to the explicit connection of spirituality and culture or to its connection to culturally relevant education. The many authors who have contributed to Kazanjian and Laurences's (2000) book on religious pluralism and spirituality in higher education implicitly touch on it, given that many of the authors are also of different cultural groups; yet their focus is more on religious pluralism. In a book edited by Jablonski (2001) that deals with the role of spirituality in students' lives and how student affairs practitioners might draw on it, only Chavez (2001) even touches on the connection between spirituality and culture in her discussion of having a Mestiza consciousness about spirituality. Although few books explicitly deal with the connection of spirituality and culture, this has been a focus in journal articles, book chapters, and conferences (Dillard et al., 2000; Curry & Cunningham, 2000; Hernandez-Avila, 1996; Tisdell, 1999; 2000a; Tolliver & Tisdell, 2001a; Simmer-Brown, 1999). These contributions and discussions have been made largely by people of color or those who are explicitly interested in cultural issues. As hooks (2000) suggests, these authors are a part of the counterculture that is trying to "break mainstream cultural taboos" (p. 82) that silence our passion and the spiritual underpinning to our cultural work. My purpose here is to further the discussion relating to spirituality and culture in adult and higher education and thus to further break that silence. But first, it is important to define as clearly as possible the terms *spirituality, culture,* and *culturally relevant education.*

Defining Spirituality

Spirituality is an elusive topic. Different people define it in different ways, but all definitions somehow seem to be incomplete. Nevertheless, it is important to define what is meant here by the term *spirituality* and how it relates to work in multicultural and culturally relevant education. Based on interviews with thirty-one adult educators and as discussed in some prior work with colleagues (Tisdell, Tolliver, & Villa, 2001; Tolliver & Tisdell, 2001a, 2001b), I make the following seven assumptions about the nature of spirituality in relation to education:

1. Spirituality and religion are not the same, but for many people they are interrelated.

2. Spirituality is about an awareness and honoring of wholeness and the interconnectedness of all things through the mystery of what many I interviewed referred to as the Life-force, God, higher power, higher self, cosmic energy, Buddha nature, or Great Spirit.

3. Spirituality is fundamentally about meaning-making.

4. Spirituality is always present (though often unacknowledged) in the learning environment.

5. Spiritual development constitutes moving toward greater authenticity or to a more authentic self.

6. Spirituality is about how people construct knowledge through largely unconscious and symbolic processes, often made more concrete in art forms such as music, art, image, symbol, and ritual which are manifested culturally.

7. Spiritual experiences most often happen by surprise.

Although a more detailed discussion of several of these aspects of spirituality will be presented in far greater depth in later chapters, a brief discussion of each of these is provided below.

Spirituality and Religion Are Not the Same

As Lerner (2000) observes, religion is an organized community of faith that has written doctrine and codes of regulatory behavior. Spirituality, however, is more personal belief and experience of a divine spirit or higher purpose, about how we construct meaning, and what we individually and communally experience and attend to and honor as the sacred in our lives.

For those who were socialized in a religious tradition, spirituality and religion often are related. After all, the ongoing spiritual development of most of us as adults cannot be completely separated from how we were socialized religiously as children. In most cases, such childhood exposure was the foundation of spiritual development. In thinking about the four stories presented in the last chapter, it is clear that there are many adults, like Marcus Washington and Aiysha Ali, who find spiritual meaning in and remain committed to the religious tradition in which they grew up. But there are many who live in North America, like Julia Gutierrez, who have moved away from the religion of their childhood or left organized religion altogether in search of a more meaningful adult spirituality. Even so, their childhood religious socialization still served as a spiritual foundation. Even those who were not socialized in a religious tradition, like Lisa Riddle, still often spiral back to what was foundational to their earliest socialization or experiences around spirituality. This is probably why Lisa's sense of wilderness as a spiritual source growing up in Alaska is so central to her adult spirituality. Hence a first aspect of the working definition of spirituality as it is used here is that spirituality and religion are not the same, but for many adults they are at times interrelated. This idea might be depicted pictorially as intersecting Venn diagrams, where there is a religion sphere, and a spirituality sphere, and the two intersect when spiritual experiences happen in the context of one's religious life or religious community. Yet spiritual experiences often happen completely outside the context of a religious tradition; similarly, there are many experiences of organized religion that have nothing to do with spirituality.

Spirituality Is About an Awareness and Honoring of Wholeness

As Lisa Riddle stated when I asked about her definition, "Spirituality is some sort of an aware honoring of the Life-force that is happening through *everything*." I like Lisa's definition. It picks up on some themes that other researchers and writers have discussed in trying to define *spirituality*. For example, participants in a study conducted by Hamilton and Jackson (1998) noted that spirituality was fundamentally about three main themes: the further development of self-awareness; a sense of interconnectedness of all things; and a relationship to a higher power or higher purpose. Such a definition gives a sense of the psychological aspects of spirituality as broadly related to meaning-making. Lisa's definition highlights these aspects as well, but also gets at something more. Her definition emphasizes some intentionality on the part of the meaning-maker about spirituality. An "aware honoring" indicates that one takes action, however subtle, and cultivates an attitude, a way of being, a way of honoring the Life-force. Further, to say that the Life-force is "happening through everything" also connotes that this Life-force is primarily about wholeness, a wholeness and order to the universe, a wholeness that is beyond human understanding. This concept of wholeness experienced at times through the ever-present Life-force is an important component of spirituality.

Spirituality Is About Meaning-Making

Spirituality, as many have noted, is fundamentally about how we make meaning in our lives (English & Gillen, 2000; Hunt, 2001; Vella, 2000), particularly as related to our overall life purpose. Many adults indicate that it is a major organizing principle that guides their life choices, including choices of lovers and intimate friends and the kinds of work that they see as their vocation as they make meaning of their life experience. For some, spirituality is more individualistic; for others, like those whose stories were featured in the last chapter, spiritual commitment requires that they actively work for social justice. In either case, individuals do what they feel called to do—what gives their lives meaning.

Spirituality Is Always Present in the Learning Environment

Given that the Life-force is everywhere and the process of meaning-making is happening all the time, people's spirituality is always present (though usually unacknowledged) in the learning environment. Vella (2000) discusses the relevance of spirituality in teaching and learning in her discussion of a "spirited epistemology" (a view of knowledge that incorporates the spiritual). She states: "Every education event is movement toward a *metanoia*, the passage of spirit from alienation into a deeper awareness of oneself. A spirited epistemology is based on the belief that all education is directed toward such a transformation" (p. 10).

Although not all educational events are transformative, many educational events are or can be transformative if they are guided

by Vella's "spirited epistemology." As will be discussed in far greater
depth in Part Three, Vella is not necessarily suggesting that educators
need directly to discuss spirituality in those terms in the classroom to
make use of a pedagogy that is based on a "spirited epistemology";
rather she is suggesting that educational moments that are a movement toward a *metanoia* implicitly draw on spirituality.

Spiritual Development Constitutes Moving Toward Authenticity

The notion of spirituality as moving toward a sense of greater
authenticity or a more authentic identity is strongly related to the
concept of *metanoia* as discussed by Vella (2000). If people undergo
a *metanoia*, literally a "change of heart," about their view of themselves and their world and move to a less alienated state and a
deeper awareness of themselves and others, they are invited further
into their own authenticity. *Authenticity* in this sense means having
a sense that one is operating more from a sense of self that is defined
by one's own self as opposed to being defined by other people's
expectations. Joan Borysenko (1999), a theorist of women's development, discusses this theme of authenticity and wholeness in her
examination of women's spiritual development. Nearly all of the
people I interviewed talked about spirituality as related to this growing sense of greater authenticity or a more authentic identity, which
was strongly related to a sense of God-within, a higher self, the Life-
force, or spirit alive within.

Ava Valdez, a Latina born in Central America who immigrated
to the United States as a young adult, talked a lot about spirituality in relationship to her cultural identity. After discussing some of
her mixed cultural heritage and her Mayan ancestry, she explained,
"I think that spirituality is *to know who you are, and to be able to define who you are*, wherever you are, despite the changing conditions
of your life." What Ava was suggesting is that it is easy to fall into
a sense of identity mostly defined by fulfilling others' role expecta-

tions. But when one is grounded more in one's own spirituality, one has a greater sense of embracing an identity more congruent with who one is. Beverly Ward, an Alaska Native woman, explained that her spirituality was especially prominent when she was going through significant transitional times that helped her face difficult issues. "It certainly got me through a lot when I was going through my divorce, because I did spend a lot of time addressing issues that I had never addressed in my adult life," she explains. This sense of finding the courage to take a stand, determining what one believes and how one should be in the world, was defined by many participants as a spiritual process that brings one more in touch with one's core self, which is grounded in one's deepest spirit.

A key point here is that spirituality is about *moving toward* this greater sense of one's deepest spirit or more authentic identity. Since most of the participants were theists, they believed in a core self, or a "core essence" that was God-given and part of the divine spirit, a part of each person's uniqueness. Buddhists might call this "Buddha nature." Those in the study who were uncomfortable with the idea of a personal God referred to this idea as the higher self. Part of their spiritual journey was *moving toward* knowing and operating from this "core self," this more authentic identity. They were not claiming that they had "arrived" at "authenticity" or that they were operating all the time from *the* "authentic self." Furthermore, it would be important to be skeptical of claims to *absolute* authenticity, since this is what cult leaders often claim. Given that we are all shaped partly by culture, gender, our genetics, our various psychological and biological needs and desires, and others' expectations of us, it would be impossible to know with certainty absolute authenticity in this life. Nevertheless, if one believes in a unique essence to every human person, regardless of what one calls that essence, it is possible to *move toward* understanding and operating from that core self or authentic identity, at the same time one calls into question what that "authentic identity" is. This is the paradox: moving toward one's more authentic identity at the same time questioning the notion of authenticity. But then again, as Palmer (1980) suggests, spirituality is also about living in the belly of paradox.

Spirituality Is About Constructing Knowledge Through Unconscious and Symbolic Processes

The first five components of spirituality discussed above are related to education. They are also potentially related to culturally relevant approaches to adult and higher education. But it is the fifth and sixth components that are especially related to considerations of culture. When people are invited into their own authenticity, they are invited to explore and reclaim aspects of their cultural identity and make it more overtly present in the learning environment. This is part of being one's authentic self. This connects naturally to a sixth component of spirituality—that spirituality is about how people construct knowledge through largely unconscious and symbolic processes. This is based primarily on the insight of James Fowler (1981), who developed a theory of faith development that relied, in part, on the work of Piaget and moral development theorist Lawrence Kohlberg. Yet Fowler takes issue with Piaget and Kohlberg for "their restrictive understanding of the role of imagination in knowing, their neglect of symbolic processes generally and the related lack of attention to unconscious structuring processes other than those constituting reasoning" (p. 103). Indeed, we construct knowledge and make meaning in powerful and unconscious ways through image, symbol, music, art, metaphor, and ritual. Heron (1996) refers to this as imaginal or presentational knowing. But these aspects of how we construct knowledge, who we are, and how we make meaning are also cultural and thus connect us back to our cultural selves.

Spiritual Experiences Happen by Surprise

For the most part, spiritual experiences (or what are viewed as "spiritual experiences" by people) seem to happen by surprise. These moments of catching a glimpse of the wholeness of Life, the inter-connectedness of all things, and one's more authentic self generally cannot be planned. It may be possible to engage in practices whereby one is more likely to experience such moments, such as through practicing regular meditation, listening to inspirational music, spending time in the natural world, or attending ritual celebrations. But whether or not anyone has what might be called a "spiritual experience" in any of these situations varies from person to person and almost happens as an unexpected gift. Similarly, an educator might also create an environment that further invites people into their own authenticity and increased understanding of themselves and other people, which may or may not result in a "spiritual experience" by engaging the cognitive, affective, and symbolic domains in the educational process. For example, the educator might incorporate critical reading and engagement of new ideas (cognitive domain), consideration of how such ideas relate to one's life experiences (affective domain), and a space for celebrating and integrating new learning through the use of original or available music, art, poetry, or metaphor (symbolic domain). As Fowler suggests, this incorporating of the symbolic domain (which is often cultural as well) may begin to attend to the spiritual for some people, but whether what goes on in the learning environment is actually experienced as "spiritual" depends on the individual.

Defining Culture

The term *culture* is nearly as difficult to define as the term *spirituality*, but it is nonetheless important to be clear about what is meant by the term as it is used here. Indeed, *culture* has many meanings in our society. As Guy (1999) notes, "everyday usage includes *high culture, popular culture, organizational culture, ethnic culture, subculture,* and *uncultured*" (p. 6). He traces the various historical uses of the term in the United States and notes the long-standing influence of nineteenth-century British cultural critic Matthew Arnold's definition of culture as that which is associated with the most elite in beauty, intelligence, and perfection. Adult educators Horace Kallen and Alain Locke in the first half of the twentieth century had a more inclusive conception of culture as that which is connected to the lifeblood of a people. They considered the implications of such a definition in a culturally pluralistic society, using the term *cultural pluralism* to refer to "a society in which different cultural groups would democratically and peacefully coexist" (Guy, 1999, p. 7). Guy notes that this more inclusive definition of culture focusing on the lifeblood of a social group probably did not really take root, however, until the 1960s. The now more popular definition of culture refers to the "shared values, attitudes, beliefs, behaviors, and language within a social group" (p. 7). This is what is meant by *culture* as it is used in a general sense here.

But what is meant by *culture* when it is being used with a broadly descriptive adjective in front of it, such as American culture or U.S. culture? After all, there are several social groups living in the United States, with their own beliefs, values, norms, behaviors, language, or dialect, not just one. The 2000 U.S. census report reveals a white population declining to approximately 72 percent and an increasing percentage of communities of color. African Americans make up the largest, at nearly 13 percent, and Latinos, including Puerto Ricans, Cubans, Mexicans, and Colombians, each with their own unique cultures, only slightly behind at 12.5 percent (U.S. Census Bureau, 2000). In addition, there are the indigenous people of the United States and groups from the Mid-East, Africa, the India-Pakistan subcontinent, and various Asian or Asian American communities, including those whose families have lived here for several generations and those who are more recent immigrants. Each of these groups has its own unique culture and, often, religious tradition as well, which also has an impact on their values, beliefs, and behaviors. Diana Eck (2001) reports that America is now the most religiously pluralistic country in the world: "[T]here are more Muslim Americans than Episcopalians, more Muslims than members of the Presbyterian Church USA, and as many Muslims as there are Jews—that is, about six million. We are astonished to learn that Los Angeles is the most complex Buddhist city in the world, with a Buddhist population spanning the whole range of the Asian Buddhist world from Sri Lanka to Korea, along with a multitude of native-born American Buddhists. Nationwide, this whole spectrum of Buddhists may number about four million" (pp. 2–3).

This complexity of the interplay between religious pluralism and cultural pluralism makes it difficult to determine what is meant when people refer broadly to American culture, since American culture is actually very pluralistic. In general, though, it seems that when this term is used what is likely being referred to is the *dominant* culture, which in the United States is white, of European ancestry, middle class, with a tendency toward individualism, and informed by the values of various Christian denominations. This is the largest single group in America. As Guy (1999) notes, this is the group that has had the most structural power in society in terms of greatest access to money, property ownership, and public decision-making power as manifested by their greater presence in managerial positions and in elected bodies such as in the U.S. Congress. In educational circles, members of this cultural group have also historically had the power to determine what must be included in the U.S. educational curriculum. Thus, in the following discussion, I will specifically use the term *dominant culture* when I am referring to those who are white, middle to upper-middle class, and Christian. Those with the most power in this dominant culture tend also to be male, heterosexual, and moneyed. I will use the term *larger culture* to refer to the plurality of cultures in America. In sum, then,

- *Culture* refers to a specific social group with a shared set of values, beliefs, behaviors, and language, such as African American culture or Puerto Rican culture.

- *Dominant culture* refers to those in North America, who are white, of European ancestry, moneyed, of Christian

background, heterosexual, able-bodied, and often male
as well.

- *Larger culture* refers to the plurality of cultures that
  make up all of North America.

Defining Culturally Relevant Education

It is also important to define more clearly what is meant by *multicultural education* and *culturally relevant education*. There have been
many discussions about multicultural education in the past fifteen
years. To be sure, there are strong proponents of it, but there are also
critics of it both from the left and the right of the political spectrum
(Nieto, 1995). The critics on the right tend to see *multicultural education* as an overly politicized term that is divisive and destructive
to the cultural fabric of America (D'Souza, 1992; Hirsch, 1988).
Some on the left see it as a term that has been coopted by mainstream white educators who have little understanding of power relations between dominant and oppressed groups based on race,
gender, class, sexual orientation, and ableness. Indeed, some of the
confusion lies in the fact that different authors and theorists mean
very different things by the term *multicultural education*, and elsewhere I have discussed at length some of the differences among various models of multicultural education (Tisdell, 1995). Some
versions simply focus on individual differences among people of different cultural groups, primarily from a psychological perspective.
These approaches aim to help those who are marginalized by race,
class, culture, or gender to fit more successfully into the dominant
culture and educational systems without necessarily challenging
what privileges some over others in these systems. In fact, as Sleeter
and McLaren (1995) observe, in some of these approaches racism
is never mentioned, nor is it dealt with as a phenomenon in society; rather the emphasis is on cultural differences with no attention
to power imbalances. Other versions explicitly deal with how power
relations based on the structural systems of race, gender, class, sex-

ual orientation, and ableness, based on the critical pedagogy work of Paulo Freire (1971), tend to privilege some groups over others (Banks, 1993; Sleeter, 1998). These versions of multicultural education, often called *critical multiculturalism* are explicitly trying to challenge those structural systems in order to create greater equity in education and society.

Closely related to the discourses of critical multicultural education are the discourses of resistance postmodernism. There are many complicated discourses of postmodernism (Lather, 1991; Sleeter, 1996). All versions of it focus to some extent on the notion of deconstruction—to take apart or examine how each of us has been at least partially "constructed" through our socialization and our "positionality," or how we are positioned in society relative to the dominant culture by virtue of the multiple factors of gender, race, class, sexual orientation, age, and national origin. Some versions of postmodernism, often called "ludic" postmodernism, focus almost exclusively on deconstruction and seem to play word games that are accessible to almost no one except elite academics. Such versions would likely have no interest in spirituality, and would be likely to suggest that it is impossible to know one's self, much less one's more "authentic self," apart from the way one has been socialized through the limitations of language and by social structures of race, class, and gender that privileges some over others. Other versions (usually called "resistance postmodernism") focus more on the *resistance* of particular marginalized groups to the dominant culture in a way that helps them claim and define their own individual and group identity on their own terms. At the same time, resistance postmodernists are mindful of the danger of absolutizing any category of identity manifested in such absolute statements such as "women are this, men are that" or "white people are this, people of color are that." The discourses of resistance postmodernism are roughly parallel to the discourses of critical multiculturism, and many resistance postmodernists would recognize the role of spirituality in fueling people's passion to resist.

A difficulty with any version of multicultural education, even a critical multicultural or a resistance postmodernism approach, is that when dealing with a plurality of cultures and multiple systems of privilege and oppression in a classroom or learning situation, sometimes not enough in-depth attention is given to any one system to provide any real understanding of how social systems work. This lack of more specific attention can inadvertently maintain the status quo. This is another reason why some are leery of the term *multicultural education* and of postmodernism in general, and why some authors specifically focus on how one structural system, such as race or gender, affects teaching and learning. For example, Peterson (1996) and Colin (1994) specifically examine race from an Africentric perspective; Sheared (1994, 1999) and Johnson-Bailey (2001) focus on educational issues for African American women. In a similar vein, Abalos (1998) and Darder, Torres, and Gutierrez (1997) focus on Latinos, whereas others focus on gender (Hayes & Flannery et al, 2000; Hart, 1992; Tisdell, 1998) or sexual orientation (Grace, 2001; Hill, 1995; Pagenhart, 1994). Some educators use the term *culturally relevant education* to refer to and highlight the importance of understanding the culture of a particular social group. The term *culturally relevant education* was made more popular by Gloria Ladson-Billings (1995) in her discussion of successful teachers of African American children, and how they made use of approaches to education that were culturally relevant and responsive to these children. Talmadge Guy (1999) and the many authors in his recent edited book have used this term to discuss culturally relevant adult education approaches with specific population groups. As Guy (1999) states: "A principal focus of the educational experience, from the perspective of cultural relevance, is the reconstruction of learners' group-based identity from one that is negative to one that is positive. . . . For adult educators interested in addressing the ways in which cultural domination affects learners in adult education settings, educational strategies must be developed to minimize the potential for further exclusion and marginalization of learners" (p. 13).

He goes on to suggest that instructors employing culturally relevant education approaches need to increase their own cultural self-awareness, be aware of the learners' cultural identity, create an inclusive curriculum that challenges power relations, and attend to instructional processes in the classroom. Although Guy does not discuss spirituality, it seems that it can play a part in culturally relevant approaches to adult and higher education.

Toward a Spiritually Grounded Approach to Culturally Relevant Pedagogy

There has been little discussion of the role of spirituality in culturally relevant education thus far. To be sure, most attempts at culturally relevant education in adult and higher education settings happen in groups—in classrooms or in community-based and other group settings. And while everyone's spirituality is uniquely her or his own, the spirituality of most people connects to what they value and how they behave in the world. Thus there is a communal dimension to spirituality as well. Further, for many people, there is also a sense of communal responsibility to their spirituality that requires that they work for social justice or greater equity in the world. Rabbi Michael Lerner (2000) refers to this as an "emancipatory spirituality" (p. 165), and suggests that a specifically *emancipatory* spirituality highlights a sense of awe and wonder, the cultivation of mindfulness, and a love and care for the universe, but that it is manifested in actively working for environmental sustainability and a focus on the transformation of the world. He states: "To achieve and sustain this transformation, Emancipatory Spirituality encourages people to work together in social and political movements, and to fill those movements with a powerful spiritual practice that includes meditation, celebration of the universe. . ."

(p. 169). He goes on to discuss the importance of a sense of love and respect, not only for those of a similar political and spiritual philosophy, but also for those who do not share that philosophy. An emancipatory spirituality, in contrast to what he refers to as a "reactionary spirituality" (p. 174), recognizes the value of pluralism and the many manifestations of spirit within different cultures and traditions. For Lerner (2000), emancipatory spirituality includes an emphasis on working for social justice, with some attention to cultural pluralism and difference, which are elements not always highlighted in more general discussions of spirituality.

A basic premise of this book is that when educators attend to cultural issues, are more their own authentic selves (including more aware of their cultural selves), and invite others into their own authenticity by attending to cultural issues, they are engaging in culturally relevant education. Culturally relevant education is sometimes grounded in what Lerner refers to as emancipatory spirituality and might be made manifest in the learning environment in different ways. When one engages the cognitive, affective, and the symbolic domains of learning, learning itself becomes more holistic, thereby increasing the chance for learning to be transformative. This may be a spiritual experience for some people. Given that spirit is always present in the learning environment (Dirkx, 1997), attending to spirituality and its relationship to culture does not necessarily mean discussing spirituality directly, and it certainly *is not about pushing a specific religious agenda*. It can simply mean creating an environment and a space where people can bring their whole selves into the learning environment and acknowledge the powerful ways they create meaning through their cultural, symbolic, and spiritual experience, as well as through the cognitive. Such a "spirited epistemology" may result in a *metanoia* around cultural issues and facilitate greater understanding about one's own culture and that of other people. This is primarily why spirituality may have relevance to critical multicultural and culturally relevant approaches to education. When one engages in social justice issues on behalf of oneself or others as a result of this *metanoia*, culturally relevant education is also emancipatory education. Thus this concept of emancipatory spirituality has something to offer the theory and practice of culturally relevant education. It is my hope that the remaining chapters in this book will illustrate how.

3

Spirituality, Religion, and Culture in Lived Experience

Overlaps and Separations

Fifteen adults sit in a circle on the first day of a master's level course entitled "Spirituality and Culture in Adult Education." Some are of mixed European American descent, some are Puerto Rican, a few are African American, one is African, another is Japanese, and yet another is Native American. They are Catholic, evangelical Christian, Muslim, Jewish, Unitarian, Buddhist, and of no religious background. Some still practice the religion they were raised in; others define themselves as "spiritual but not religious." They have each written their definitions of *spirituality, religion,* and *culture* on three separate sheets of paper and posted them around the room. Then they grapple in the subsequent discussion with the similarities and differences among them. Most of them developed their working definition out of their lived experience of spirituality, religion, and culture.

Naturally, those who were religious found more of an overlap between their spirituality and religion, regardless of their cultural background. In general, the people of color felt more of a connection between their spirituality and their culture than the European American participants did at first. This is not surprising, for as Kincheloe, Steinberg, Rodriguez, and Chennault (1998) observe, lots of people from white European American or dominant cultural communities aren't as consciously aware of their culture as people of color are. Finally, those who strongly identified with particular ethnic communities (regardless of whether they were European American communities or communities of color) *and* were religious saw a strong overlap among their religion, culture, and spirituality. For all of us, this exercise of defining terms, examining our lived experience of these three separate but interrelated phenomena, observing the diagrams and pictures that were created throughout the discussion, and analyzing our lived experience helped us all make sense of our cultural, religious, and spiritual experience in new ways.

I begin with the discussion of this early exercise in the class because it brings to the forefront some issues of difference and similarities among the *lived experiences* of spirituality, religion, and culture. Although one would rarely *directly* discuss spirituality or religion in teaching classes, except when it is a direct part of the course content, as it was in the above case, the scenario does demonstrate how one might help participants examine and discuss their own knowledge and experience in constructing and reconstructing knowledge about these areas of their lives. Such an exercise begins to ground participants' learning in their own cultural and other experience and brings their own histories and life experience into the center of the discussion. This is part of culturally relevant education. In higher education settings such as this one, participants also read and evaluate books and articles as well as write papers related to these issues, activities that also contribute to how they think about and beyond their own life experience.

The last chapter focused on defining spirituality, culture, and culturally relevant education. This chapter focuses more on similarities and differences in the *lived experience* of spirituality and religion, and how we construct knowledge through these symbolic mediums that are so connected with culture. I begin by considering the intersections and divergences between spirituality and religion. I then discuss the role of imagination in narrating spiritual experience, which is then often given further expression through culture. This discussion will provide a backdrop to understanding the connection between spiritual experience as a way of constructing new knowledge made manifest in culture and creativity.

Spirituality and Religion: Overlaps and Differences

As noted in the last chapter, spirituality and religion are not the same. Organized religions have institutionalized components to them—written doctrine, codes of regulatory behavior, and organized communities of faith. Spirituality is more about how people make meaning through experience with wholeness, a perceived higher power, or higher purpose. All of the verbal definitions of spirituality among those I interviewed, as well as those of the participants in the above exercise, highlighted this theme of meaning-making. All referred to either a divine spirit, a higher self, a higher power, the Life-force, God, karma, the Great Spirit, or the Realm of Mystery. Most were theists. Although not all believed in a personal God, or otherwise felt that the concept of the personification of God was too limiting, all did believe in an order to the universe, a sense of wholeness and interconnectedness, and a higher *something*, whether that was a higher self or a higher power.

These verbal definitions were made more concrete in the examples they gave of spiritual experiences, which focused on times they caught a glimpse of something of what that wholeness was about, or of what they saw as their authentic identity. Not surprisingly, some of these experiences were related to life and death—being present at the miracle of the birth of a child or in the process of dying and death of a loved one. Other experiences were related to sexuality—experiences making love whereby somehow a sense of wholeness, connection with a soul mate, one's deepest identity, and a unity of body, emotion, and spirit with another found new and sacred expression. Many also discussed physical or psychological healing experiences that resulted in the courage to take new action. Still others described significant experiences in meditation, nature, synchronistic meetings, dreams, and in creative activity whereby a piece of art or music seemed to emerge from some higher part of one's being. Many also referred to spiritual experiences during sacred rituals or religious services, in which a life transition was marked as a rite of passage, or personal or cultural identity was affirmed or given expression in a new way. But at bottom, it seemed that spiritual experience was about *catching a glimpse* of an understanding of the wholeness and interconnectedness of all of life, and honoring that experience as sacred.

It is interesting that *wholeness, holiness,* and *health* all have the same root: *hal,* "to be whole" (Sanford, 1977). The drive of spirituality is the drive to wholeness, to holiness, to health, and to making meaning of that wholeness. Fundamentally, this is what spirituality is about.

As William James (1902/1982) observed at the beginning of the last century in his classic *The Varieties of Religious Experience*, there are many types of spiritual experience. Although there are times when spiritual experience intersects with religion, often it does not. Because religions are organized communities of faith, most of them preach a particular message and have direct discussion of what constitutes "salvation" or a "correct" way to live. Some religions have fundamentalist interpretations of what they see as their holy texts, whereas others have broader interpretations in light of the historical and cultural context. Nearly all religions have an official creed as determined by those with the most power and authority to do so. In many cases, organized religions also have various injunctions about appropriate behavior based on gender and sometimes for various class and cultural groups as well, which seem to indicate a hierarchy of entitlement. These aspects of religion often have a lot to do with the imperatives of organizational and political structure and little to do with spirituality.

The Intersection of Religion and Spirituality

Most religions, however, also provide their members with important aspects that do connect with spirituality. They provide a structure for people to organize their spirituality in their daily or weekly lives. What one person might experience as too many behavioral injunctions about how to live, others might find freeing and a gateway to the sacred. For example, Ahmed Hasan, an African American Muslim man, discusses the importance to his own spirituality of the injunctions of one of the five pillars of Islam—to pray five times a day. He notes that for him, the regularity of stopping and centering at predictable intervals during the day helps keep him more focused on what's important in his life and on how his daily activities relate to matters of ultimate purpose.

Sociologist of religion Martin Marty (2000) discusses some common characteristics of all religions and considers the important role they fill in many people's lives. In particular he notes that they provide: (1) a focus on matters of ultimate concern relating to the meaning and purpose of life; (2) a sense of community to gather, celebrate, and mourn; (3) behavioral injunctions of how to live; (4) myth and symbol that tell ultimate truth through allegory, story, metaphor, or art; (5) ritual and ceremony that celebrates in community some of life's most important transitions, such as birth, entry into adulthood, love or marriage, and death as the final transition.

Religious rituals are often important markers for people because they provide comfort at times of sorrow or a way of ritualizing and celebrating profound and significant events in their lives. Many religious people make deeper meaning through those rituals and often the symbols attached to them. Furthermore, many people have also had important spiritual experiences in the context of particular religious rituals. Hannah Adanah, a Jewish woman in her late forties who has been very involved as an educator in the reform Jewish community, described a significant experience that she often goes back to that is related to her spirituality, her Judaism, and how she sees her life purpose. She reflected back and related the story of her Confirmation as a sophomore in high school, at a time before it was common practice for Jewish girls to have a Bat Mitzvah. "I surprised even myself with the experience of being up there facing the Torah in that moment in a way that had never before moved me," she explained.

> *I will never forget the thrill of that feeling that God was right there choosing me for some special task for the Jewish people which I had no real sense of at the time. It was visceral thing. It was a physical thing. It was kind of electric and very personal. I was sure that God was right there with me. That feeling has stayed with me all of my life. I am still learning about what that moment meant. I was not a religiously oriented teen at the time. Those feelings and that way of knowing God came to me as a complete surprise.*

This was an important spiritual experience for Hannah, and one that took place directly in the context of her religious and cultural tradition.

Among the most important places where spirituality and religion intersect are in the rituals, images, symbols, prayers, and music of religious traditions that provide a gateway to the sacred. Human beings construct knowledge and meaning in powerful and often unconscious ways through these mediums and other forms of art. Faith development theorist James Fowler (1981) speaks to this point and notes, the "forming of an image does not wait or depend upon conscious processes. The image unites 'information' and feeling; it holds together orientation and affectional significance. As such, images are prior to and deeper than concepts" (p. 26). So too are some of the rituals, mythic stories, symbols, prayers, and songs that people grew up with that may be part of their religious traditions, celebrated in their churches, synagogues, temples, or mosques, as well as in their own family rituals. As Sharon Daloz Parks (2000) notes: "Religion, at its best, provides a dynamic distillation of images (symbols, stories, smells, sounds, songs, and gestures . . .) powerful enough to shape into one the chaos of existence—powerful enough to name a community's conviction of the character of the whole of reality that its members experience as both ultimate and intimate" (p. 118).

Many people have strong affective and symbolic ties to such songs, stories, and rituals that are far deeper, and often more unconscious than they realize, than can ever be expressed in words. Although several of the educators I interviewed no longer regularly practice in the religious tradition of their childhood, many of them very occasionally go to religious services for weddings, funerals, the birth or naming of a child, or simply to find a sacred space in which to worship, sort things out, or provide support to a friend. Most of them spoke specifically about the importance of the music, its power to inspire, and the unconscious positive memories associated with it in which they still often take comfort when they attend such religious services. To be sure, music and ritual can hold a lot of affective and spiritual power and meaning for people on a conscious and often an unconscious level.

This point of the power of religious ritual, at its best, to name and experience both the ultimate and the intimate has been driven home to me on a number of occasions, probably most significantly for me personally when my mother was dying. For nearly five days, my father, my brothers and sister and I, and some extended family members kept vigil by my mother's bedside. Although many of us no longer practice the Catholicism of our youth, I would venture to say all of us found tremendous meaning in the rituals we conducted in the process of her dying. We sang songs (both Church songs and songs she sang to us growing up), we prayed rosaries, we read her favorite psalms—things that were an important part of her spirituality and things that were formative to our own. Perhaps it made us feel safe or helped us know what to do; after all, five days is a long time. But among the most significant of those rituals was when her good friend and favorite priest, Father Denny, came and led us in anointing her in what was once called the "Last Rites" in the Catholic Church (now called "Anointing of the Sick"). He anointed her with oil; some of us followed his lead, anointing her hands, her feet, and her forehead—in love and in thanksgiving for the great gift of her life that she offered to us. We sang more songs, and encircled her with love. Some of us cried. We waited.

I think if you asked us in advance, many of us probably would have thought the ritual of her anointing wouldn't have been particularly important. But all of us found tremendous meaning in the ritual itself. Perhaps it was its familiarity, the symbol of the holy oil in the sacred honoring of my mother's life, and the fact that we took such an active part in the ritual itself. Perhaps it was our bonding to my mom and each other that was present in our gathering that also made it sacred. To this day, I hold the image sacred in my head, as do my brothers and sisters. It was indeed, as Parks (2000) suggests, an experience of both the intimate and the ultimate. So while some family members may no longer check the box marked "Catholic" in those hospital forms, all of us still find some meaning in those Catholic rituals that we first learned about in classes similar to Sister's in *Late Nite Catechism* described in the first chapter. Indeed, we often spiral back.

Divergences Between Religion and Spirituality

Yet as already discussed, in spite of the overlaps between spirituality and religion—particularly in the ways many of us have constructed important meaning through symbol, image, and ritual that is part of our religious backgrounds and cultural traditions—religion and spirituality are not the same. Clearly, many leave the religions of their childhood for good reasons, primarily because they are rejecting the codified rules and regulations of their religious traditions. They generally are not leaving because of the positive ways they have constructed meaning in those traditions, rituals, and symbols. Sometimes, they are rejecting the negative messages they appropriated (rightly or wrongly) from various leaders within those traditions about their badness, their inferiority to others of a different status, gender, or culture. Some leave because they are ashamed of the role their religions played in a history of colonization, in the Holocaust, or in committing human atrocities in the name of "God." They may be leaving for the ways representatives of their religious institutions have tried to claim something as the "will of God" when it appeared to be more about maintaining the power of some over others. Furthermore, some leave simply because there is too much of a dichotomy between their personal beliefs and the official creed or ideology of their religious traditions. Others leave because the message preached seems totally irrelevant to their lives. And of course, many remain within the tradition of their childhood, either out of habit or because it does indeed nurture their spiritual growth, and they are committed to their communities and the cultural tradition that is part of that religious tradition. To be sure, many continue their spiritual development in profound and significant ways within those traditions.

At this juncture, it is important to note that there is much that is misunderstood by many people in North America about the core teachings of many religious traditions, sometimes of their own, but certainly of those other than their own. Many people's formal religious education stops when they graduate from high school (Groome, 1999; Parks, 2000). In some cases what was learned was strictly from the perspective of whatever religious representative happened to be located in their hometowns. Perhaps what was taught or learned was accurate, or perhaps the message was a distortion of what the tradition actually teaches. Furthermore, as Diana Eck (2001) observes, most of us were raised with little or no information about the teachings of other religions. Such lack of information or misinformation about other traditions results, at the very least, in distorted assumptions about "the other" and at times outright religious bigotry. We have seen evidence of this in the post–September 11, 2001 era, in which in the minds of some Americans, Islam became erroneously equated and confused with terrorism. Indeed, as many Muslim scholars and imams have explained, terrorists who are also Muslim have a very distorted understanding of Islam, in much the same way that members of the Ku Klux Klan had (and still have) a distorted understanding of Christianity and the teachings of Jesus. It is not my intent here to explore the complexity of the current world political situation, as the political, religious, and cultural issues that are part of the background context of many current world conflicts seem far afield from the nature of spiritual experience. Nevertheless, as Charaniya and West Walsh (2001) have noted, the complexity of religion and culture, so apparent in the unfolding of the world's events, does point to the need for interreligious dialogue and for an examination of how religious pluralism intersects with cultural pluralism and what interreligious dialogue suggests for learning in a the context of adult and higher education.

We live in a complex world, beset with power relations based on economic systems, race, gender, class, and religion. As we have seen, religious institutions are a mixed bag. In some ways, as Marx observed, they serve as "the opiate of the people" and are used as a justification for those in power in governments and institutions to do what they want and to invoke the name of "God." They are human institutions, beset with politics and division. But religions institutions also provide meaningful avenues to the sacred and a strong sense of community for many. The earlier stages of spiritual development and people's earliest spiritual experiences are often named and given early meaning and definition in the context of that religious tradition (Wuthnow, 1999). This early religious formation remains a part of their spiritual and cultural history, whether they remain within that religious tradition, leave organized religion altogether, or identify with a different religion.

It is also important to note that many aspects of spirituality have nothing at all to do with religion. As Wuthnow (1998) observes, many people in America were not socialized in any particular religious tradition, yet they have a well-defined spirituality. This was the case for Lisa Riddle, the singer-songwriter and educator who was introduced in the first chapter. To be sure, religious traditions and institutions do not have a corner on the market of who does and does not have spiritual experiences. As I discuss later in this chapter, it seems that most of the primarily significant spiritual experiences that interviewees reported experiencing had little or nothing to do with their childhood religious traditions but were imbedded in their life experiences and relationships with others, the earth, and the larger cosmos. Often these experiences were given further expression and manifested through ritual, symbol, art, music, and other forms of cultural expression. This is the point where religion, spirituality, and culture intersect.

Spiritual and Cultural Knowing Through Image, Ritual, and Symbol

Human beings construct knowledge and meaning in powerful and often unconscious ways through image, symbol, and ritual. It is consideration of how we do so that is often absent from discussions of cognition, learning, and education. The "symbolic processes" and the "unconscious structuring processes" that Fowler (1981) refers to are within the realm of what I mean by spiritual knowledge construction processes, and what Heron (1996) refers to as imaginal or presentational knowing. These processes are deeply connected both to imagination and to culture. A consideration of culture as the expression of spiritual experience will make more sense in light of the role of imagination in spiritual knowledge construction processes.

The Role of Imagination in Spiritual Experience

Just what is happening when people *catch a glimpse* of the wholeness and interconnectedness of things and have what they refer to as a "spiritual experience"? To be sure, it is difficult to know exactly what is going on here, for as Fowler notes, these are unconscious processes, and it is hard to make visible what is not totally conscious. Sharon Daloz Parks (2000) proposes a paradigm of what may be going on in such spiritual experiences. She discusses the role of imagination in knowledge construction processes and notes that imagination acts in three dimensions in the formation of meaning: (1) it facilitates a process as we initially imagine possibilities, (2) it attempts to make whole in its act of naming, and (3) it activates people's creative power and sense of participating in "the ongoing creation of life itself" (p. 105). In this sense, imagination is not to be confused with fantasy. She argues that imagination is a "composing activity" of putting together insights, images, and ideas in a way that approximates or comes close to the real and that speaks to a larger reality that is about meaning-making; fantasy, however, is more about knowing and recognizing what is unreal. "The task of the imagination," she says, "and particularly of the religious imagination, is to compose the real" (p. 106). Some postmodernists likely have trouble with the notion of "the real" since, according to the views of postmodernism, each person's version of "reality" is socially constructed amid conflicting power relations based on race, gender, class, sexuality, religion, and other structural systems of privilege or oppression, and it is difficult to know reality outside of those constructs (McLaren, 1994; Sleeter, 1996). In any event, Parks is not a postmodernist, and would probably argue that there is an ultimate Truth and an ultimate Reality, though our understanding of that Truth or Reality is always partial, since to some extent the role of imagination is to narrate and compose an approximation of something of the truth of this larger reality, whereas this is not the intent of fantasy.

Building on the work of theologian and psychologist James Loder (1998), Parks (2000) suggests that the way this process of imagination works in the knowledge construction process is in five "moments," which include (1) conscious or unconscious conflict, (2) pause (or a move away from consciously dealing with it, although there is probably continued unconscious or semiconscious dealing with the conflict), (3) image or insight whereby the conflict is resolved and recast in some way, (4) repatterning and release of energy, whereby "the vast reaches of one's knowing and being may be reordered in light of the new insight, as there is a re-patterning of the connections among things" (p. 120), and finally (5) an interpretation or testimony about the experience. She uses the example of Nobel prize-winning genetic biologist Barbara McClintock, who by her own account, after days of working to solve the mysteries of genetics in the meiotic cycle, took a break to sit under the eucalyptus trees at Stanford University and suddenly came to new insight and new scientific discovery. In reflecting on the pause under the eucalyptus trees, McClintock noted, "I don't know what I asked myself; all I knew was that I had to go out under those eucalyptus trees and solve what was causing me to fail" (cited in Parks, 2000, p. 115). This new insight, the solving of the intellectual problem, was also manifested in the discovery of new patterns in science, the releasing of that energy and the testimony, not only of the new scientific information, but also of the process that gave rise to it— of seeing the interconnectedness of all things. Whether or not McClintock described this as a "spiritual experience" is unclear. But she did talk about the importance of wholeness, of paying attention to hearing what the material is saying as though the data has a living message of its own, and of cultivating a mindset of being open enough to hear it. According to Parker Palmer (1998), it appears that McClintock wasn't just tending to the relationships between the genes; her attention "included the relationship between the genes and the scientist who studied them" (p. 55).

The apprehension of a new insight after a conflict, and the result of a "pause" under a eucalyptus tree or some other space, is not always manifested in something as concrete as a new scientific discovery, as in the case of Barbara McClintock. Sometimes the conflict isn't so much an intellectual problem to be solved but a conflict in relationships with others or with various parts of one's self as one is recovering from pain or loss or facing a dilemma or difficult choice. Sometimes the repatterning that is the result of spiritual experiences or other unconscious structuring processes is manifested in ways other than words: more symbolically in art, music, poetry, movement, or other forms of symbol making. As many of the people

I interviewed noted, it is often difficult to put spiritual experiences accurately into words. Anna Adams, a fifty-three-year-old African American professor of education who discussed the significance of the ancestral connection to her own spirituality, spoke to the fact that spiritual experience is often beyond words and beyond cognition. Using her spiritual understanding of ancestral connection as an example, she noted:

> *When I say that, to me, the connection to ancestors and the connection to ancestral culture is a spiritual process, it's a spiritual thing because I don't cognitively know all about it; there's a lot of it that I just kind of intuit, and that I accept on a spiritual level—I feel it, . . . It's past language! That's one of the things that really points to how spiritual music is—it reaches people beyond boundaries and language.*

Because of the limitations of language, people express their spiritual experiences symbolically and through other forms of expression and creativity.

Parks (2000) discusses the significance of image and symbol in knowledge construction processes in general and in faith or spiritual experiences in particular. "Because the task of faith is to shape into one the whole force field of life, whenever an image functions to give form to meaning at the level of faith, it necessarily engages a degree of complexity only held by symbol" (p. 116). Using the term *symbol* broadly, she goes on to note that the symbol could be a concept, a person, a physical object that has a particular meaning, or a movement or gesture. We map onto those symbols meanings that go beyond words, but convey something deeper than rational explanations. And of course, everyone attaches somewhat different meanings to the same symbol. Although there may be a general common cultural or religious understanding of symbols such as the American flag, or bread and wine in certain contexts, a menorah, mezuzah, La Virgen de Guadalupe, Aretha Franklin, *hijab*, the Yin-

Yang symbol, or other symbols common to a particular cultural group, to some extent each person maps her or his own particular meaning onto the symbol, or no meaning at all to it if one has no personal or cultural relationship to it. Thus, image and symbol are always partial. "Since the image only gives *form* to the truth it attempts to convey, it can only *represent* the truth; it cannot fully reproduce or embody it"(Parks, 2000, p. 119). Nevertheless, image and symbol, in their many manifestations, often speak louder than words in the ways human beings narrate spiritual experiences. And images and symbol do connect to culture.

Symbol and Music as Mediated Through Culture

Parks (2000) and Fowler (1981) have contributed enormously to our understanding of the role of the imagination and the unconscious knowledge construction processes through imagination, ritual, image, and symbol. But most who have discussed spiritual or faith development have not considered the role of culture in those processes in any great depth. In the first chapter, I illustrated the interplay between my culture and religious background in my own life in the story of my experience of *Late Nite Catechism*. I tried to make the distinctly cultural aspect of the story visible. Further, I illustrated the connection between religion, culture, and spirituality in the experience of my family during the rituals surrounding my mother's death. These experiences may be fairly typical for those who grew up white and of Irish- or Italian-Catholic descent. But they are the experiences of a white woman, with a white cultural backdrop. Although the white cultural backdrop may seem very incidental to the stories, it is nevertheless part of the background and thus is never really incidental.

Culture is almost never incidental. Most people of color never forget about their cultural identity, and it probably never even seems incidental to the stories they tell. If they live in North America, they live in a society where their race or cultural identity is inscribed within a context where white culture is the dominant norm.

As I discuss further in Chapter Seven, very often a part of their spiritual journeys is about developing a positive cultural identity in a world where they probably have experienced some oppression because of their race, color, or ethnicity. In addition, their spirituality is what gives many people further inspiration to stand up against injustice. This was particularly evident in the civil rights movement and is an example of where spirituality, religion, culture, and working for social justice intersect. Symbols, music, and cultural forms of knowing are often a part of those experiences. This is why Marcus Washington (whom we met in the last chapter), in reflecting on his connection and disconnection with neo-Marxist thinking, noted that in his experience in African American Christian churches, religion was not an opiate. Religion was what animated members of his community; there was a sense of mission rooted in a cultural experience, enforced through the power of the word, and given soul and spirit in the animating power of the music that still speaks to his own heart and soul. This is why he continues to be involved on a regular basis with African American Christian churches.

Anna Adams, unlike Marcus Washington, has long since moved away from the African American Christian religious tradition of her childhood. She does not affiliate with any organized religion but has developed her own individualized spirituality that is still very much connected to her cultural background. In particular she refers to Aretha Franklin as an important spiritual symbol for her that connects to her cultural identity and her spirituality, a spirituality that has become more important to her as she has gotten older.

> I don't think I understood why they called her the "Queen of
> Soul" when I was younger, but when I listen to her sing now,
> I feel her! I feel her soul; she sings right into mine! There's a
> connection . . . she takes me into heights, she hits those notes
> and there's something about the power of her voice that connects me to something beyond myself, and that for me is the

spirituality of Aretha Franklin, that takes me places that I can't go without her.

In further reflecting on the connection of Aretha's music to her own cultural identity, Anna explained:

I grew up in a black community doing and understanding and experiencing things of black culture, so when I say Aretha takes me back, she takes me back to my childhood and the things that I understood then—things like music and dance, and the way of walking, the way of talking, the way of knowing, the interactions, the jive talk, the improvisations, you know all those things that I learned coming up—the music of the church, the choir that I sang in, all of that. And because I was raised in that community with that knowledge her music takes me back even farther than I know, because I don't know where all of those things come from. As I've gotten older, the more I am able to let go of the material plane and accept things on a spiritual plane that I am in touch with spiritually, but I'm not in touch with necessarily materially. . . .

And finally, in hinting at the connection of Aretha and her music to her ancestors, she summed up:

The way that Aretha sings is very old, so when I go back to my childhood, it's really connected to my parents' childhood, and so on, and so on, so Aretha takes me back to places I don't even know that I know about. There are ancient roots that are beyond my memory of this time and place. . . . When I listen to Aretha sing—all of those songs are songs of struggle . . . about how to survive, how to resist oppression, and I got to thinking about other spirituals that I know, and they're all at that level. . . . Music is an expression of a spiritual journey, and Aretha Franklin's voice, and the way she sings her songs, to me expresses that spiritual journey.

Obviously, for Anna, Aretha Franklin's music is a great source of inspiration because of its connection to her ancestors, her own spirituality, and its rootedness in her own cultural experience.

Whereas Marcus Washington and Anna Adams spoke about the power of music in their own spirituality and cultural experience, Julia Gutierrez spoke of the journey of reclaiming a positive cultural identity as a spiritual experience, and the role of the cultural symbol of La Virgen de Guadalupe in that process. Julia has long since moved away from the Mexican-Catholicism of her youth, but in reflecting back, she notes:

> I think part of my journey is going back to my heritage, my Aztec and indigenous roots. . . . Ana Castillo (1996) gives a different picture of what La Virgen could represent in terms of powerful women. . . . But there's another side to it. . . . I don't always just go with "this is the way that it is" because I do question, was that a way for the Spaniards to . . . convert the Aztecs into Catholicism? Or is it really an Aztec goddess? . . . But I do believe it's a spirit—a spirit that kind of watches over me.

Further, she discusses some of the affective significance she holds to this image of La Virgen de Guadalupe in her family and cultural history:

> We have this ritual in my family—every time I go home, and when I'm getting ready to leave, I ask for my parents' blessing, and so they'll take me into their room, and each one of them will bless me. . . . And I don't feel complete if I don't do that. . . . So my father will bless me, "te encomiendo a Dios Padre, y a La Virgen de Guadalupe" . . . and ask my grandmother and La Virgen to watch over me, and so I feel like my Grandmother's watching over me!

For Julia the importance of the cultural symbol is in its significance to her ancestral connection, to her cultural roots, and the
affective dimension associated with the family ritual of blessing.
Authors Gloria Anzaldua (1987) and Ana Castillo (1996) have also
discussed the similar cultural and spiritual dimension that the symbol La Virgen de Guadalupe has for many Chicana feminists as a
liberational image and as a sign of feminine power.

Many writers of color have discussed the importance of the interplay between spirituality and culture. Asian American writer
Naomi Southard (1996) discusses the significance that Kuan Yin,
the feminine wisdom figure and Buddhist symbol of compassion, has
for Asian American women of both Christian and Buddhist background. Mohja Kahf (1999), a Muslim woman of Syrian origin who
grew up in New Jersey and rural Indiana, discusses the spiritual and
cultural significance that *hijab,* "the head scarf associated with
Islamic notions of womanly propriety" (p. 421), took on as a symbol of her cultural, gender, and religious identity as an adolescent,
and the power it still holds as a spiritual and cultural symbol for
some Muslim women in the United States today. These symbols
may have religious roots, but often they are deeply associated with
one's culture. They hold spiritual significance because they create a
grounding place for cultural identity, which is also an important way
we make meaning out of our lives. Often, there is a strong affective
component we attach to these cultural symbols of our identity.

Spiritual experience is not only about constructing knowledge
through image and symbol. Spiritual experiences and the manifestations of these significant experiences anchor our lives in specific
ways, and are generally related to how we live with others in the
world. Attempts to live in accordance with a spiritual path have
an orientation toward community, particularly if, as Lerner (2000)
notes, one is attempting to develop an emancipatory spirituality.
American Indian writer Paula Gunn Allen (1992) speaks further
to this point in her discussion of the connection among culture,

spiritual symbol, and the "personal choice-community responsibility" dialectic in American Indian communities. She notes: "it is an ineradicable orientation toward a spirit-informed view of the universe. . . . This view is not merely private, for it is shared by all the members of tribal psychic reality. It is not exactly personal. It is however subjective, for . . . all matters of the nonmaterial realms of being must be experienced within the subjective mind of each individual at least as much as within the particular part of the tribal gestalt that is activated by ceremony, ritual, and vision" (p. 165).

What Allen suggests is that in American Indian communities, knowledge is constructed through ritual, symbol, and ceremony, but it is constructed by individuals in a cultural community for the development both of the individual and that community. It connotes ways of living in the world and working for justice in a holistic way that honors the earth and the creatures and people in it (Deloria, 1992). Such holistic life practices or ways of living based on one's spirituality can take many forms—perhaps in dietary habits, music, meditation practices, emphasis on mindfulness, particular ways of working for justice in the world, and ways of accessing inspiration to do so. But such practices cannot be torn from one's cultural background or the sociocultural context and usually spill over to how one lives all aspects of one's life.

Summary and Brief Thoughts for Practice

In this chapter I have tried to lay a foundation for how one might begin to draw on the *lived experience* of spirituality in order to consider how to develop culturally relevant educational approaches. I began with a brief scenario from my own class to ground the discussion in educational practice as well as to explore in greater depth the convergences and divergences among religion, spirituality, and culture in *lived experience*. I also considered the ways in which image and symbol, including both its cultural and particular dimensions, inform and narrate spiritual experience.

As Parks (2000) suggests, spiritual experiences that facilitate a new understanding of the wholeness and interconnectedness of all things often arise by surprise as a result of a new experience or an internal conflict (intellectual, emotional, or spiritual). Such an experience is given new meaning after a pause and is restructured in some way through the power of imagination, thereby creating a new wholeness or a map of a new reality. This new wholeness is often manifested symbolically in many ways, such as in dreams, images, or creative new insights. The energy of this remapping is released and expressed through various means. It may be ritualized or experienced in the context of a religious tradition. It is at this point that spirituality and religion intersect. Or this energy may be manifested through ongoing creative activity in art, music, poetry, writing, and creative living. Such symbol-making and symbol-manifesting activities that draw from the new wholeness that has arisen from myriad fragments are necessarily cultural expressions. This is the realm in which spiritual experience connects to culture.

What does all this suggest for developing a culturally relevant approach to adult and higher education? I discuss the specific implications for practice in detail in Part Three, but briefly: people construct knowledge in powerful ways through imagination to make order out of chaos, wholeness out of fragmentation. As Dirkx (2001) notes, the role of imagination in this sense has been given little attention in the literature on adult development and learning, yet we connect all new forms of knowledge to what is already stored in our memory and use the power of imagination, both to access what we already know and to connect it to the present to create new knowledge. There are a myriad ways to explore the role of imagination in development and learning. One way would be to encourage participants to discuss the role of imagination in their own lives—in problem solving, in creating new meaning, in experiences that get at the interconnectedness of all things, or in making a life decision. Of course, this activity would be relative to both the context of the subject and the institutional context of the learning activity. Once participants were able to identify an experience of imagination, they could consider how this new knowledge was manifested, how it was expressed, or how it was symbolized. Some people may consider these experiences of imagination to be spiritual; some may not consider them to be spiritual experiences per se, but significant in some other way. But generally such experiences are manifested culturally. Thus, participants might then explore the cultural manifestations of this particular expression of imagination and further imagine or find out how someone of a different cultural group might express it. This exercise might help them examine what has been and is culturally relevant for them as individuals and what might be relevant for others. Clearly, it is not necessary to determine whether the experience is "spiritual." Rather, it is important to consider the particular ways it is possible to draw on the imagination and symbolic knowing processes that often touch people on another level in trying to further develop approaches to culturally relevant education.

4

Between the Cultural
and the Universal

Themes and Variations
of Spiritual Experience

Life can be chaotic. At times we seem to be in harmony with the universe; at other times, all seems discordant. In large measure, spirituality is about making sense of our chaotic lives, making harmony out of disharmony, or jazz out of discord. "Jazz reduces the 'chaos of living to form.' The effect of this transformation can be profound," writes religion scholar, Sharon Welch (1999). Drawing on the power of jazz to create order out of chaos, she goes on to note that jazz pianist Mary Lou Williams "occasionally interrupted her performances to implore inattentive audiences, 'Listen, this will heal you'" (p. 19). Indeed, the interruption helped her audiences listen in a new and different way.

There are many varieties of spiritual experience. Like many classical or jazz music pieces, where there is a primary theme with several variations, spiritual development often has a primary theme with improvisational variations. As suggested in Chapter One, a main theme is moving forward and spiraling back. Related to this process is an important variation running along simultaneously with this theme: the ongoing development of identity. Many have described significant spiritual experiences relating to particular milestones in their identity development or other important aspects of their life experience, such as understanding their life purpose, dealing with a death of a loved one or working through some other painful life experience, or celebrating some special joy. What all these types of experiences have in common is that they offer hope, healing, or affirmation. And just as Mary Lou Williams may have interrupted her performances to get her audience's attention, these significant spiritual experiences spontaneously interrupt the chaos of our ordinary or inattentive lives as if to say, "Listen! This will heal you!" These experiences cannot be planned; rather, they usually happen quite spontaneously. But as Hays (2001) notes, they stand out as "shimmering moments" in our lives—moments that we often go back to with awe and wonder. The power of their "shimmer" endures in the ongoing meaning-making of our lives. These are often moments of significant learning.

This chapter is primarily about the varieties and types of spiritual experience—the specific moments and events that are experienced as sacred, primarily as reported by the people I have interviewed, although I also draw from my own experience and from some of the literature on spirituality as well. As you read these stories, I encourage you to think of some "shimmering moments" of your own and to bring yourself into these stories. To be sure, such moments often facilitate development. The literature on adult development and spiritual development generally focus on development as *change over time*, rather than on specific moments themselves. In this chapter I will specifically focus more on the experiences themselves and the cultural context in which they are experienced and expressed. In Chapter Five I will consider the implications of these experiences for adult spiritual development as *change over time*.

Spiritual experiences come in a variety forms, including what is perceived as a physical or emotional healing, dreams, synchronistic experiences, or other events that seem to get at the wholeness of life. Some of these experiences have a lot to do with cultural background and identity, particularly in the expression of those experiences. I briefly considered some of these experiences and how they relate to culture in the last chapter—a point I will come back to in depth in Chapter Seven in considering how embracing a positive cultural identity is interwoven with spirituality for many people.

Other types of spiritual experiences are not so obviously about culture, but rather seem to center more on the types of experience that are common to all human beings, experiences in birth and death, in dreams and visions, in nature and in meditation. These types of experiences or sacred moments sometimes offer hope, healing, or direction in times of difficulty and despair, or elation and joy in times of celebration, or they may facilitate or affirm a life decision. Still other moments offer a sense of a centering presence or of being one with the universe, what some refer to as experiences of bliss, that might happen out in nature or in meditation. There is always a cultural backdrop to such experiences, although the cultural element of the experience is often not central. What is more central in these types of experiences is the sense of interconnection of the whole universe and all of creation. This chapter focuses on these types of experiences potentially common to all human beings in all cultures, although they may be given further expression in specific cultural communities in a variety of ways.

Dreams and Synchronicities

One of the powerful ways that we make new meaning through image and symbol and the unconscious processes that Fowler (1981) and others refer to are in dream experiences. Throughout the ages, many have reported the transformative and spiritual power of dreams, from before Joseph in the Old Testament to Carl Jung in his many works to the many authors who have written about dreams and its uses in therapeutic and soul work. I also heard many stories from the people that I interviewed and many others over the years about the power of their own dreams in helping them make decisions. Of course, dreams are full of symbols that arise and are narrated through the unconscious self and brought into consciousness and given further meaning by the conscious self.

Most of those I interviewed do not consider *all* their dreams necessarily spiritual per se; however, the dreams that were described as spiritual experiences were those that stood out as particularly transformative and that were either predictive in some way or that promoted healing or aided in making a life decision. These dreams seemed to come at times when the dreamer was in conflict, on the verge of or in the midst of a transition of some kind. From this standpoint, the dream seemed to appear at what Sharon Parks refers to as the first "moment" (discussed in Chapter Three) in the process of constructing knowledge through imagination: the moment of conscious or unconscious conflict. Sleeping, in this sense, is "the pause" of the second moment, whereas the actual dream itself is the third moment in which the chaos of the conflict is recast in some way. In the fourth moment, some of the releasing of the energy of the dream is making conscious sense of it in its wholeness, including its images and symbols, whereas in the fifth moment, one might literally narrate the significance of the dream perhaps by speaking about it, but more important, in living out the energy of the dream.

Providing Direction

Some dreams seem to provide direction in times of transition. Patricia, a psychology professor in her early forties, described what she referred to as a spiritual dream experience that took place at the time she was going through a divorce from her husband of fifteen years. While she and her partner were no longer living together, they still loved each other and were struggling with how to negotiate aspects of their relationship. It was then that Patricia had a dream where she was hanging by her fingers on a treacherous cliff. To the right she could see the water crashing up against jagged rocks; she couldn't see a way down or back up to safety, and she was sure she would die. She had been at a picnic and could hear friends and family, who sent a little boy over to check on her. Although he couldn't really help her, in the process of his getting her attention, she looked in another direction, and saw that to the left there was a path of sand, and that she could just turn and walk away across the sand.

When she awoke, she felt that the dream had been a gift. It let her know that in spite of the foreboding cliff, with the background support of her friends and family she could look in another direction and walk away in order to move forward to start a new life. The dream helped her make sense of both the divorce and the transition. It helped her repattern her life in a new way. In reflecting back she notes, "During that time period, all my dreams were about walking away; none of them were about staying." This particular dream and the consistent messages and meanings she made of her dreams during that period provided important direction in a time of transition and assured her from a spiritual perspective that this was the right decision to make.

Providing Love and Healing

While some dreams seem to provide direction, others seem to provide healing and reassurance from those who love us. One of my own that was a rather intense spiritual experience that helped me repattern my life comes to mind. It is similar to Patricia's in that it came in the aftermath of the breakup of a thirteen-year relationship, but the dream was so full of images, symbols, and an overwhelming sense of love and care that I will never forget it. The dream came a couple of weeks after the final breakup. It was incredibly sad for both of us to say goodbye to this relationship as we had known it, and for me, to one that I had loved like no other. It was like cutting out part of my soul. I had been grieving a lot off and on, and after two weeks I was tired of my own sense of grief and loss and wondered how much longer I would feel so miserable. I woke up in the middle of the night, cried some more, and tossed and turned until I finally drifted back to sleep. Then my mother, who had passed away about eight months prior, came to me in the dream. I was standing in a doorway. She asked me why I looked so sad and why I wasn't packing for the family trip. I made some vague comment about being upset that she was dead. And she turned and said, "Oh honey, that's not why you're so sad. You and I both know it was time for me to go. You're sad about your breakup, and you're going to be sad for a while still. But in fifty days you really are going to feel better!" And she kissed me on the cheek and touched my face like she used to when I was a little girl, a touch so loving and gentle that I will feel it forever. Then she was gone.

When I awoke up I felt so much better—refreshed and repatterned in a mother's love, feeling my right cheek still tingling in her gentle touch. Of course, not long after I awoke I went to find my calendar to figure out that in fifty days it would be October 26! Although nothing miraculous happened on October 26 that year (1999), I did feel a whole lot better by then, and I went to the movies that night with someone I had recently met; I was ready to move on. And to this day, whenever anyone touches me ever so gently or so lovingly on my cheek, I am reminded of a mother's love and abiding presence that lasts way beyond October 26 of any year. It lasts for all eternity!

Solving a Mystery

Patrick Morton (2000) discusses a very different but very significant type of dream that he had when he was working on his Ph.D. thesis in mathematics. He notes that the dream served as a defining moment in his life, one that was "particularly magical" (p. 70) and in which he understood wholeness in a new way. He had been trying for a full year to solve a particular math problem that was central to his thesis, and he simply kept coming up blank. In the dream he is talking to his thesis advisor and pacing back and forth, when the thesis advisor tells him to use abelian fields. Then the two walk over to a pedestal where there is a spinning mass of energy that turns into a human head, which tells them, "You've found the answer!" When Morton awoke he wrote the dream down and for three days worked on the problem by making use of abelian fields. He explains the three-day aftermath of the dream thus:

> I did not at any point have a conscious understanding of what the dream meant, nor did I by any stretch of the imagination know the answer to my problem, as the dream head claimed, but I had an intense feeling that something was bubbling up inside me. I could feel the energy, like something about to burst forth or waiting to be born, but for three days it just stayed inside. I knew the answer was there and had no idea how to get at it. . . . By the third day I had found the key, which was to look at a certain equation and interpret it in two very different ways. Once I worked out the details it turned out those "abelian fields" the dream mentions did show up in the theorem I proved. (p. 70)

What was significant for Morton was not only the wonder of the dream itself and the ability of the spirit, or his unconscious self, to release the imagination in the "pause" state of sleep and to find incredible creative problem-solving capacities in the resultant dreams and images. What was also significant was that the dream also became a defining moment in how he understands his vocation as a math professor. As he notes, many people, including educators and academics, have similar experiences of the wholeness and unity of things through dreams, in altered states of consciousness, and through the wonder of creative imagination, but most academics rarely talk about these experiences. His current understanding of his vocation is to help his math students release their imagination and creativity to see and experience the wholeness of things in order to engage their own deepest problem-solving capacities. Indeed, this "particularly magical" dream not only affected how he solved this particular mathematical dilemma, but also how he thinks about the world and how this thinking influences his own teaching.

Finding Order in Chaos: Synchronicity

Related to dreams are the uncanny coincidences that happen in many people's lives at various times—the kinds of experiences in which someone who has been on your mind but you haven't spoken to in years suddenly calls you; or when two people have the same or similar dream on the same night; or when you meet someone for the first time who gives you the answer to a question you have been wrestling with when you hadn't even verbally asked. As the adage goes, "When the student is ready, the teacher appears!" Synchronicity, the term Carl Jung used to describe these uncanny and meaningful coincidences, was discussed at great length by Jung (1961) in many of his works. He attributed synchronicity to the collective unconscious and the unity of all things. One famous example of synchronicity that Jung described was of a woman patient he was working with in therapy who he didn't feel was making much progress due to her many rationalizations that he felt were evidence of resistance. He was hoping that something would happen that would move her and their progress together to a different level. Then at one session the woman was relating a dream that she had had the night before about someone who had given her a piece of jewelry, a golden scarab. As the woman was relating the dream, there was something tapping on the window, and Jung got up to see a huge flying insect—he opened the window and caught it as it flew in; it was a golden-green colored scarab beetle. "I handed the beetle to my patient with the words, 'Here is your scarab'" (Jung as cited by Bolen, 1979, p. 15). He reports that this incidence of synchronicity broke through the woman's many rationalizations and from there they made great progress in their work together.

Many of those I interviewed discussed synchronicities that they experienced and described them as among their significant spiritual experiences. Ahmed Hasan described a situation where he had met in passing a young woman. For a moment, he had the flash of a fantasy about what it would be like to be married to her. Aside from their brief meeting, he never saw the woman again. Two and a half years later he was in counseling, discussing very serious problems in his then-current marriage and its difficulties due to his wife's diagnosis as a paranoid schizophrenic and her very erratic behavior with him and their three children. He left the counselor's office trying to determine what to do—whether to stay in the marriage or get a divorce.

> I remember thinking "Dear God, give me a sign about what I'm supposed to do." And I get on the bus, and who gets on two stops later but this woman who I hadn't seen for two and a half years. I remember putting my head down so she wouldn't see me, and I was so shocked, and I thought "this must be a sign."

Ahmed didn't actually speak to this woman that day, but nearly a year later, after he was actually divorced, a friend of his told him that he and his wife would like him to meet someone, and invited them have over for dinner. It turned out to be the same woman Ahmed had seen on the bus, and whom he eventually married. He describes the experience as a significant spiritual experience, one of the most significant in his life. Ahmed is also Muslim, so he speaks about this and other spiritual and synchronistic experiences in specifically religious terms, relating such experiences specifically to God: "One thing I constantly remember in saying prayers, remembering God's Oneness, or the Oneness of his creation, or the Oneness of humanity."

Although most who described synchronistic experiences did not specifically use language referring to God per se, they did refer to how synchronicity and significant dream experiences speak to the Oneness of all creation. And they did report these synchronistic experiences as spiritual experiences.

The Unbroken Circle: Birth, Death, and Close Calls

Among the most commonly cited spiritual experiences of those I interviewed were related to birth, death, and near-death experiences. These experiences spoke to the great miracle of life and its never-ending circle.

The Miracle of Birth

Janine Lu, a Chinese American woman born and raised in Hawaii, describes the conception and birth of her daughter Meena as the single most profound spiritual experience of her life.

> *That's the single most spiritual thing; the very fact that she was conceived; I was over forty, and had gone for years in my marriage without practicing birth control.*

As Janine assumed she would never have children, Meena was a completely unexpected gift. It was not just her conception that was a spiritual experience; it was also in the various experiences that Janine had during a somewhat difficult pregnancy that kept little Meena alive in spite of the threat of significantly premature labor, as well as the wonder of the experiences Janine has had in raising Meena.

Greta Schmidt also describes the significance of her daughter's birth as one of the most profound experiences of her life:

> *The most cosmic spiritual transformative events of my life are strongly related to the body. One was giving birth to my daughter, which was just such a cosmic event. I don't think I've ever, ever experienced such profound COSMIC JUBILATION; it transcended all boundaries!*

This sense of "cosmic jubilation" was not only experienced by the women I interviewed who had given birth, but also by some of the men who witnessed the birth of their children. Jason Dunbar, in reflecting on being present at the birth of his two sons, noted,

> *Those were incredible spiritual experiences that filled me with an incredible sense of wonder and awe—a very humbling experience, because I was witness to an event or act which was just incredibly mysterious—full of mystery and wonder; nothing I could make sense of from the point of view of thinking about it, or analyzing it. It had its own beauty, its own wonder!*

Death

Spiritual experiences surrounding the death of a loved one were cited perhaps the most often as profound and significant spiritual experiences. Anna Adams described a transformed presence of her mother when Anna was traveling home on the train to the funeral.

> *I was watching the telephone poles go by, and a black bird flew past the window and came real close, and in my ear, I heard my mother's voice say "I'm free!" And it was like a major relief because I'd been grieving and crying and as soon as I heard that voice say "I'm free" it was OK. To be totally dependent those last years of her life was just horrific for her. So when I heard that voice say—and you know, it's not that I was thinking it—it was* HER VOICE; *and it came out of nowhere!*

As noted in the last chapter, Anna had emphasized the significance of the ancestral connection throughout our conversation. She went on to describe similar experiences that her own mother had at the time of a death of a loved one.

> *My mother had told me about a similar experience when her mother died. She and her sister were going to visit her mother*

*in the hospital; she was very close to death. They looked up
at her window and her mother was sitting in her window and
she waved at them. And they said, "Oh, she must be better."
So they went up to her room, and she was dead! But both of
them saw her waving in the window. It wasn't like one
of them saw her and the other one didn't, both of them looked
at her. So there's histories of things like that in my family.*

To be sure, experiences surrounding birth and death, where the
great mystery of the Life-force is present in all its fullness, are
extremely spiritual. Of course many only feel the pain of grief and
loss during the time surrounding the death. But some people have
spiritual experiences in the aftermath of dealing with that sense of
grief and loss, as they make meaning of the experience in new ways.
Elise Poitier described the sadness and loss associated with having
a miscarriage. Not only did she have to deal with her own loss as a
mother, but the experience stirred up the complicated difficulties
she had with her own mother. She described a significant spiritual
experience shortly after her miscarriage in going to a meditation
service led by a woman leader of one of the Yoga traditions:

*Well I closed my eyes and everything was silent, and for the
first time there is no internal dialogue. . . . And all of a sudden there's a voice in my head that is not my voice that says,
"Why are you upset with your mother? I am the mother.
Why blame her?" . . . After the program was over, . . .
I went up and when I did this woman said to me "you've
been working very hard" and immediately I broke out into
tears . . . and I was just weeping and weeping and weeping,
and at that moment my life changed.*

Elise then went on to describe how this facilitated some work on
the healing of her relationship with her own mother.

Close Calls

Many of those that I interviewed also reported the significance of accidents and near-death experiences, moments in which they became aware that "we're but moments in eternity" (Terkel, 2001, p. 352), or times when they got more in touch with what their real commitments were. Greta Schmidt, who had been in a very serious car accident in which she had almost died, described how the experience changed how she thinks about her life.

> It somehow stripped away all those layers of illusion and disillusion, and things you make up and rationalizations, and pretenses—they were ALL GONE. And all of a sudden you're THERE, and you're really just THERE, and you look around and realize what a gift it is to be there.

She went on to discuss how she found herself living differently as a result of this very serious accident, following the many months it took to recover. In a similar vein, Aiysha Ali, who was introduced in the first chapter, also discussed the role of a serious car accident in helping her think of her life differently and staying true to what she sees as her life purpose. She noted that she often reflects back on that accident, especially when faced with a major life decision.

Raul Guerrero, a Filipino man in his early fifties, is a sociology and education professor who was granted political asylum in the United States when he fled from the Marcos regime more than twenty years ago. He describes the power of a memory of a close call that helped him redefine and remember his spiritual commitment to social action. A very gentle soul, Raul has always embraced the call of moving from silence to language and action, and was forced to leave the Philippines after being detained and interrogated as a result of being involved in organizing efforts on behalf of the poor and oppressed. His commitment then and now arose out of a spirituality that he describes as "a journey toward wholeness" and explains that "a metaphor of journey is always action." Just as he had done as a very young man in the Philippines, he continued his work of community organizing, and had worked for years on college campuses getting students involved in community action projects concerned with everything from homelessness to domestic violence against women to antiracist work to environmental justice movements. Raul considered this an important part of students' out-of-class education to complement their in-class education of studying social theory and critique. Raul is a pacifist, and his commitment to working for social justice is rooted in his understanding of the Christian social gospel based in Latin American liberation theology, his understanding of who Jesus was as a man of nonviolence, and in the nonviolent action of both Martin Luther King and Gandhi.

Raul described a relatively recent spiritual experience that took place when he brought a group of students to a rally focusing on nonviolent social action. He described listening to a woman give a talk on nonviolence. He explained that she didn't speak English very well and kept touching her forehead trying to remember various English words. All of a sudden a long buried memory came flooding back in the gesture of this woman's touching her forehead:

> *I remembered my own interrogation in the Philippines. I was taken to a detention center and at night a soldier came in with a .45 caliber pistol and was asking me questions, but he said, "but I don't want you to answer the questions until I make the question mark." So he would ask his question, and he would come up, and he would do this question mark on my forehead with the .45 caliber pistol cocked.*

Raul paused, and explained:

> *So it was a memory that really shook me and I started to cry, but it's one of those memories that you can smell the person*

next to you . . . could remember his skin and how his fingers
were on the trigger, and I was just overwhelmed, so it was
that remembering that had been powerful for me.

He explained that what he was doing there with this group of
students was really acting on his commitment to who he is as a spiritual being and as a (nonfundamentalist) Christian and to doing
justice in the world. He was acting just as he had in the Philippines,
in a way that got him into trouble to the point that he found himself gazing down the barrel of a .45 caliber pistol. But he could not
not do this work for justice. This was fundamentally who he was in
all his authenticity.

He went on to talk about the spiritual part of this experience
for him:

> *The spiritual part of that . . . I play with the words the*
> *cross—the sign of the cross—is the sign of the question mark,*
> *so the sign of the cross is like the question mark drawn on my*
> *forehead, and so to me that was that connection—I was in*
> *this journey and there is a journey of justice and I have to*
> *carry this cross, and even now this cross is in my forehead,*
> *this question mark is in my forehead and it will always be*
> *there; I will always remember it.*

In essence, as Raul explained, he could not *not* do his community
work and challenge systems of injustice through nonviolent means.
It might lead him to future signs of crosses and question marks on
his forehead, or gazing down the barrel of a .45. But not to embrace
who he was and what he believed would never let him escape even
bigger questions. Revisiting the memory of this close call was painful
yes, he explained. But in reclaiming this long buried memory, he
felt that he had moved a little further along his journey to wholeness. For him the spiritual was present in the symbols, in the experience, but much more in the journey of embracing the living of life
of reclaiming wholeness.

Many have written about coming to terms with their life purpose in a new way as a result of near-death experiences or an illness that puts them in touch with their mortality. For example, African American feminist writer Audre Lorde (1984), who eventually died of breast cancer, wrote how confronting her own mortality had helped her recognize the importance of breaking silences and moving from silence to language to action. As she wrote, "I was going to die, if not sooner then later, whether or not I had ever spoken myself. My silences had not protected me, and your silences will not necessarily protect you" (p. 41). She calls on her readers and audiences to live their lives as if they were to die the next day, to break those silences and to stand up for what they believe in. Indeed, such encounters with mortality often facilitate the courage to take new action. Former Cherokee chief Wilma Mankiller speaks to this point in reflecting on her involvement in a serious car accident. "The accident in 1979 changed my life. I came very close to death, felt its presence and the alluring call to complete the circle of live." She describes the experience as a spiritual awakening, resulting in her taking on "a very Cherokee approach to life—what our tribal elders call 'being of good mind'" (Mankiller & Wallis, 1993, pp. xxi–xxii). She did indeed find the courage to take new action: she became the first woman chief of the Cherokee nation!

Spiritual Experiences in Meditation and Nature

There is probably nothing that can evoke a sense of the incredible majesty of the universe more than experiences in nature. To be sure, most of the people I talked to about their spiritual experiences discussed significant moments in nature and in meditation. Many, however, struggled with how to capture in words the power of those moments. But they did speak about a majestic sense of awe and mystery at the cosmic wonder of a glorious sunset, or of the ecstasy of watching a moon rise amid a sky glittering with the majesty of a million constellations.

Eco-theologian Thomas Berry (1999) reminds us that such experiences in the natural world put us in touch with the great connection between "the wild and the sacred" (p. 48). He suggests that it is this connection that animates all of life, both our survival efforts and our creativity in our celebration of life. "This [connection] is the same inner tendency that evokes the insight of the poet, the skill of the artist, and the power of the shaman. Something in the wild depths of the human soul finds its fulfillment in the experience of nature" (p. 51). But Berry also warns that if we disrespect this connection we become spiritually impoverished. In speaking about the wholeness of the entire universe he notes: "We see quite clearly that what happens to the nonhuman happens to the human. What happens to the outer world happens to the inner world. If the outer world is diminished in its grandeur then the emotional, imaginative, intellectual, and spiritual life of the human is diminished or extinguished. Without the soaring birds, the great forests, the sounds and coloration of the insects, the free-flowing streams, the flowering fields, the sight of the clouds by day and the stars at night, we become impoverished in all that makes us human" (p. 200).

This sense of wonder and oneness of the universe seems to be what those who regularly engage in meditation practice occasionally encounter in deeply significant spiritual moments. Michael DiMarco, a forty-eight-year-old artist who has been regularly practicing transcendental meditation for more than twenty years, described a meditation experience in which he encountered the universe in a new way:

> One day I was sitting in meditation in the lotus position and I started getting this cramp in my leg. Rather than straighten it out as I ordinarily do, I sat in it for a while, and then the pain started washing away. . . . As it dissipated, it felt like a wave, and as each wave washed over me the pain got less and less. And that wave turned into the creation and destruction

*of the universe—that from moment to moment the universe
was being created and destroyed. And that became my experience: I was being created and destroyed from moment to
moment, on a relative level—that we're here one moment
and then gone the next. In that experience, I couldn't be anything other than what I was created to be, and that I was
being created from moment to moment. So I didn't have to
aspire to anything; I was already it. And then from that experience, I started seeing the universe, and then I saw the universe inside me . . . and I realized that everything of the
universe is us: we are the universe and the universe is us.*

To some extent Michael was speaking metaphorically about the
interconnection of all things. Although he doesn't live in that
experience of being at one with the universe all the time, he notes
that it is a spiritual experience that he often goes back to, and its
aftermath affects the way that he lives and thinks about his life. In
that experience more than fifteen years ago, it seems that he understood something about his higher identity and his interconnection
with everything. He explained with an example: "I realized I didn't
have to struggle so much anymore: to be my mother's son, my
father's son; to be an artist; to be Michael DiMarco, because
Michael DiMarco was. He *is.* So don't worry about it so much." As
he noted, it is of course impossible to stay in that space, but he
often goes back to it:

*I forget that I don't have to struggle. But I remember too!
And as time moves on I struggle less. . . . I kind of exist along
side my relativeness. I kind of have an absolute Michael and
a relative Michael. Sometimes the relative Michael is bigger,
and sometimes the cosmic Michael is bigger.*

The relative Michael is the very human Michael who gets caught
up in the worries of life; the absolute-cosmic Michael is the one that
is his higher self at one with the universe. In that at-one-ness, when

the more cosmic Michael is operating, he feels that he potentially has access to everything that he needs to know.

> *The fact that I can know anything I want to know is also there too. And I use that in my work: that we really know everything. We just don't know we know everything. But if you ask the right question and you know how to listen to the answer, then the information comes. And I forget that too.*

Michael went on to describe specific experiences in which he was able to access some forms of knowledge by getting himself in a meditative space wherein he was able to center more on the sense of at-one-ness of the universe. He continues his daily practice of meditation because he feels that it is only through regular practice that he can live in the present moment, continue to develop a sense of mindfulness, and try to bring greater unity between the "relative Michael" and the "cosmic Michael." Indeed, many have written about the importance of regular meditation practice in order to be able to access that sense of oneness. Those who do it regularly seem to occasionally experience, in the center of their being on a soul level, the lived insight so well stated by Thomas Berry (1999): "The universe carries in itself the norm of authenticity of every spiritual as well as every physical activity within it. The spiritual and the physical are two dimensions of the single reality that is the universe itself" (pp. 49–50). It seems that people's most significant spiritual experiences are when they are able to catch a glimpse and live for a moment inside of that great reality.

Summary and Brief Thoughts for Practice

In this chapter I have tried to lay a foundation for how spirituality might relate to the development of culturally relevant education by exploring some of the varieties of spiritual experience and by expanding on the role of imagination in spiritual knowledge construction processes discussed in Chapter Three.

Significant spiritual experiences are those that seem to get at the interconnectedness of all things. They seem to happen especially when the energy of the Life-force is most obvious, as in birth, death, and near-death experiences; at times of transition in dreams and synchronistic experiences; or at significant moments in nature and meditation. These types of experiences are common to all cultures and are part of all human experience. In that sense and on the surface, they do not seem to be obviously related to culture. But the meaning of those experiences is not only valued differently by different cultural communities, it is also manifested and given further expression symbolically differently in different cultures—in art, music, or ritual—expressions that are obviously cultural and sometimes religious as well.

Although all learning might involve imagination or the symbolic domain on some level, as noted in the last chapter, all forms of imagination are not necessarily "spiritual experiences" for people. Furthermore, it would probably be only in quite specific contexts that one would discuss significant spiritual experiences directly. In those contexts, it might be possible to specifically encourage the sharing of significant spiritual experiences that seemed to get at the wholeness of life in a new way and to explore both its particular cultural manifestations and the universal interconnectedness of all life in those moments. In this way participants might come to a new understanding of the unity within the diversity, of the specifically cultural, and the interconnected wholeness that perhaps is universal. As my colleague Derise Tolliver (in Tisdell, Tolliver, & Villa, 2001) notes, such an activity might move beyond the strictly rational view of the world apparent in Descartes' phrase, "I think; therefore I am," to the wisdom of the wholeness and interconnectedness of all of life more apparent in the African proverb, "I am because we are; we are, therefore I am."

Finally, it is always helpful to think about one's own experience related to the phenomenon under discussion. I have been reminded of my own experiences of wholeness, and inspired by the rich and generous sharing of significant spiritual experiences of those I interviewed. These have helped me think about and share, not only their stories, but some of these rich, "shimmering moments" of my own. I hope sharing some of these stories has helped you think of some "shimmering moments" in your own life, the times when something stopped you in your tracks as if to say, "Listen! This will heal you!" and how they connect with and were given further meaning in your own cultural context. And I hope they help you further use your imagination about new ways of drawing on these moments to engage in culturally relevant education.

Part II

Claiming a Sacred Face
Identity and Spiritual Development

*What a long time it can take to become the person one has always
been! How often in the process we mask ourselves in faces that are
not our own. How much dissolving and shaking of ego we must
endure before we discover our deep identity—the true self within
every human being that is the seed of authentic vocation.*

P. Palmer (2000, p. 9)

Discovering one's deepest identity that Palmer speaks of is a
process of unmasking the faces not our own. For many of us,
it is also a spiritual process connected to aspects of our being in all
its gendered and cultured dimensions. So often we wear faces that
others have taught us to wear, and we play roles based on gender,
culture, birth order, and a host of other factors that have been
defined by others—parents, teachers, institutional religions, or the
dominant culture. Unmasking these many dimensions and reclaiming who we are on our own terms is, according to Latino writer
David Abalos (1998), part of claiming our sacred face. Abalos also
suggests that this process of claiming our sacred face is intimately
connected to understanding and claiming our personal, historical,
and political faces and is part of reclaiming our cultural identity.

Part Two focuses on claiming a sacred face, or the ongoing development of identity related to spiritual development in a culture
and gendered context. Part One laid the groundwork for discussing

the interplay of spirituality and culture and the specific spiritual experiences that people have had at *particular moments in time*. Part Two examines what those moments and other spiritual experiences suggest for spiritual development in a cultural and gendered context, specifically as *change over time*.

Chapter Five sets the context by providing an overview of spiritual development as *change over time* by using the metaphor of the great spiral to understand spiritual development as a process of moving forward and spiraling back, a process that is also related to gender and culture. Chapter Six takes a more narrative approach to spiritual development and focuses more specifically on the contextual dimensions of culture and gender that are always a part of anyone's story of spiritual development. Chapter Seven provides a more in-depth examination of the idea of claiming a sacred face by looking at the role of spirituality in claiming a positive cultural identity. Finally, Chapter Eight examines the complexity of intersecting identity and its role in crossing cultural borders to further one's spiritual development.

We study spiritual development or any aspect of the ongoing identity development of adults as change over time not simply to be informed about developmental theory. We do it because it has relevance not only to our work with adult learners, but also to our own lives as developing adults living and working in the world. It has relevance for working in the present moment as the "seed of authentic vocation" (Palmer, 2000, p. 9) continues to unfold in our own lives. In my own classes and workshops with adult learners, I often begin by asking them to think about or dialogue with another person about the following questions:

1. How has your own spirituality changed and developed over time?

2. How does it relate to your childhood religious tradition (if you grew up in one)?

3. In what ways is it connected to your gender, race, ethnicity, or cultural background?

4. What important historical events affected your development overall?

5. What are sacred or important symbols for you, and how did they come to be sacred for you? Do any of these sacred images or symbols relate to your cultural background?

6. How do you seek inspiration, and how has this developed over time?

7. When do you feel most alive and most authentic? And what, if anything, does this have to do with your current spirituality?

These questions are the focus of Part Two. Keeping these questions in mind, and how your own answers to them might be similar to or different from those of the adult learners with whom you work, might offer a clue as to how you might draw on what follows to develop culturally relevant approaches to adult and higher education.

5

The Great Spiral

*Spiritual Development as a
Process of Moving Forward
and Spiraling Back*

The great spiral, a theme alluded to in Part One, is perhaps a
metaphor for development. But it is more than metaphor. As
many scientists have noted, the spiral is a repeating pattern in the
universe itself. From the spiral shape of many a galaxy (including
our own) to the spiral of the chambered nautilus to the double helix
of DNA (a double spiral that constitutes life itself), the spiral man-
ifests itself repeatedly in physical ways in the natural world. As
many have noted (Bateson, 1995; Graves as cited by Wilber, 2000a;
Kegan, 1982; Wilber, 2000a), it is perhaps an apt metaphor for
understanding development.

In our attempts to understand and make sense of our lives and in
the ongoing development of identity, we often spiral back. Yet we
don't *simply* spiral back; we also *move forward*. And we always do so
in a cultured and gendered context. We stand in the center of the
great spiral in the present moment. We look back to make sense of
our lives *now*, hoping that the making sense of the *now* will yield a
hopeful or fulfilling future. The perspective of the present moment
is central here. It reminds me of a favorite expression used by a Jesuit
professor of a year-long course on Zen Buddhism I took nearly fifteen
years ago. Amid explaining central elements of Zen, such as the concepts of mindfulness and the Eight-Fold Path, and encouraging us
in the meditation practice of *zazen*, he would regularly slip in the
following reminder: "The present moment is pregnant with God."

The simple but profound singular import of these words, spoken in nearly every class, are forever etched on my mind and are relevant to our discussion here on spiritual development, whether one can relate to the pregnancy metaphor or whether one is a theist or an atheist. So often we miss the wonder of the present moment. So often we're lost in the memory of the past or worrying about the future. This is one of the most important things I learned from the study of Zen and the practice of meditation and mindfulness: an emphasis on being in the present moment.

A basic premise of this chapter is that spiritual development is a process of standing in the present moment and spiraling back to explore significant events and spiritual experiences that shaped both one's spiritual journey and life journey and identity thus far in order to move forward to the future. Part of what spiritual development is about is the ongoing development of identity. This, of course, always happens over time, and takes place in a culture and gendered context. But focusing specifically on *change over time* raises the questions of whether spiritual development unfolds in stages and what its relationship is to other aspects or "lines" of development, such as cognitive development, moral development, or cultural identity development. Merriam and Caffarella (1999) and Clark and Caffarella (1999) have recently discussed the need for more integrative perspectives that connect the threads of these various lines of adult development. Further, they have pointed out the need for greater attention to how the sociocultural context informs development overall.

How one views spiritual development, and whether there are identifiable stages to it, depends in part on how one defines spirituality. In reviewing various theorists' explanations of it from both the East and the West, Ken Wilber (2000b) notes that there are approximately five ways in which spiritual development has been discussed, each of which has different assumptions of what spirituality is and how it affects development overall (Wilber, 2000b, p. 129). These are that spirituality is:

1. The highest of any of the developmental lines; or
2. The sum total of the highest levels of all the developmental lines combined, such as moral development, cognitive development, and so on.
3. Is its own developmental line.
4. Is an attitude of openness at any stage.
5. Is about peak experiences, not stages.

Although Wilber himself takes a more integrative approach, by "developmental lines" he is referring to the assumption made by many theorists that various aspects of development (such as cognitive, moral, psychosocial) unfold in a sequence of stages. He is posing the question of whether or not spiritual development is itself a separate developmental line that can be separated from other developmental lines. I would suggest that it is of course impossible to *completely* separate out one aspect of development from another, since a human being always works as an integrated whole. But it is possible to focus on integration. Perhaps spiritual development is itself that integration. Yet it is always informed by the sociocultural context in which it takes place, a point explored in detail in the next two chapters.

The focus in this chapter is on the spiral shape of spiritual development as a process of moving forward and spiraling back. This is where I will begin. Next I consider how this spiral process of spiritual development propels us to the future in attempting to live true to our life purpose.

The Spiral Shape of Spiritual Development

Many adult development authors and theorists have discussed various life phases or stages of development and have suggested, either overtly or implicitly, that the process of development is probably more spiral-shaped than a sequence of linear and clearly defined stages or phases. In Robert Kegan's (1982, 1994) discussion of the evolving self, he describes five "orders of consciousness" in constructing new knowledge of the self that result in more complex constructions of meaning based on interaction with other people and the environment. Kegan (1994) suggests as one moves through these "orders of consciousness" as a result of such new experiences, there is a "personal unfolding of ways of organizing experience that are not simply replaced as we grow but subsumed into more complex systems of mind" (p. 9). Implicit in this statement of Kegan's discussion of development overall (as opposed to spiritual development in particular) is the assumption that one does indeed spiral back and make new meaning of old experience.

Mary Catherine Bateson (1995) also discusses the process of adult development and learning as a spiral process. In discussing "spiral learning," she suggests that we often go back and make new meaning of old events, symbols, and experiences. What may have once been peripheral to those experiences may become an important meaning-making experience at a later date through the process of "spiral learning." Just as events and experiences of the past can be infused and remapped with new meaning, so too can symbols and music. As noted in Chapter Three, this is partly why the symbols of religion and the culture that we grew up with are forever etched on our often unconscious memory, both laden with the old meaning and refreshed and with new meaning as we continuously spiral back.

Although neither Kegan nor Bateson discuss spiritual development specifically, they both discuss the spiral learning that comes with all aspects of experience that results in further development. As noted above, Ken Wilber (2000a) does discuss spiritual development in particular, but he discusses it from a more integrative perspective and does not separate it from other aspects of development. Further, although he refers to "stages," he actually discusses spiritual development as a spiral process. Following the pioneering work of Clare Graves and the more recent work of Beck and Cowan (1995) on "spiral dynamics," as well as the work of many developmental theorists, Wilber ultimately argues that there are eight general stages to our development that include the spiritual, but he also makes use of a more fluid definition of stages as more spiral-like. These stages "are not rigid levels but flowing waves, with much overlap and interweaving, resulting in a meshwork or dynamic spiral of consciousness unfolding" (p. 7). Each stage includes and expands on the development of earlier stages.

Most developmental theorists, including Wilber, who write about spiritual development as change over time do in fact connect it with other aspects of development. Some focus on what seems to be happening at particular points in the life cycle. For example, Parks' (2000) focus is on the spiritual development of young adults, whereas Loder (1998) discusses it from a theological perspective in adolescence, young adulthood, the middle years, and after age sixty-five. Borysenko (1999) discusses women's spiritual development more from the perspective of salient themes, such as a sense of mystery, spiritual identity and healing, and the role of ritual and prayer. As noted earlier, whether or not spirituality unfolds in a series of stages is a matter of some debate, but it is James Fowler's (1981) six-stage theory of faith development that is most often sighted in considerations of spiritual development. Because there are elements of Fowler's theory that are relevant to our discussion here, I will briefly summarize his theory and then examine how it fits into consideration of spirituality as a spiral process of moving forward and spiraling back.

Fowler's Theory of Faith Development

James Fowler (1981, 2000) developed his six-stage theory of faith development from studying a sample of 359 people (interviewed in the late 1970s and early 1980s), of whom 97 percent were white and identified with the Judeo-Christian faith traditions. Although he offers a broader, more inclusive definition of "faith" as related to meaning-making *beyond* religious tradition, his theory is actually based on a sample whose "faith" is deeply informed by a specific religious tradition. Nevertheless, his work offers some important insight for spiritual development. Although he draws heavily on Kohlberg's and Piaget's theories of moral and cognitive development, he notes their overreliance on rationality in cognitive and moral development, and he brings to the fore the role of image and symbol and the unconscious in knowledge construction processes.

Briefly, Fowler's (1981) faith development stages are as follows: (1) intuitive projective faith, (2) mythic–literal faith, (3) synthetic-conventional faith, (4) individuative-reflective faith, (5) conjunctive faith, and (6) universalizing faith. The first two of these stages relate only to childhood so will be given no further consideration here. But in that the last four are related to spiritual development over the course of adult life, some explanation here is in order.

Fowler suggests that the third stage, synthetic-conventional faith, emerges in early adolescence. In this sense, *synthetic* means pulling together pieces and synthesizing one's identity into a coherent whole. But this faith identity is typically conventional in that it is developed in light of the approval of significant others and authorities. In essence, in this stage, one's beliefs and values as passed on through parents and religious authorities are integrated into a coherent whole but are rather unexamined and accepted with little question. Although some adults stay in this stage, many move on to the next stage, individuative-reflective faith, in early adulthood. In this fourth stage, life circumstances present dilemmas that make it necessary for adults to "examine and make critical choices about the defining elements of their identity and faith" (Fowler, 2000, p. 49). Roles and relationships as defined by others are called into question in favor of determining one's own belief and value system. This is where many later adolescents and young adults question and often move away from their childhood religious tradition.

In the next stage, conjunctive faith, which Fowler suggests often emerges at midlife, adults are able to hold the tension of opposites. In addition to being critically reflective, those in this stage are sure enough of their own belief system that they are able to hold as valuable the truths of different traditions and communities—in essence these ideas become "conjoined" with their own. There is an ability to deal with paradox and to be able to resolve the tension of accepting and seeing as valid many different points of view while maintaining one's own more expanded position. Fowler's final faith development stage, universalizing faith, is a bit undefined; only one person in his own sample was described as being in this stage, and he also uses Gandhi as representative of someone in this stage (Courtenay, 1994). But Fowler notes that those in this stage move beyond the self to a universalizing concern for all of humanity and a realization that all are one in God or a higher power.

Fowler's stages of faith development offer us some insight into spiritual development but have some limitations. Indeed, there are many people who are probably representative of these stages as he has defined them. But any aspect of human development is probably not as linear as what Fowler (or others) have defined. For example, some might exhibit most of the characteristics of the conjunctive faith stage but in times of crisis or threat exhibit elements of earlier stages. Further, many of us for various reasons seem to need to spiral back for a time, and revisit elements of our lives at earlier stages. This is why I believe development is more spiral-shaped than it is linear. But despite some limitations of Fowler's study, it contributes to our understanding of how people construct knowledge through image and symbol, an area that has been ignored by most development and learning theorists. All the educators that I interviewed were probably at least at Fowler's conjunctive faith stage in that they were able to deal with paradox and the tension of accepting and seeing as valid many different points of view and spiritual paths, while being true to what they saw as their own spiritual path. Their development seemed to be an ongoing process of moving forward and spiraling back at different times in their adult life, beginning with their later adolescence and early adulthood.

Questioning and Moving Away

Late adolescence and early adulthood are periods of experimentation, questioning, and for some a period of outright rebellion (Erikson, 1980; Loder, 1998; Perry, 1970; Parks, 2000). These aspects of young adulthood are important for identity development. Further, when one is confronted with new ideas and ways of thinking about the world, through travel, higher education, involvement in social or political movements, or interaction with people who are different, one is likely to rethink some of one's own previously held assumptions and ideas. This is true at any stage of adult development. But it is especially true in early adulthood, when many are first exposed to new ideas and ways of viewing the world, perhaps because this is the first time they have been away from their family or culture of origin. Young adulthood is a time of big questions and of trying to develop worthy dreams (Parks, 2000). Examining one's values, what one has been taught as a child, and having new experiences are part of the process of developing "worthy dreams." Further, questioning one's childhood faith or what one has learned about the nature of spirituality is essential for most young adults, for as Parks (2000) notes, "for faith to become mature it must doubt itself" (p. 19). Otherwise one is likely to be simply parroting back what one has been taught, or perhaps living someone else's worthy dream. In Fowler's terms, this is when many young adults are in the process of moving from the synthetic-conventional faith and into the more individuative-reflective faith stage.

This process of questioning the way one was socialized around religious, cultural, or spiritual issues can take different forms. I had many serious questions around religion and spirituality during my college years. As I discussed in the first chapter, I wasn't sure that I "bought" any of the Catholicism of my youth. The way I dealt with these questions was to get more involved in the community, take classes, and really study the religion in which I was socialized. In short, as a young adult, I was able to continue my own spiritual

development from within the tradition itself, though there were significant places where my own beliefs were in conflict with official
Catholicism.

Many adults follow a similar path. They may engage in serious
questions or have serious disagreements with their religious tradition in young adulthood and throughout their lives but may remain
committed to the religious community in which they grew up,
though they may not be in agreement with all aspects of its doctrine. Aiysha Ali, for example, has remained strongly identified with
Islam throughout her life, though she certainly questioned aspects
of it, and always places various passages from the Qu'ran in context.
In a similar vein, Chris Larson, a music professor in his early thir-
ties, grew up Mormon in Salt Lake City. Although he went through
a period of questioning in his early young adulthood, he had significant spiritual experiences within the context of questioning his
faith that helped him confirm his commitment to the traditions of
the Church of Jesus Christ of the Latter-Day Saints. Chris's questioning didn't result in a complete move away from the faith of his
childhood, but he did feel a need to move away from being
immersed in a nearly totally Mormon community of Salt Lake City.
Thus his was a move away from living in a monocultural setting to
a more culturally and religiously pluralistic environment. He values
the cultural and spiritual insights gained from interacting in a
racially, culturally, and religiously diverse community.

Unlike Chris Larson and Aiysha Ali, many people deal with
pursuing these questions about spirituality and meaning by moving
away from their childhood religious tradition, either temporarily or
permanently. Some simply drift away in their early adulthood
or later because they are more concerned about other things that
seem more pressing to their development, such as launching their
careers or developing long-term intimate relationships. Marcus
Washington, whose childhood and adolescent social life centered
had around events in the African Methodist Episcopal (AME)
Church, in reflecting on his early adulthood noted:

> *I was going to carve out my own identity. I wanted to do things*
> *my way, so there were years where I just didn't go to Church.*
> *I broke away from it; I wasn't interested in it; I didn't think*
> *about it.*

For a period of time, he simply drifted away.

Still others were much more intentional in specifically moving away from the religion of their childhood, and did so for very thought out reasons, because the places of disagreement were simply too great. As Wuthnow (1999) and Parks (2000) note, these specific points of departure may be either temporary or permanent. Nancy Epstein grew up both religiously and culturally Jewish but actively and intentionally left much of her Judaism behind in her young adulthood. Her discontent with Judaism was mounting during her adolescence. Her "final" break with Judaism came as an early young adult, at the time shortly after her father died. At Yom Kippur that year she attended services, hoping to find some peace about her father's death, but found herself agitated with the rabbi instead. "That was it. That was the end of it; I couldn't get any solace. That was when I left, and I've never gone back," she noted. More recently however, in dealing with the dying process of her mother, she has found some comfort in the Jewish mystical tradition of the Kabbalah.

While Nancy Epstein couldn't find much personal meaning in her Judaism, others found that their own developing personal beliefs were too much at odds with the traditions of their childhood. This was the case for the gay and lesbian participants who grew up in fundamentalist Christian church. As they became more sure of their sexual orientation and were convinced through their own spiritual search that they needed be true to this aspect of their identity, they found themselves at odds with their own childhood traditions and sought spiritual support elsewhere. As I discuss in greater depth in the next chapter, in a similar vein many women have found the patriarchal aspects of their childhood religious traditions incompatible with their own emerging spiritual beliefs, and so they move away either temporarily or permanently to forge an adult spirituality that is more meaningful and affirming to them as women. Greta Schmidt also talked about her move away as being very intentional and related to the development of her political and social consciousness:

> This was the '60s, and I renounced my Catholicism and became officially an atheist. It was like a liberation. At first I thought, "I am going to die in hell," and then I became interested in all the events that were going on . . . '60s stuff was happening and it was very political. This was the beginning of my Marxist phase, not very spiritual.

Like Greta, several participants referred to going through an atheist phase as part of their spiritual development, but a phase that didn't last forever. Still others never went through an "atheist phase" but intentionally left the religious traditions of their childhood in order to search out other traditions, because something was just missing in their childhood religious traditions and it didn't resonate with them. For example, Ahmed Hasan is an African American who grew up in a largely white Episcopalian church and community. He noted that his leaving was also more intentional, primarily because the religion of his youth simply didn't have much meaning for him, spiritually or culturally. As a college student in the early 1970s, he went on a spiritual search and explored a variety of spiritual traditions, including various black Christian traditions, Buddhism, other Eastern traditions, and the martial arts. Although he resonated with many of the Eastern philosophies, he eventually got involved with the Nation of Islam because it spoke both to his spirituality and to his cultural identity, as he was in search of a spirituality that would also respond to his social justice concerns. The Nation of Islam was a much better fit for these reasons. While his spirituality has developed over time and he has come to embrace a more traditional view of Islam, Ahmed remains committed to Islam, as we saw in the last chapter.

Spiraling Back

Even though most adults as they develop either move away or question their childhood religious tradition (if they grew up in one), nearly all who believe spirituality is important to them spiral back to "re-member" the life-enhancing elements of their religious tradition and their culture of origin while developing a more meaningful adult spirituality (Tolliver in Tisdell, Tolliver, & Villa, 2001). In Fowler's terms, this might also be a part of being able to deal with paradox and the tension of opposites that is typical of the conjunctive faith stages and beyond. Part of "re-membering" what was important from one's childhood traditions is probably part of that process of spiritual development. In this sense "re-membering" is different than simply remembering, and connotes a reevaluation process, a reworking of such childhood symbols and traditions and a reshaping to be more relevant to an adult spirituality. Frederich Buechner, in considering how memory works in relationship to spiritual development, notes: "[Memory is] more than a looking back to a time that is no longer; it is a looking out into another kind of time altogether where everything that ever was continues not just to be, but to grow and change with the life that is in it still" (as cited by Wuthnow, 1999, p. 141).

As most adults reflect on their religious and spiritual background, they reflect on elements of their past that still have life in them. This reclaiming and "re-membering" earlier aspects of one's foundational spirituality seems to be a pattern both among adults like Anna Adams, whom we met in Chapter Three, who place a high emphasis on spirituality but do not formally associate with any organized religion per se, and those like Hannah Adanah, who now very strongly identify with an organized religion or community of faith. Hannah went through a divorce in her late twenties, which prompted a spiritual search and a reclaiming of her Judaism, and eventually a strong formal personal and professional relationship with Reform Judaism and many Jewish organizations in the United States. Like Hannah, Marcus Washington returned to the African Methodist Episcopal Church because, as he says, there was "a part of me that was missing." And as Cimino (2001) notes in his study of Catholics, Protestants, and Jews, many who left their childhood traditions have returned and found a renewed nurturing spirituality through movements based on the Taizé music and prayer communities, the Call to Action community that blends social justice work with a Christian emancipatory spirituality, the Jewish renewal, or other religiously affiliated movements that attempt specifically to nurture its members' spiritual development.

Even those who never really return to their childhood religious traditions spiral back at times in their own spiritual development. Although neither Julia Gutierrez nor Greta Schmidt have any formal association with the Catholicism of their youth, both of them have reclaimed images and metaphors from their religious upbringing that continue to be important to them. Greta discusses the significance of the metaphor of resurrection to her current spirituality and worldview. In reflecting back, she notes,

> I just LOVED Easter. I think that has really profoundly affected me. That Easter, there's always some resurrection. You go to hell, you die and you're really at the bottom of mystery, but then you get resurrected. Often I think about that when I'm in bad shape, that resurrection.

Thus although Greta has no desire to reconnect with the Catholic Church, this concept of *resurrection* or new life after a dark night of the soul continues to be an important spiritual concept. Julia discussed the importance of La Virgen de Guadalupe to her current spirituality, though as noted in the last chapter, Julia has reframed *La Virgen* as a feminist activist liberator based partly in Catholicism and partly in the Aztec goddess traditions. This image grew and changed, as Buechner notes, with the life that is in it still, and with

Julia's life as a Chicana and an educator for social justice, rooted in her own particular cultural identity.

Even those who do not grow up in a specific religious tradition seem to spiral back to significant childhood experiences that were foundational for their current spirituality. For example, Lisa Riddle, a white woman in her early forties whom we met in the first chapter, a singer, songwriter, and workshop leader who grew up in Alaska, notes the continued significance of the natural world and the wilderness in relationship to her adult spirituality in having grown up "in the temple of the great outdoors." Lisa also discussed the significance of growing up and working with and alongside Alaska Native communities and the impact that it continues to have on her current spirituality. For Lisa, spirituality is partly about catching a glimpse of the unity of all things. She reflected back to describe one important spiritual experience that she had in her late adolescence that brought together a sense of at-one-ness in the context of her close relationship with Alaska Native communities. She describes watching a two-year old do the Raven dance:

> And she GOT IT. She WAS Raven, and that's what the dance was teaching—sort of a mystical spirituality where you ARE coyote or you ARE whatever this is, and it transforms the way you are—your consciousness is different. And it was a WONDERFUL moment, seeing this little tiny being who was already there.

Reflecting back on the sense of the at-one-ness of the embodiment of Raven in the dance of the two-year-old was key for Lisa. It is a memory that is still very alive for her. So although Lisa was not socialized in a religious tradition per se, the importance of wilderness and her connection to indigenous cultures has been extremely formative to her adult spirituality, and obviously has some connections to the culture in which she grew up.

There is both a cultural and a spiritual energy to this kind of spiraling back. It seems that if spirituality is important to a given individual, whether one grows up and is socialized in a religious tradition or not, there is a tendency to spiral back and to "re-member" a given aspect of one's childhood religion or significant earlier spirituality and to allow it, as Buechner says, "to grow and change with the life that is in it still." Furthermore, as we have seen, connections to what is most alive for people are often (though not always) related to their cultural background.

This tendency to "re-member" and reclaim what has life from childhood traditions or cultural backgrounds is not to suggest that adults, in fashioning an adult spirituality, do not also develop new aspects of their spirituality as they have new experiences, encounter new traditions and ideas, and have new life experiences. Indeed, some, such as Ahmed Hasan, have moved toward other spiritual traditions in order to grow and develop, either as a young adult or later in middle adulthood. Sometimes a life crisis prompts a spiritual search, as a result of anything from alcoholism or drug abuse to overwork, a health crisis, or a divorce. Maureen Nelson, a professor in her mid-fifties, grew up Methodist and is now also involved with a Yoga community. She reported that she needed to find a way to experience a deeper form of meditation that she didn't find in her Methodist background. But Maureen notes that her Methodist background and her involvement with the Southern Christian Leadership Conference in the sixties as a young adult was foundational to her current work and spirituality. "It was from this crucible of spirituality and social action that my own sense of identity and core beliefs were formed," she said. Thus, it seems that we move forward partly by "re-membering" the life that is still in foundational spiritual experiences, at the same time that we develop new insights from encounters with other spiritual traditions.

Moving Forward to the Future: Balancing Inner Reflection and Outer Action

So what does understanding of spiritual development as a spiral process have to do with standing in the present moment and moving forward to the future? As noted, it seems that for those who value spirituality, spiritual development is strongly related to claiming of a more authentic identity. It is also about the search for wholeness and integration. This is why I would suggest that spiritual development is about the integration not only of the developmental lines of our lives, as Ken Wilber (2000b) suggests, but also of the wholeness of our lives. Part of that integration and search for wholeness appears to be about being able to live with the integration and the paradox of the tension of opposites, which adults seem to be able to do more successfully in midlife and beyond (Loder, 1998), a point that I will return to in the next chapter. For those I interviewed, the integration was also about trying to live true to one's life purpose as one understands that life purpose on a daily basis. It is by finding the ability to stand in that present moment that we are paradoxically able to live more authentically in a way that propels us to the future. For nearly all I spoke with, this required attempting to embrace spirituality as a way of life that requires inner reflection and outer action.

Trying to live out an ethic of life that is consistent with how one sees one's life purpose in light of one's spiritual development isn't easy. Jason Dunlap, a professor in his early fifties, describes some of the work of integration in his own life as being committed to doing what he refers to as *soulwork*. "Soulwork for me is a matter of coming to grips with those aspects of myself, the sort of shadow parts that I'm not well in touch with, but I tend to act out in relations with others." His commitment to doing soulwork is partly so he doesn't project these "shadow parts" onto others, in his classes or in other aspects of his life. There is an energy both inward, in exploring the "shadow parts," and an energy outward, "in relations with others," in his commitment to soulwork. This balancing of energy both inward and outward appears to be an important component to the dynamic of spiritual development. For Jason Dunlap, this *soulwork* is a way of life that requires a balance between inner reflection and outer action.

Matthew Fox (1996) discusses the connection between spirituality as "inner work" and the revisioning of our work in the world as "outer work," and the importance of ritual and celebration in the creation of a new cosmology as the great paradigm shift of our time. Many of those I interviewed seemed to be living in the midst of that paradigm shift in their own lives. They valued inner reflective meditative work in order to find the courage to embrace the shadows (in Jason Dunbar's terms) and to connect with their center, or what was referred to as the Life-force, God, the Realm of Mystery, or the divine spirit. But this inner work also pulled them out of themselves toward others and helped them do their outer, community work from a more centered perspective.

Greta Schmidt spoke specifically to the importance of her spirituality to her teaching and community work, and how this inner work and outer work connect. There is an "ethical underpinning" to why she values spiritual practice:

> One of the things I've learned over the years is that if you practice a certain way it's like you become ONE—you don't have the mind-body split anymore; there's kind of a sense of oneness; and the sense of oneness for me translates into, or is strongly related to, in the world. Everybody is separated, split, fragmented, except in bits and pieces. [The point is] to try to translate a sense of oneness—to live that out when you're not in a meditative state.

Similarly, Nancy Epstein, who practices primarily in one of the Yoga traditions, talked about the importance of meditation to her work in the world as a university faculty member and former department chair. She talked specifically about the role of Japa, the repetition of the mantra om namaha shivaya, which in Nancy's words means, "I honor the God within me, or I honor my higher self." She explained how regularly practicing meditation that includes Japa affects her practice: "I can be in a meeting, especially when I was department chair. I could be with a faculty member who was in my face and angry. Before I would always interrupt or say something that would maybe escalate the conversation." But since regularly practicing meditation for the past seven years, she notes that in similar situations, "I would silently do Japa, or repetition of the mantra, and it would change the interaction."

What both Nancy and Greta are suggesting is that the regular practice of meditation helps them center and come to a work space with a greater sense of "at-one-ness," which affects their interactions with people both in their workplace and in all aspects of their lives. They were less likely to become defensive, and more likely to be able to facilitate a positive sense of community when operating from a more centered space. Although nearly everyone values this sort of inner work that affects one's outer work in theory, trying to live this way in practice is always a struggle. Most of those I interviewed emphasized that ideally it requires a way of life, and generally they found the outer work easier than the inner work. This of course is partly because of the great pressure in North American culture to spend a lot of time "working" for productivity. But outer work based on spirituality is not about productivity. It is about an approach to life that integrates spirituality, work, living, loving, learning, and social activism. According to many I interviewed, this requires regular practice of meditation or centering, because practice cultivates an attitude that affects all of life. In drawing on the analogy to her work as an educator and teacher in a community college setting, Shirley Johnston explained that her spirituality permeates everything, "like I will keep going to work because this is the best place for me to be teaching, but I'm teaching whether I'm at [the community college] or not."

Embracing the inner work of spirituality at midlife seems to have the paradoxical effect of moving many people outward to work in the world. But working with communities around social justice issues grounded in a spiritual perspective and one's own cultural identity seems also to have the paradoxical effect of calling one back inward and developing more of a global consciousness beyond one's self. Julia Gutierrez spoke to this point:

> *It's bigger than just being Chicana. I'm also a member of a global community—it encompasses more. For me, working for social justice isn't just done five days a week; it's in every part of my life . . . it's a way of living. I call it spirituality.*

The integration of the tension of opposites—such as the tension of the inner work of self exploration and the outer work of building community from a spiritual perspective, and bringing all aspects of one's identity into a coherent and consistent whole—is a life-long process. Being able to do that more successfully at times and to live more for what seems to be most important may be a part of midlife generativity. It seems that when these components are most balanced that there is a greater sense of at-one-ness, which Greta spoke about, that connects inner work and outer work. As Matthew Fox (1996) suggests, learning to live in that place and in that balance is perhaps the great paradigm shift of our time.

Summary and Brief Thoughts for Practice

This chapter has focused on spiritual development as *change over time*, largely from the perspective that spiritual development is the integration of the developmental lines and connects to cognitive development, moral development, and cultural and gender identity development. The spiral shape of spiritual development as an ongoing process of moving forward and spiraling back was the centerpiece of this chapter. In order to develop a more authentic identity that is also grounded in one's spirituality, most adults need to move away or deeply question their childhood religious tradition (if they grew up in one) as they are exposed to new ways of thinking about spirituality and new ideas about the world that also develop their critical thinking skills. Typically this moving away and questioning happens in early adulthood. Some move away and never return, while others can pursue these questions from within their religious traditions. Among those who come to value spirituality, some return to the religious traditions of their childhood, while others pursue another spiritual path, and still others develop a more eclectic spirituality. But it seems that nearly all who come to value spirituality spiral back to "re-member" and reclaim concepts, images, and symbols from their childhood religious traditions as they continue on their spiritual journeys with the influence of many ideas, other spiritual traditions, and their own spiritual and other life experiences.

Most of those interviewed and quoted in this chapter were in their forties and fifties, and thus were at midlife. They were at or beyond what Fowler would consider the conjunctive faith stage of spiritual development, where there is an ability to deal with paradox and embrace the tension of opposites. Although some may have had this ability earlier in adulthood, it seems to be further integrated and more characteristic of the generativity of those at midlife who have questioned, doubted, and explored other spiritual possibilities with openness and have gone on the journey of reclaiming and spiraling back. As will be explored further in the next chapter, this journey of moving forward and spiraling back also appears to be part of the integration process, which also results in a firmer commitment to live according to what one sees as one's life's purpose and most important work. Although actually living out this commitment is difficult, it was described as a way of life that required inner reflection that also led to outer action and a connection to other people and a sense of communal responsibility.

What does this suggest for culturally relevant practice in adult and higher education contexts? The most obvious suggestion would be the relevance of the themes of this chapter to classes or activities dealing with adult development and learning. Engaging learners in some activity related to the questions at the beginning of Part Two could help them explore the relationship of their own culture, gender, religious background, and historical context to their own development, or to what they see as their life's purpose and that engages their passion. As Matthew Fox observes, the re-visioning of work that engages our spirituality and our passion is perhaps the great paradigm shift of our time, and it requires ways of celebrating and creating ritual in our lives. Thus it might be interesting to explore how learners celebrate and use ritual in their own lives as a way of honoring some of life's transitions and significant moments. The sharing of such passion and ideas might be a way of experiencing being in the present in a new way. Another important suggestion for practice might be to follow the example of many of those I interviewed, in terms of finding a way to stand in the present moment by developing a regular centering, prayer, or meditative space and time. Perhaps this inner reflection will lead to new and creative outer action.

In addressing the themes of this chapter during the month or so of writing it, I have had the occasion to probe more deeply into the dynamics of my own spiritual development. I was struck with the fact that I began this chapter by relaying the story and favorite saying of my Jesuit Zen professor from fifteen years ago, "The present moment is pregnant with God." It thus seemed clear that I should be more intentional about attending to my own present moment. I have always tried to find a way to attend to the spiritual dimension of my life through various practices and through cultivating an attitude about life. The reality is, however, that while I think meditation and mindfulness are a good idea, my actual practice of meditation itself over the years has been somewhat sporadic. Since the way I began this chapter suggested that I needed to focus more on the present moment myself, I returned to the regular daily practice of meditation. The form of mindfulness meditation that I typically follow is somewhat eclectic, but it is based primarily on my own version of the practice of zazen that I learned in that Zen class some fifteen years ago. It encourages focus on the present moment by counting and centering on breath. Where did this very regular practice in the past month take me? And am I moving forward?

On one level, it didn't take me anywhere all that profound; I had no earth-shattering insights or visions that made me want to quit my job or change my life in obviously significant ways. Of course, if one is a purist, this isn't the purpose of mindfulness meditation; it is rather to be in the present moment as it is. In many ways, my experience was and is quite ordinary. I hear the planes overhead, the traffic outside, the heater coming on. There are often the many distractions of the chatter in my own head about what I need to do that day, who I need to call, and so on, which are more about anxiety and getting things done than about anything particularly spiritual. But there is also a comfort in this stillness, an ordinary rhythm that promises the regularity of moving forward. Indeed, all these elements are often a part of my present moments, as I try to get centered.

Yet in another way, the experience of mindfulness meditation has also been quite profound in its ordinariness. But perhaps that's what spirituality is: finding the extraordinary in the ordinary business of life. On a deeper level, in focusing on and meditating on my own breath, I am reminded of the fact that *spirit*, *respire*, and *inspire* all have the same root: spirit is in fact the breath of life. I have felt that spirit alive within me. I could feel the power of my own breath, my own aliveness, the sense of a deeper energy in my own body. Although I tried to center on the present moment, even at times when I was most in the present moment I could feel vestiges of myself spiraling back. At times I would have a sense of the Holy Spirit, an image from my Catholic background, as the breath of life. At other times, I was reminded of how I was taught to work with that spirit-energy, the *shakti* or *chi*, in my therapeutic massage training through the power of my own breath. At still other times, the redundancy of counting my breaths reminded me of the redundancy of saying the fifty Hail Mary's of the Rosary that I was taught by my mother as a little girl. Sometimes during those "present moments" I felt like my mother and all who have gone before me are somehow very much with me in that energy. Further, I felt like I am drawing on the energy of all those who have shared their own stories—people like Shirley Johnston, Ahmed Hasan, Julia Gutierrez, Jason Dunbar, and others who have offered me their own spiritual insights and wisdom. Somehow, in that present moment, in sharing in and counting this breath of life, in a strange sort of profound way, I feel myself at-one with all that is and ever was. While I am only one person, a small speckle of the infinite number of people and creatures who have walked this way and will walk this planet, in sharing in this great breath of life, this Great Spirit, I am deeply connected to all of these. It makes me want to take better care of myself to honor this life within me; it makes me more aware of my connection to others and to want to be careful to treat them well. It makes me want to cherish and honor the earth. The present moment is indeed ordinary; but it's also quite extraordinary.

There is a sense of community in this. It is not the same sense of community that one might experience in attending a communal worship service. Rather, it is the paradoxical experience that in the solitary is the communal. In my aloneness and grounding in the energy of the Great Spirit, manifested in this breath of life in the present moment, I indeed connect with others. So before I leave this meditation space, I also try to send forth some of this energy of the divine spirit in me to particular people that I love, to those I know need special care, to those suffering the terror of New York and Washington, Afghanistan and Pakistan, to the universe in general. I also try to take in and be receptive to the energy of the Great Spirit also being manifested and sent forth by others. I take comfort in knowing others try to connect with me in this way at times. Although I'd like to say that my motivation to engage in this daily practice is strictly my own, I admit that having others close to me agree to engage in a similar practice increases my motivation to keep doing it. Further, knowing that one in particular has agreed to try to meditate at the same time every day with me, in spite of the fact that on many days we are in different parts of the world from one another further increases my motivation. Somehow I believe we draw on each other's energy in that sacred space. Perhaps all of this is only my imagination. Or perhaps finding inspiration in the simultaneous meditation practices of others is indicative of my own lack of spiritual development. But I like to think that it is part of the communal nature of spirituality and of finding the communal in the solitary.

"Spirituality is some sort of aware honoring of the Life-force that is happening through everything," says Lisa Riddle. I think that spiritual development is becoming ever more aware of the dynamics of the presence of that Life-force in its many manifestations. Although we never can really grasp its multiple manifestations, in our own development, as we move forward and spiral back, we "re-member" the grounding of our own spiritual and cultural traditions "that still have life in them" at the same time that we are strongly influenced by the spiritual and cultural traditions of those with whom we come in contact. Indeed, as discussed in Chapter Four, there are many varieties of spiritual experience that are key to our ongoing development. But perhaps by standing in the great spiral of our own present moment, discovering our connectedness with others as well as our own grounding places, we discover new ways "the present moment is pregnant with God." In so doing, we move forward to the future.

6

Gender, Culture, and Spiritual Identity in Midlife Integration

S piritual development always takes place in a cultural, gendered, and historical context and happens over time. The last chapter touched on these issues but focused more on the spiral shape of spiritual development. This chapter and the next focus more on how gender and cultural context shapes the spiritual development of individuals.

Given that spiritual development is about the ongoing development of identity, it is intimately connected to how we understand all aspects of identity, including our gender, ethnicity, culture, and class background. The difficulty with some of the stage or phase theories briefly touched on in the last chapter is that in looking at general tendencies in human development, often cultural and gender differences are either placed in the background or ignored completely. This is why Merriam and Caffarella (1999) and others call for more integrative models and more cultural and gendered models of development (Chavez & Guido-DiBrito, 1999; Ross-Gordon, 1999; Sheared, 1999).

In responding to the need to attend to the cultural complexity of development, Pamela Hays (2001) offers a model that she calls the ADDRESSING framework to analyze how multiple dimensions of people's lives affect development in a sociocultural context. She includes spirituality as a component to understanding that development. She notes: "The ADDRESSING framework offers a system for organizing and addressing these cultural influences and groups in the form of an acronym: Age and generational influences, Developmental and acquired Disabilities, Religion and spiritual orientation, Ethnicity, Socioeconomic status, Sexual orientation, Indigenous heritage, National origin, and Gender" (Hays, 2001, p. 5). Hays' purpose is to help counselors, teachers, therapists, and adult learners who are attempting to facilitate ongoing adult development of either others or themselves to grapple with the cultural complexity that informs each person's life.

Just as Hays' ADDRESSING framework gets at the complexity of the sociocultural context, Rossiter (1999), Clark (2001), and Brooks (2000) argue for the importance of narrative perspectives on development. In her work on narrative learning, Clark (2001) notes, "personal stories are not merely a way of telling someone (or oneself) about one's life; they are the means by which identities may be fashioned" (p. 87). This is why Baumgartner and Merriam (1999) put together an edited book of multicultural stories that deal with issues in adult development: because the stories foreground issues of culture, gender, and sexual orientation that were a central part of the identities of the characters and could not be ignored in understanding their development. Indeed, identities are fashioned partly by the cultural and gendered context in which they develop.

In order to make the significance of the importance of the cultural, gendered, and historical context particularly vivid, I begin this chapter by first examining the role of spiritual development in fashioning identity in a cultural and gendered context by focusing on one woman's narrative of spiritual development. This will be followed by an analysis of the interacting elements of her identity that are central to understanding her story. Third will be a particular examination of gender issues in the identity and spiritual development literature. Last will be a discussion of the integration of the tension of opposites that appears to be an important part of spiritual development for many people at midlife.

A Spiritual Development Narrative: Shirley Johnston

Shirley Johnston is an African American woman in her early fifties. She is a tenured faculty member at a community college, and teaches reading and writing to a multicultural group of students from a variety of ethnic and class backgrounds. She attempts to teach in a way that is culturally relevant to her students by drawing on current events and issues directly related to their lives. In discussing the role of spirituality in her life now, particularly as to how it informs her work, she weaves together a story of her own spiritual development in light of the cultural and historical context in which it took place.

Shirley grew up in a racially segregated working-class neighborhood in the Midwest, where her family had a long-standing relationship with the black Baptist Church. She noted, "My family was active in the struggle for the rights of workers and justice under the law for Black people." There were many ministers in her family. Although her formal religious background is Baptist, her family did not embrace the "no card-playing" or "no dancing" aspects of the tradition. She explained that the focus was on

> the main piece—there's God, there's justice and mercy, and that your main responsibility in the world is to . . . share your blessings with others. And to stand up . . . and be brave in the face of injustice because you're backed up by a power that's stronger than government and armies, as long as you are doing the right thing.

She was heavily involved in activist work even as a child and states that her family, as well as her church, "was one where the pastor preached liberation theology. We raised money for the movement, supported boycotts, and hosted visitors who traveled to raise money and consciousness for the civil rights movement." Thus,

Shirley had a long legacy of activism, particularly around civil rights, often organized through the church.

Shirley went to college, where she began studying black history and questioning her childhood Christian beliefs. "I became convinced Christianity was a trick—the oppressor to keep us humble and in bondage. . . . Even the terminology 'Lord,' 'Master'—I had serious issue with it, and stopped going to church." During this time, she became involved with a part of the Black Power movement that was not particularly informed by spirituality and was challenging the civil disobedience that required nonviolence. She moved away form the organized church for a long time. She noted, however, that eventually, "I was confronted with the notion that I really believed in a power, a positive power and a negative power, and I was calling it by different names, but in reality it was the same power that I had known about as a child." Over the years in addition to raising her two children and being married and divorced, Shirley was involved in many different social justice activities, in both her paid and nonpaid work. Virtually in all of these activities as an educator for organizations such as the Urban League, Black Women's Health Project, and adult literacy programs, she was involved in cross-cultural conflict mediation and the development of more culturally relevant educational programs.

Shirley currently does not belong to a church per se. Her partner is a Christian, and she sometimes goes to church with him; she has connections to the Muslim community and sometimes worships there. She meditates daily, centering on the notion, "God is love." Although she reports that she likes many of the prayers in organized religion, she noted:

> Some of the word images, such as "father," "he," are barriers . . ., some of the pictures and images can take me away from centering. . . . I find that I'm able to be more connected in silence and solitude, but I do like the evoking of the spirit that happens through the music.

In thinking about how spirituality informs her work she explained:

> *The purpose of life is to restore and maintain the balance,*
> *which is . . . order, justice . . . and truth. My intention is to*
> *walk my convictions, and to be authentic, and to show love,*
> *to teach how to do that through my actions and evoking of*
> *spirit, of love, of courage, and justice. Especially in working*
> *with women's groups in telling the truth and being as real as*
> *I know how to be, and trying to bring forth the power of God*
> *in myself, I can touch that in other people.*

Her daily meditation centers on this. In considering how religion and spirituality intersect, she noted, "I am certainly a student of the teachings of Jesus. . . . When people ask me, I say I'm Muslim because a Muslim is one who submits to the will of God," but membership in organized religion is not important for her.

Shirley has a strong commitment to equity issues that is based partly on her spirituality. In her current work as a community college faculty member, she directly deals with cultural issues, including issues of race, class, and gender as these issues arise in the everyday lives of herself and her students. She seldom discusses her spirituality directly in classes with students, although people know she celebrates Ramadan and Kwanzaa and that she is mostly vegetarian, for spiritual as well as health reasons. She also works at raising consciousness about diversity and equity issues with coworkers on campus, and sometimes spirituality will come up in these conversations. She and a multicultural group of her women colleagues meet in each other's homes explicitly for discussing campus diversity issues, where they share both their own vulnerability and knowledge about race, class, and gender. In addition, their work together has overflowed onto the campus in the form of workshops and conversations about diversity. She notes that there are "spiritual moments" in these conversations, and she describes one experience at a campus diversity workshop that "showed the power of being authentic and telling the truth out loud." In her closing thoughts on the connection between spirituality and education for social justice and cultural relevance, she stated:

> *I just think it's absolutely connected. . . . I've been going to church a lot more, because I like this church, but my spirituality is separate from that. . . . Like I will keep going to work because this is the best place for me to be teaching, but I am teaching whether I'm at [the community college] or not. . . I think all people have a spiritual part to them. For me it's the main part. I believe that there is a higher power that keeps the universe in balance. It's like the intellect—it's not as muscular in some people as it is in others, but it's there in everyone whether they know it or not.*

In reflecting on her own spirituality in relationship to being an African American woman and her involvement in social justice efforts, her tolerance and perseverance are inspired in part by the notion that "black women are the mothers of humanity." In closing she noted:

> *I think my responsibility is great because I know what people went through so that I could have the freedom and the power to move forward in the world, so I must get up! And I must dig deep! And I must do good! And to not do that would be an affront to my ancestors who stayed alive, and stayed strong, and stayed spiritually connected through centuries of brutality and everything, beyond slavery. That's what it is for me!*

The Interacting Elements in Shirley's Narrative

The value of narrative perspectives on any aspect of development is that the significance of the context and the interacting elements of the narrative and the person's identity become the centerpiece of the analysis of story. As noted earlier, stage and phase theories tend to either ignore or marginalize factors of gender or culture that are so central to contextualizing people's stories.

If we take Shirley's story as one example, there are a number of background interrelated contextual elements that are central to understanding how her spiritual development has unfolded. First is her *particular cultural background*. This is not incidental; the fact that she is African American is absolutely central to her story. Second is the *historical context* in which her story unfolds. A third element is her *childhood religious background*. Shirley's growing up and young adulthood took place within the historical context of the civil rights movement, where many African Americans and those who were their allies bonded together in a social movement to fight racism. Further, the involvement of her family in the black Baptist church that emphasized working for justice in the context of the civil rights movement informed by a spirituality that required social activism was extremely formative to who Shirley is today. Her understanding of who she is and a part of her life's purpose were indeed constructed in the midst of this important sociocultural, historical, and religious context.

A fourth element that is central to understanding Shirley's story is the *gendered context* that has given rise to and shapes Shirley's identity and spiritual development. Shirley's gender, of course, cannot be separated from her cultural background, as Shirley is simultaneously both African American and a woman. Obviously, her life was very different from those of white women who grew up in the same era, so the fact that she is an African American woman in particular is important to her story. As many have noted, this race-gendered perspective of being "both and" cannot be separated one from the other (Etter-Lewis, 1993; Johnson-Bailey, 2001) and has given rise to black feminist thought (Hill Collins, 2000; 1998; hooks, 1989; 1994), and womanist perspectives on the life experiences of black women. As Vanessa Sheared (1994, 1999) notes, the term *womanism* was initially made more popular by Alice Walker

(1984), and emphasizes the impacts of race and gender in the lives of women of African descent, largely from an Africentric perspective. Religion scholars Delores Williams (1993) and Katie Cannon (1996) have each discussed the spiritual development and experiences of black Christian women in a sociocultural, historical, religious, and gendered context in their work on womanist theology, and make clear how all these factors interact in the lives of black women of Christian background. Of course, not all African American women are Christian or necessarily grew up in the Christian tradition. Further, like Shirley, many have moved away from a strictly Christian spirituality and have developed a more eclectic spirituality informed by Christianity, Islam, Buddhism, or other perspectives. The recent edited anthology by Gloria Wade-Gales (1995) about African American women's spiritual experiences offers a broader perspective on the multiple ways spirituality is manifested in the lives of women of African descent.

A fifth important element that has affected Shirley's spiritual development is her *educational background* and her *educational experience*. Shirley is well educated; she values education from life experience, as well as from formal post secondary education. Her view of education and her involvement in community-based and formal education programs as both a learner and an educator increased the likelihood that Shirley would critically reflect and question some of what she was taught to believe from her childhood religious tradition. To be sure, formal education is neither required nor a guarantee that one will critically reflect on one's life assumptions. However, given that students are often called upon to critically examine underlying assumptions within different positions in higher education settings, this questioning stance often carries over to an examination of other aspects of their lives, including their childhood religious backgrounds. As noted in Chapter Five, given the obvious connection between these processes, nearly all who discuss spiritual or faith development as change over time tie it very much to cognitive development (Fowler, 1981; Loder, 1998; Parks, 2000).

People's more complex thinking processes, which are part of cognitive development and affected by both formal education and life experience, will affect their spiritual development and their development overall.

Shirley's spiritual development was certainly affected by her cognitive development. As she notes, she began studying black history in depth as a young adult and college student. Presumably, learning to see what had been left out in the mainstream history as it was presented in schools while she was growing helped Shirley see that the presentation of any history, any story, is always from a particular perspective. Further, Shirley also saw that the way that history had been presented to her in school primarily served the interests and agendas of the dominant culture. Learning black history, including the history of taking action, and further developing her own critical thinking abilities as a result of her ongoing education and life experience that examined multiple perspectives had the simultaneous effect that Shirley also questioned whose interests were served by a particular presentation of Christianity. This is exemplified in her statement that at least for a time she "became convinced Christianity was a trick to keep us humble and in bondage." It was during this time that Shirley first moved away from the church of her youth.

The spiral shape of spiritual development discussed in Chapter Four is also evident in Shirley's narrative. For example, although Shirley moved away from Christianity as a young adult, she did later also spiral back to reclaim and reframe those aspects of Christianity that continue to be important to her. We see evidence of this reframing in Shirley's comment above about returning to the notion that she really believed in a power that she had called by different names over the years, but as she says, "in reality it was the same power that I had known about as a child." Further, as she notes in reflecting on her current spirituality, she refers to the fact that she is "a student of the teachings of Jesus" though she doesn't claim Christianity as her religion. To be sure, this process in her spiritual

development—of questioning her childhood religious tradition—
was very clearly affected by her cognitive development and probably other aspects of her development as well.

It is clear that these five interacting elements of Shirley's life—
her cultural background, gender, the historical era in which she grew
up, her educational background, and her religious upbringing—all
affected Shirley's spiritual development and the development of her
identity. There are, of course, other elements that are factors in
Shirley's spiritual development story. But I want to highlight the
importance of these background factors because most people who
discuss spiritual development have spent little or no time considering how sociocultural context informs development, but instead
focus primarily on the psychological and individual dimension of
spiritual development. This is why Clark (2001) and Rossiter
(1999) are calling for narrative perspectives on development. Narratives (such as Shirley's) tend to make apparent the *particular* cultural, historical, and gender factors that affect development. These
elements were apparent not just in Shirley's story but also in the stories of all those I interviewed; they are also apparent in the many
recent anthologies that focus on the role of spirituality in people's
lives. In essence, such anthologies provide narrative perspectives on
spiritual development (see, for example, Mandelker & Powers,
1999; Sumrall & Vecchione, 1997; Wade-Gales, 1995) and make
clear that it is difficult to separate spiritual development from the
particularities of one's cultural background, gender, or overall identity development.

Gender, Spiritual Development, and Authentic Identity

A salient theme among nearly all those I interviewed was the central role of spirituality in their ongoing identity development. (It is
important to keep in mind here that I interviewed only those whose
spirituality was very important to them; those who do not value

spirituality obviously develop their own identity as well.) Many of them referred to their spiritual journeys as a move to living more authentically in accord with their true or "authentic" identity.

Toward a More Authentic Identity

The subject of the role of spirituality in claiming a more "authentic" identity was briefly touched on in Chapter Two; there I used the examples of Ava Valdez, a Latina from central America who defined spirituality as "to know who you are, and to be able to define who you are, wherever you are, despite the changing conditions of your life." Ava was referring to the connection between spirituality and her overall identity development, but she was also discussing its role in developing and maintaining a positive cultural identity as an immigrant in the United States. The connection between spirituality and cultural identity development was such a strong theme, especially for the people of color, that I focus primarily on that topic in Chapter Seven, where I consider it in more detail.

This emphasis on authenticity is also very apparent in Shirley's narrative above, where she discussed her life's purpose: "My intention is to walk my convictions, and *to be authentic,* and to show love, to teach how to do that through my actions and evoking of spirit, of love, of courage, and justice. . . . telling the truth and *being as real as I know how to be*" (italics added). She made further reference to spirituality as part of authenticity when she referred to the important "spiritual moments" in some of the diversity workshops and conversations, which "showed the power of *being authentic* and telling the truth out loud." Further, Shirley's belief that she must carry on the legacy of her ancestors rooted in a spirituality that works for justice is grounded in her cultural story and spiritual legacy that she must "get up" and she must "dig deep." As she says, "to not do that would be an affront" to her ancestors. Obviously, this spiritual purpose is absolutely grounded in her cultural identity.

Identity is never static and is always expanding (Flannery, 2000). As Sheared (1994) notes in her discussion of womanism and its relationship to education, our lives are lived in the midst of what she refers to as "polyrhythmic realities." We not only have a race and gender, we also have different roles as teachers, students, mothers, fathers, sisters, and so on. Our spiritual development and identity unfolds amid these polyrhythmic realities as a result of new life experiences, changes in relationships, and from life's various transitions. Sue, a Korean American woman, described living for a time overseas away from her husband and finding a more solid independent identity apart from her husband as a spiritual experience that facilitated her authentic identity. Furthermore, she noted that her spirituality, in helping her develop her own more independent and authentic identity, helped her be more accepting of her daughter's lesbian identity. Michael DiMarco, the artist who was introduced in Chapter Four, discussed spirituality and his regular meditation practice as being foundational to his ongoing identity development because it is in those moments that he occasionally catches a glimpse of who he really is—of his own authenticity. Indeed, spiritual development is partly about forging a more authentic identity. As noted in the last chapter, this greater authenticity seems to be found in the spiritual development process of moving forward and spiraling back.

A Gendered Spirituality

Although most who write about spiritual development as change over time tend to give little attention to sociocultural issues, more have given attention to identity development based on gender in spiritual development. These discussions rely, in part, on the pioneering work of Carol Gilligan (1982) in women's moral development and Belenky, Clinchy, Goldberger, and Tarule's study (1986) on how women come to know and learn. A primary theme is the connection of spiritual development to moral and cognitive development, with a particular emphasis on the importance of connection and relationship for women while also developing critical thinking processes. Another important theme is how growing up in a patriarchal culture relates to and affects women's spiritual development (Plaskow & Christ, 1989; Winter, Lummis, & Stokes, 1995).

Nearly all the women I interviewed discussed the role of spirituality as related to their gender, and spoke explicitly or implicitly of challenging patriarchal notions of divinity. Some of the men referred to some of these gendered issues in spirituality but spoke of them somewhat differently. For example, David Preston, a man in his late fifties who now practices a form of Hinduism called Vedanta, talked about the significance of feminine figures in Vedanta. He explicitly talked about the important role of Holy Mother within that tradition, which he finds important and compelling and considerably different than the Catholicism in which he grew up and remained very devoted to until his mid-forties. But David noted that he has not given much direct thought to his own gender specifically in relationship to his spirituality beyond valuing the feminine presentation of divinity available in other traditions.

The women, however, talked much more about the role of spirituality specifically in relationship to their gender and identity development. Perhaps this is so because many of them were more negatively affected by the explicit or implicit message of women's inferiority in some patriarchal religious traditions. In the process of developing a woman-positive gender identity through their spiritual development, many of these women challenged some of the patriarchal notions in a variety of ways. Shirley, for example, in reflecting back on her young adulthood, noted, "Even the terminology 'Lord,' 'Master'—I had serious issue with it, and stopped going to church." She also referred to how some of these exclusively masculine divine images affect her currently when she attends religious services: "some of the word images, such as 'father,' 'he' are barriers." Further, many of the women took offense to the interpretations of some religious traditions that suggest that the evil of the world were the result of women's deeds. An example might be a literalist interpretation of the Genesis story in which Eve's eating of the forbidden fruit in the Garden of Eden results in the pain of the world.

Developing a life affirming spirituality is one that affirms and nurtures a positive identity development overall, including a culture-positive and gender-positive spiritual development (Bolen, 1994; Borysenko, 1999; Cimino, 2001; Loder, 1998). People develop such spirituality in different ways. As we saw in the last chapter, some develop it by leaving their religious traditions and seeking out other spiritual paths that are more identity-affirming and congruent with their own beliefs. Others develop a more eclectic spirituality in much the way Shirley has done by drawing on a variety of spiritual traditions.

Many women and some men in trying to develop their spirituality draw on the work of feminist theologians who have explored the feminine face of God in various religions and cultures by examining feminine images, or the blending of patriarchal traditions with indigenous spirituality or matriarchal traditions over the course of history that happened as a result of conquest and colonization. (See, for example, Rodriguez, 1994; Ruether, 1996; Christ & Plaskow, 1992; Isasi-Diaz, 1993; Moody, 1996; Plaskow & Christ, 1989.) Some theologians center more on what is relevant to women of particular cultural groups. For example, womanist theologians (Cannon, 1996; Williams, 1993) center on the life experience of African American women, while others focus on Latinas (Castillo, 1996; Isasi-Diaz, 1993; Rodriguez, 1994), Asian American women (Nakishima Brock, 1989), and American Indian women (Gunn Allen, 1992). Many women from various cultural groups take great inspiration in the work of such feminist theologians and spiritual writers in developing a woman-positive and culture-positive identity. And as Miriam Winter, Adair Lummis, and Allison Stokes (1995) note, based on the results of their survey of seven thousand Christian women who have been concerned about the place of women in their religious traditions, many fashion a positive gender and cultural identity from within the context of their religious traditions. The women in their study continued to practice within those traditions but took responsibility for their ongoing woman-positive development by also developing their own prayer circles, rituals, and celebrations that celebrate their womanhood.

The literature on women's spirituality that connects to identity development is voluminous, far too extensive to go into in much detail here. What most of it has in common is that it deals with the important notion of image and symbol, with an emphasis on reclaiming positive images of women, beyond the dualistic image of virgin-seductress that has been the emphasis of many patriarchal traditions. This emphasis is reminiscent of what James Fowler pointed out about the powerful ways people construct knowledge through image and symbol, which have basically been ignored by cognitive and moral development theorists. In earlier chapters, the power of feminine figures in women's spiritual development was obvious in some of the women's stories. For example, Aretha Franklin and her music were very important in Anna Adams' story. Elise Poitier, who described recovering from her miscarriage, which facilitated her own healing and the healing of her relationship with her mother (Chapter Four), discussed the significance that this experience was facilitated through a woman leader in one of the yoga traditions:

> I needed that woman energy! I needed it! I needed a mother.
> I didn't need a tangible mother. I needed to know and experience that love energy, that nurturing energy that my mother could not give, so I could forgive my mother. The actual quotation [she used] was "I am God the father and the mother" but the part that was for me—the mother part. And that's the part I latched onto, because I really needed a mother and I didn't have it. So to be able to have that experience was part of my personal development.

Although the experience itself was only one moment in time, it did facilitate Elise's ongoing development, and the feminine presence and imagery were important to that development.

Spiritual Development and Midlife Integration

Most of the people I interviewed are now at midlife and trying to live out what they see as their life purpose, strongly informed by their spirituality. Trying to live out one's life purpose is obviously related to one's identity in all aspects, including one's gender, race, class, culture, national origin, and sexual orientation. Although this is true for everyone, whether fully conscious of it or not, it is particularly true for people like those in this study who are quite conscious of these issues and consider that a part of their life purpose is to deal with one or more of these issues in their own work with adult learners.

From a spiritual development perspective, all the participants in this study would probably be in what Fowler (1981) described as the conjunctive faith stage (as described in the last chapter) or beyond. One of the characteristics of those in or beyond this point in their lives is that they can see and integrate the tension of opposites. Parker Palmer (1980) suggests that it is the living within and embracing the paradox of these tensions of opposites that pulls people open to a sense of spirit and to living more authentically. Erikson (1980) would perhaps describe this as midlife generativity; thus, perhaps spiritual development also facilitates generativity. Anna Adams, at age fifty-three, reflected specifically on the integration of opposites. She used the example of the role of neo-Marxist thinking in her spiritual development and her social justice work:

> I think Marxism is a form of spirituality because it really is about connections with other people; it's a rather earthly bound nature of connections, but it's still about looking back and looking forward, and taking care of each other. . . . So I guess in my Marxist period, which lasted until I was in my thirties, it was a transformation of God being outside of me who controlled all things [to] an inside internal controlling force. I think in retrospect, my spirituality was still there.

In going on to describe a spiritual experience and her integration of it now at midlife, she explained:

> It was kind of like an epiphany. I guess I had come full circle, from thinking that humans were all powerful in my Marxist period, and [now] back to knowing that we are only a part of the great fabric of whatever it is—that we are interconnected on many different levels, and that whatever God is, is a part of those interconnections.

The seeming tension of these positions—of a Marxist perspective with its emphasis on human agency in taking care of the world, and a perspective that draws on the spiritual and divine spark both within and beyond us and in the connection with her African American ancestors (as noted in Chapter Three)—is integrated into Anna's present spirituality. Loder (1998) discusses at length the ability of midlife adults who are generative to integrate and live within the openness of the tension of opposites. Perhaps the moving forward and spiraling back process that is the shape of spiritual development is part of the integration process at work.

Another component of this process of integration and of living in the present moment among those I interviewed (most of whom were educators specifically teaching classes that focus on justice issues) is the expansion of their spirituality beyond their own self-interest toward other people. This is why most of them were engaged in the work they do as educators for equity—to engage as fully as possible in the interconnectedness of all things grounded in a spirituality of wholeness that is also connected and relevant to their cultural roots. The purpose of their work is to bring about a better future by also focusing on the present. In essence, there was a concern for the creation of some sense of community that focuses on both the present and the future. In this respect there was a lot of similarity among those I interviewed to what Daloz, Keen, Keen, and Parks (1996) found in their study of community and commitment among those working for what they referred to as "the common good."

In some respects, this aspect of spiritual development as the integration of wholeness and concern for both the present and the future is also reflected in the insights of Ken Wilber (2000b), whose work on spiritual development was introduced in the last chapter. Wilber examines the sociocultural context in which spiritual development is taking place in this new millennium, although his focus is more on the spiritual needs of the culture as a whole (primarily from a distinctly North American perspective), as the larger culture is evolving at this point in history. His is a cultural evolutionary perspective (inadvertently more focused on the white dominant culture), rather than one that emphasizes the connection of one's particular culture to identity or one's work in the world. In any event, Wilber argues that from a cultural evolutionary perspective, spiritual development (of the whole, and of the individual) evolves as a result of a significant portion of the whole culture going through phases or levels of spiritual development. Each level includes and expands on the development of earlier stages and "becomes more inclusive, more embracing, more integral—less marginalizing, less exclusionary, less oppressive" (Wilber, 2000a, p. 25) in its move toward greater integration. An important strength of Wilber's work is his attention to how the larger culture as a whole is affected by some of the realities of our time, such as technology and increased contact with people from all over the world. Yet he doesn't attend much to how different cultural and class groups are affected differently by what is going on in that larger culture in light of a global economy.

This move toward integration and wholeness encompasses all aspects of one's being, including one's cultural identity. Thus, to gloss over the fact that people are situated differently relative to what is going on in the larger culture, as Wilber (2000a; 2000b) does, can miss an important component of what integration and the move, grounded in one's life purpose, to create community is all about. As Anna Adams noted in discussing her spiritual development:

> *Spirituality as connection to past and present that I find in other African Americans is a powerful piece of my sense of self. . . . There is a collective consciousness there, so in terms of social justice, when I am doing social justice work, when I am making revolution, I am paying homage to a spiritual connection.*

Her desire to create community and move beyond herself is deeply connected to her cultural identity, as well as her identity overall. Her sense of her life purpose emerges from the integration of all aspects of her identity: her personal and cultural history, the history of African American people, and her cognitive development. At this point in her life, she notes that she cannot not do this work.

> *It is the reason really I am here, on a spiritual plane, but on a real plane, I have no alternative. There is really no alternative to doing this work because of the devastation, I mean what else do you do? It is my responsibility, my duty, my reason, my history, my spirit, my soul.*

At this point in Anna's life, in having integrated some of the tension of these opposites, she must be true to what she sees as her life purpose. This was true of others as well, although obviously people live out their life purpose and move to greater integration in different ways. As we saw in the last chapter, Jason Dunlap describes some of the work of integration in his own life as being committed to doing what he refers to as *soulwork*, of coming to grips with and getting more in touch with shadow parts of his own self so that he doesn't project it onto others. But this work and integrating the tension of opposites requires a way of life that requires inner soulwork, or space for quiet time and meditation, that also leads outward to work in the world. Thus, being able to deal with paradox and the tension of what is seemingly opposite, such as Anna Adams' neo-Marxist thinking with a strong sense of spirituality, is part of the process of ongoing spiritual development, which may be especially characteristic of midlife.

Summary and Brief Thoughts for Practice

This chapter brought a narrative perspective to spiritual development by focusing on the narrative of Shirley Johnston's personal spiritual journey. Stage and phase theories of various aspects of adult development have tended to ignore or downplay the significant gendered, cultural, and historical context that informs that development. Narrative perspectives, in contrast, tend to foreground and make visible the particular contextual factors in which that development takes place, factors such as gender, culture, historical period, religion, and educational background (Baumgertener & Merriam, 1999; Brooks, 2000; Clark, 2001; Rossiter, 1999). Although these elements were particularly evident in Shirley's story, they are equally important in anyone's story and are central to understanding how anyone's identity unfolds.

In addition to analyzing the culture, gender, religion, and historical period in which Shirley grew up, this chapter focused on the connection between Shirley's educational background or cognitive development and her spiritual development. All these factors clearly affect how she sees her life purpose and the ongoing development of her more authentic identity. Further, the spiral shape of Shirley's spiritual development was also noted in connecting with some of the themes of the last chapter.

Although the next chapter focuses particularly on the importance of culture in understanding spiritual development, an important focus of this chapter was the issue of gender not only in Shirley's particular story but also in the spiritual development literature overall. Gender is as important to men's spiritual development as it is to women's, although it appears that women are more fully conscious of it than are their male counterparts. Nearly all the women I interviewed discussed the significance of gender in their spirituality. Some of the men did as well, although the men and women discussed it in different ways. The men talked more about the need to get in touch with the femininity of God as a nurturing presence, whereas the women talked about gender more from the perspective of the oppression of the patriarchal religious traditions in which many grew up. The women spoke more of needing to discover the feminine face of God to be able to discover that spark of divinity in themselves, as part of their ongoing positive and more authentic identity development. Further, many resented the exclusive male language to refer to God that is part of most organized religious traditions. Many found inspiration in feminist theology, in feminine images of a divine presence, or in seeing a spark of divinity in important women role models who were also members of their own or a similar cultural group.

Another central element of this chapter was the ability of people to deal with paradox and the integration of the tension of opposites that is part of spiritual development. Although this ability may be apparent in some people in earlier adulthood, it appears to be especially characteristic of spiritual development at midlife. This finding would need to be the subject of further research, but it was indeed very characteristic of all those I interviewed, all of whom (with three exceptions) were in midlife in their forties and fifties. This ability to deal with paradox and the tension of opposites prevalent in those I interviewed may also relate somewhat to the finding that people become more interested in spirituality as they age (Loder, 1998). Unfortunately, since I only interviewed one woman who at sixty-nine had moved into her senior years, I can make no claims about spiritual development beyond midlife. This also would need to be the subject of further research.

What do narrative perspectives of development suggest for the practice of culturally relevant adult education? Although Shirley's narrative focused in particular on her spiritual development, it is obvious that the factors of gender, culture, educational background, historical era, and childhood religion cannot be separated from her story. In teaching about or doing an activity relating to any aspect of adult development, one might consider having learners analyze some aspect of their own adult development and examine how elements of Hays' (2001) ADDRESSING framework, discussed in this chapter, relate to or affect that particular aspect of development. One could foreground any aspect of development, such as gender identity, and then examine how the factors highlighted in the ADDRESSING framework affected gender identity. Further, learners might interview each other or interview another person outside of the class about their spiritual or other aspect of their development and present a case study highlighting the interaction of how these factors affect development. Using such a narrative perspective on development might help learners see how inextricably tied together all aspects of development are. Examining all aspects helps one have a greater sense of the whole. Yet as the old adage goes, "the whole is greater than the sum of the parts." Understanding spiritual development is an attempt to move closer to that whole.

7

The Role of Spiritual Experience in Developing a Positive Cultural Identity

All of us want to free our "sacred face." But how can we know what our sacred face is outside of the cultural-political-historical context of what we have been taught is sacred by our families, cultural or religious traditions, and the dominant culture? David Abalos (1998) speaks directly to this point. He notes: "The process of transformation takes place first of all in the individual's depths. . . . But each of us as a person has four faces: the personal, political, historical and sacred. . . . To cast out demons in our personal lives and in society means that we have freed our sacred face" (Abalos, 1998, p. 35). At times, we seem to catch a glimpse of a truer sacred face, grounded in our *own* authenticity rather than who we were told we should be. These moments might be when we seem to transcend our fear and stand up and say, either literally or behaviorally, "No! I will not be treated this way anymore!" Or "This is who *I* am, and this is *good*, even if it's not who *you* want me to be." Sometimes concurrent with these moments may be the insight and recognition that we have been mistreating others because of how badly we felt about ourselves. As Abalos suggests in the above quote, when we recognize these "demons" and take a stand and begin to cast them out of our personal and communal lives, we are beginning to free our sacred face.

Freeing our sacred face is an ongoing process that often involves unlearning the ways we have uncritically absorbed what others told us we should be. Most of us were taught "appropriate" ways of behaving, being, and loving for people of our gender or cultural background. Some of these messages were very explicit, such as "girls don't call boys to ask them out on dates" or "boys don't cry." Other messages were more covert but no less powerful, manifested in the curriculum we were taught in schools that emphasized what white people (especially males) did in history, English, and math and science, as though what others did were not important. In any event, all of us have received messages from the dominant culture, religious institutions, and our families about who we are, how we should behave, and what types of behavior will ensure our survival or greatest happiness. Claiming and reclaiming who we are now, according to our own beliefs and values, is a process of ongoing identity development that many have described as a spiritual experience or spiritual journey. As noted by educator and spiritual writer Parker Palmer (2000) in the opening quote of Part Two, it takes a long time to "become the person one has always been!" Indeed, as he says, in the process of life, "we mask ourselves in faces that are not our own" (p. 9). Claiming our own "face," our own identity, involves much learning and unlearning in search of what he calls our more "authentic vocation."

To find the seed of authentic vocation and to experience personal and cultural transformation, David Abalos (1998) suggests that we must unmask the faces that are not our own. He discusses this process of unmasking as a theory of transformation, most specifically for the Latino community in the United States, though I believe his theory is relevant for nearly all individuals and cultural groups. He argues that for La Cultura Latina to experience ongoing transformation and develop a positive cultural identity, the individuals and various Latino cultural groups within it need to reclaim four interconnected faces of their being: the personal, historical, political, and sacred faces.

According to Abalos (1998), reclaiming these faces is both an individual and a cultural process. He suggests that as individuals begin to examine their own personal stories and claim their personal face, they are also likely to engage their historical face, learning some of their cultural history from members of their own culture, as opposed to what is skimmed over or never mentioned in history books in school. Further, in claiming their own personal and cultural history, he suggests that many are moved to take a stand on their own behalf from a place of self-knowledge and power. To take action is to engage the political face, for as Abalos notes: "When we say no, we are not only responding to particular persons who represent society; on the deeper level we are breaking with the official politics, lords, stories, and ways of life enacted in that society." (p. 35). When we take a stand in our own personal action and bond with others taking a similar stand, we may create or join a movement. In drawing a connection to these ideas beyond the Latino community that is the focus of Abalos's writing, we need only think of Rosa Parks, whose individual action of refusing to sit at the back of the bus at the dawn of the civil rights movement was also a deeply political action. It was the bonding together of her personal action with the collective action of the African American community along with other allies, and their embracing of their personal, historical, cultural, and political faces, grounded for many also in their own sacred stories, that resulted in both personal and social transformation. Indeed, for many involved, there were deeply spiritual moments that were part of this process, moments that were also connected to their cultural identity and to the engagement of what Abalos refers to as the "sacred face."

The purpose of this chapter is to explore the role of spirituality in developing a positive cultural identity. It will begin by first considering the overlap of spiritual and cultural identity in "claiming a sacred face" in the lives of real people in light of models of cultural identity development. Second, it will examine the role of spirituality specifically in unlearning internalized oppression.

Claiming a Sacred Face: The Overlap of Spiritual and Cultural Identity

Many people, especially those who have been marginalized because of their culture, race, gender, class, or sexual orientation, experience learning their own history, their own cultural stories, and their move to new action at the same time that they engage with their own individual stories as a part of their spirituality. This is clearly related to their cultural identity development. The following story of Richard Navarro illustrates how.

The Case of Richard Navarro

Richard Navarro is a thirty-eight-year-old Native American of mixed tribal heritage, who describes some of his personal journey toward reclaiming a positive Native identity in relationship to his own spirituality.[1] Richard is an adult educator and program director on a college campus aimed at developing educational programs around diversity issues, particularly for underserved populations. He has engaged his political face in his activist work on American Indian issues and on issues related to diversity and equity that deal with racism, sexism, and heterosexism. His work on these issues is grounded in both his personal philosophy of education and his spirituality.

Richard explains that at the time of his growing up, rather than emphasizing Native American ways, his parents tended to emphasize "the Western way of doing things." Being able to fit into the dominant culture was seen as a way of providing one's children with a better life. He went on to explain:

1. At different times in our conversation, he used different terms to describe Indigenous people in the United States, and referred to "Native Americans," "American Indians," and at other times simply used the term "Native." He explained that this mixing of terms was intentional because different indigenous people prefer different terms, although he suggested that most within the lower forty-eight states prefer the term "American Indian," and those from Alaska prefer "Alaska Native."

They [his parents] are a product of their time—their parents
were part of the federal Indian policy of termination. These
were relocation Indians. My mom [who is Blackfoot] would
have been impacted directly by the Indian Relocation Act.
Her family literally was kicked out of Colorado where she
grew up.

He explains that his father, who is Tlingit, an Alaska Native group, was greatly influenced by the Indian Relocation Act and the Alaskan Native Claim Settlement Act, which "essentially eliminated all but one Indian reservation in Alaska." Given this historical context, Richard's parents were affected by attitudes that suggested that being able to assimilate would lead to a better life for Indian and Alaska Native people.

Although Richard's father was socialized and grew up with Tlingit spiritual traditions, in light of the fact that his family was emphasizing "Western ways of doing things," Richard was socialized religiously more in Christian traditions, the Assembly of God Church in particular. As an adolescent, he was extremely involved in church activities, in music and in Bible study, and attended a private Christian high school. Richard is a singer-songwriter and a poet today, and he attributes much of his development as a musician to his involvement with church music groups of his youth. He eventually moved away from the Assembly of God tradition, partly because of its fundamentalism, and explains: "as I got older, I was able to think some of the doctrine out; it just was not congruent for me." However, there are aspects of it that are still very important and have been foundational to who he is.

Part of Richard's spiritual story interacts with reclaiming a positive identity as a Native American man and unlearning some of the oppression that was built into an ideology that emphasized assimilation. We all reclaim our own identity through many means— through education, through significant relationships with important mentors, and, for some of us, through attempts to nurture spiritual experience. Richard began reclaiming his own identity as a Native American man partly through studying the history of Native people in college and in graduate school. This was the engagement of his historical face. He had many adult conversations with his parents and older Native relatives, and gathered information through various tribal elders about their lives and about Native traditions, experiences, and spiritual practices, thus reclaiming his sacred face. He also participated in some traditional Native spiritual practices, and describes a pivotal spiritual experience relating both to his spirituality and his cultural identity during his first sweat lodge:

> *When I was at sweat lodge, I met my father's mother. And I met my mother's mother, and they are probably the foundation for now of a spiritual tradition that is clearly synthesized from a Western paradigm, but it is also part of Native tradition, and it is very intuitive.*

This was a turning point for Richard. He felt that he not only had a significant experience of what Native spiritual practices are and how they work, but that he "met" one of his most important spiritual mentors, his paternal grandmother, who he feels continues to guide his spiritual practice.

Symbols are often a significant element of spiritual experience, either as a part of the experience itself, or as a manifestation of it. Richard described carrying a symbol that serves as a marker of this and other important spiritual experiences:

> *A part of the symbol for what has occurred for me there are things that I have gathered from this point, and now are in this [pulls out his medicine bag]. It's what we call a medicine bag. This is the stuff that has meaning, and I draw power from, and it's a source of power for me. For instance, you may have graduated and picked up a stone, or small rock that for some reason was just calling out to you. I don't find*

that unusual. The Bible says that if people don't worship
God, the very stones of the earth will cry out! So I don't think
it should be a leap that you think that rocks would talk.

With eyes dancing, and some humor, he adds, "Now, I don't mean
that they move their lips—I've never met any rocks with lips!"

Richard went on to explain how he and all of us get messages
through many avenues that we often ignore or pay no credence to.
This may be akin to what spiritual writer Gary Zukov (2000) refers
to as becoming multisensory—learning to construct knowledge not
only through the experience of five senses, but also to pay attention
to intuitive, or other multisensory forms of knowledge. Part of
Richard's spiritual journey was to learn to pay attention to these
multisensory ways of knowing, but ways of knowing that were
grounded in his own journey back to his Native cultural heritage.

In claiming these very positive and grounding ways of constructing knowledge, Richard was also doing away with some of the
negative messages that he received growing up that are inherent in
an assimilationist ideology. Thus his spiritual journey has been part
of his claiming a positive cultural identity, without completely doing
away with his earlier spirituality. For example, Richard connects
some of what he has learned through Native spiritual practices such
as sweat lodge with some of his Christian background in his reference to scripture. In trying to name his current spirituality, he notes:
"Spirituality is for me a synthesis of many things, I'm a product of
many things, and so my spirituality is a product of the many places
I've come from. I root it in Native Tradition . . . with a lot of other
influences."

In reflecting on how his Assembly of God background informs
his current spirituality, he notes:

I was very much a part of that tradition. I'm informed by it.
Still have some of that with me. . . . I believe in the concept
of Jesus. He was basically a Jewish revolutionary who had

*some very powerful practices and teachings that are still
applicable today. So I can go with that and it's how I can reconcile my belief in Jesus' ideas with where I am today. You
will not ever catch me discounting Christianity.*

Still, Richard roots his current spiritual practices more in Native
tradition because it culturally grounds him in who he is, and is part
of his claiming a positive cultural identity. Furthermore he notes
that Christianity played a role in the decimation of his culture and
his people in some of its missionary zeal, which Richard does not
discount lightly. However, he makes it a point to make the distinction that his problem is not with Jesus or what he taught, but rather
with what has been done to his people and others over the globe in
the name of Christianity throughout the course of history. His spirituality, as he says, is a synthesis of many things that he draws on in
his work as a poet, a singer-songwriter, and an educator. Further,
much of what he writes and educates about is related to his claiming
of his own cultural identity and in helping others claim theirs. For
him, this indeed is a spiritual process.

Cultural Identity Models and Spirituality

It is clear that Richard's story of his spiritual journey strongly interacts with his journey of embracing his identity overall and his
American Indian cultural identity in the engagement of the four
faces that Abalos (1998) describes. Richard's story is somewhat
reflective of what many authors and psychologists have written
about in discussions of models of cultural identity development
(Cross, 1971; Parham, 1989; Tatum, 1997), particularly of members of groups who have been historically oppressed in American
culture through the legacy of slavery or colonization. Unlike Abalos's theory of transformation that more generally describes embracing these four interconnected "faces," the models of cultural
identity development as discussed by psychologists tend to be more

linear in their explanation of how individuals go about reclaiming their cultural identity.

These race and cultural identity development models began with the work of William Cross (1971), who initially posed a five-stage model of black racial identity development: (1) pre-encounter, (2) encounter, (3) immersion-emersion, (4) internalization, and (5) internalization-commitment. Others have built on and refined Cross's work to consider how cultural identity development unfolds either more specifically for African Americans or for members of other cultural groups, such as Native Americans and Latinos, who have also been oppressed through the legacy of slavery and colonization (Tatum, 1997). According to these models, in addition to the positive views of their culture they may have inherited from their families, individuals from these cultural groups may have internalized (from the white dominant culture) some negative attitudes toward themselves. This results partially in the phenomenon of internalized oppression, an internalized but mostly unconscious belief in the superiority of those more representative of the dominant culture. In order to move to an overall positive cultural identity, according to these cultural identity development models, individuals will go through a process of unlearning what they have unconsciously internalized. Part of this process is learning their own history from the perspective of members of their own culture, reclaiming what has been lost or unknown to them, and reframing what has often been cast subconsciously as negative in more positive ways. As we saw above, this was what Richard Navarro did. Tolliver (in Tisdell, Tolliver, & Villa, 2001), in summarizing how this process evolves in these cultural identity models, notes that members of particular cultural groups "move from a position of devaluation of an oppressed identity to 'encountering' a situation that leads to a questioning of identity to immersion in activities in the oppressed culture and strong antagonism against the oppressors, to embracing a new cultural self that values the previously devalued identity, to integrating the new identity into a more universal per-spective" (p. 3).

For the most part, these cultural identity models have not dealt with the role of spirituality as it interacts with cultural identity. Garrett and Walking Stick Garrett (1994), in referring to cultural identity development among American Indians, do mention the significance of spirituality as part of the American Indian ethos. But Myers et al. (1991) directly and very specifically address the rela-tionship of positive cultural identity development and spirituality. They posit that it is difficult to develop a positive cultural-spiritual identity in a worldview that dichotomizes matter from spirit, and argue that this dichotomization ultimately results in oppressor-oppressed relationships of all types. Further, they propose an opti-mal conceptualization that sees the unity of matter and spirit with all of creation. "Self knowledge is the process of coming to know who and what we are as the unique expression of infinite spirit. With this knowledge, individuals can integrate all apparent aspects of being (e.g., age, color, ethnicity, and size) into a holistic sense of self" (p. 58). In essence, Myers et al. (1991) conceptualize the ear-lier race and cultural identity development models in light of spirit. They describe six phases (individuation, dissonance, immersion, internalization, integration, and transformation) in which a sense of spirituality is integral to self, and embracing one's cultural iden-tity and all aspects of one's identity is also seen as a spiritual process. Tolliver, in summarizing the optimal model proposed by Myers et al. notes, "As individuals increase their self-understanding and re-member their spiritual essence, they transcend the bondage of oppressions" (in Tisdell, Tolliver, & Villa, 2001, p. xx).

Spirituality in Race and Ethnic Identity Development

In my many conversations with educators and activists over the past couple of years, this sense of the development of a positive cultural identity as also a spiritual process for many people has been re-affirmed; it has been especially significant for people of color or ethnic minorities. Further, many have described learning about and claiming the positive aspects of their ancestral histories and cultural roots not only as part of their spiritual journeys but also as part of reclaiming what some refer to as their "authentic" identity. Elise Poitier, an African American woman now in her late forties, reflects back to the early days of this process when as a young adult she first began resisting being judged by white mainstream culture or standards of beauty. When she moved from the Midwest to Atlanta, she explains, "In Atlanta, my beauty was affirmed. I could walk down the street and see myself; there was a sense of connectedness . . . that I would consider a spiritual connection."

Derise Tolliver*[2] an African American psychologist and professor, described learning more of her African history and traditions as part of her spiritual journey, which relates to her authentic identity and all aspects of her life, including her life in the classroom:

> I try to bring my full, authentic self to the classroom and use all aspects of myself to inform my practice and to facilitate the learning of others. An important aspect of my being is Spirit. . . . My core understanding of Spirit is grounded in a traditional African ethos, which has been passed down, not necessarily consciously, through the generations of my people. I have lived it for a long time, although it has become a more conscious practice over the last decade.

Becoming more conscious of the African roots of her culture and spirituality was part of the process of reclaiming a positive cultural identity that helps her connect with students of all backgrounds. In essence, because she is comfortable with who she is, more fully grounded in her spiritual and cultural self and her own authenticity, she invites others into their own authenticity.

---

2. An asterisk (*) next to a name indicates that it is the person's real name as opposed to a pseudonym.

She describes this journey to her authenticity and positive cultural identity as an ongoing one, with an increased sense of how spirit and spirituality have been a part of that. Part of the reclaiming of her own ancestral history and culture has been to study the traditions and spirituality of the Akan people of Ghana. She described a significant spiritual experience for her that took place at one of the slave castles in Ghana when she had brought a group there as part of a study abroad program:

> *The slave castles were one of the last places that any of the enslaved Africans were before they were transported to wherever: these shores, the Caribbean, or South America. We were at Cape Coast castle in Ghana. After everybody else left, I went back into this particular dungeon and just took off my shoes, and just closed my eyes, and touched the walls, and just felt the energy, the terror, the pain—ALL of that. That was very, very profound to me, and I guess in terms of the connection, I think a lot of people build the connection between Africa and America in that place, because that's a port where the ancestors came through. So being in that dungeon, in that room BY MYSELF, and actually having my feet on THAT ground was quite a profound spiritual experience for me.*

Clearly, the experience had a strong affective component. It had an intellectual or cognitive component as the group had been studying the history and the culture of the area and the tragedy of the slave trade. But for Derise Tolliver it also had a spiritual component because it connected her ever more deeply with her own culture and history: for her, there was also an ancestral connection.

This ancestral connection, rooted in one's own history and culture, may be important for everyone. But it seems to have a particularly strong significance to people of color who have gone on the spiritual and cultural journey of reclaiming their history and cultural identity. Perhaps this is because the cultural history of many people of color is either entirely absent or "white-washed" in the U.S. educational system. Tito Rodriguez,* a forty-year-old Puerto Rican man who grew up both in Puerto Rico and Chicago, discusses the important role of learning the "sacred stories of the ancestors" as a significant part of reclaiming his cultural identity and of claiming his sacred face. He explained that he learned little of his own cultural history or the history of Puerto Rico beyond its status as an island and U.S. territory through the schools either on the U.S. mainland or in Puerto Rico. He described the process of later adolescence and into adulthood when he learned some of his own cultural history, which happened as a result of his involvement in dance and cultural arts:

> Then I became the most fervent Puerto Rican. I was angry with the world and discovered through the arts that Puerto Rico is more than an Island! I found out that I was Taino [the Indigenous people of Puerto Rico], African, and European. This made me happy. But I had to learn more about the history and stories of these cultures in order for me to be "whole."

He went on to explain that after many years of study and research, he understood more about Puerto Rican culture and history, and notes: "But even after learning about that, I felt empty." Knowing on a cognitive level wasn't enough. "I then look into the sacred story of my ancestors," said Tito, and explains that their sacred stories, and understanding the spirituality of his ancestors as a part of cultural experience that was passed on to him in different ways, led to a different and deeper kind of understanding that was transformative. For him, this was part of the process of freeing what Abalos (1998) refers to as his "sacred face." It also ties into his work as an educator and means

> I must first liberate myself from the ill of ignorance and open myself to . . . all my brothers and sisters. I must not judge,

but help those who have not acquired the same level of trans-
formation that I have. I'm not saying that I don't need more
transformation. On the contrary! I must live a life of contin-
ued transformation for the better of my family, my commu-
nity, my country, and all humans. I hope that by doing this,
I'm also a tool for transformation.

Thus, for Tito Rodriguez,* Derise Tolliver,* and many others, being
a tool for transformation requires that they connect with the history, culture, and spirituality of their ancestors in order to continue
their own transformative work on themselves and those with whom
they work.

Spirituality and Dealing with Internalized Oppression

The cultural identity models of Abalos, Cross, Meyers, et al. are
obviously applicable to the experience of people of color in this
country. Yet the process of developing a positive sense of one's cultural and spiritual identity is important for all of us, but especially
those who are marginalized because of their cultural background,
social class, or sexual orientation. In building on the Cross (1971)
model, others (Chavez & Guido-DiBrito, 1999; Phinny, 1990) pose
a model of ethnic identity development relative to all U.S. nondominant groups that focuses on dealing with the effects of prejudice, unlearning internalized oppression, and reclaiming a positive
identity. Although these authors don't discuss the spiritual component of this, many of those I interviewed did discuss the role of
spirituality in dealing with internalized oppression, that is, the
internalized (but mostly unconscious) belief in the superiority of
those more representative of the dominant culture.

Being Jewish and Dealing with Internalized Oppression

Activist and adult educator Penny Rosenwasser* describes her own
journey to reclaiming a positive Jewish cultural identity and its

relationship to spirituality and to her own internalized oppression against herself as a Jewish woman. She explained the insidious ways her own internalized oppression against her Jewish culture was manifested. She notes that in her many years of activist work around women's issues, race relations, antinuclear, and other social justice movements, she virtually disassociated herself from her Jewish roots.

> *Raised as an assimilated Jew in white Christian middle-class suburbs, I learned well how to blend in and belong as white. . . . I felt uncomfortable around people who looked and/or behaved in ways that were "too Jewish." When told I didn't "look Jewish," I replied "Thank you."*

She described a particularly poignant moment in this process of beginning to unlearn this lethal form of internalized oppression when she cofacilitated a council of Jewish women:

> *When one of my Jewish mentors heard me talk about my childhood, she told me there were thousands of people with experiences like mine in this country. She reflected back to me, "You lost your wail; your song is a minor key, and you've been trying to fit into a major key." When I mentioned that, as middle class, I at least had had my voice heard, another friend offered: "But not your Jewish voice." As her words sifted through me, I felt in my body the parts of me that I had allowed to be cut off: the most-Jewish parts. In brief, I had learned to internalize societal attitudes of disgust at those who were "too Jewish"; I had learned to hate who I was, and I did not even know it.*

Unlearning this internalized hatred or oppression has been a process that she describes as a spiritual journey that she really didn't come to until midlife. And in reflecting back, she said in amazement:

> *It took nearly thirty years of my life for me to embrace my*
> *Jewishness in a deep emotional way . . . as a significant part*
> *of my heritage and identity. My reading . . . along with my*
> *mentoring friendships with Jewish women activists, filled me*
> *with stories I related to, helping me access my own cultural*
> *background through women I identified with.*

Finding these women's stories and mentoring friendships has indeed
been a blessing for her that has helped her embrace all parts of her
identity, particularly her cultural identity as a Jew. In summing up
and reflecting on how this relates to her spirituality she noted,

> *My spirituality is all about how I relate to my world and oth-*
> *ers, how I make meaning of life. From Jewish prophetic tra-*
> *dition and mysticism (via the Kabbalah), comes the concept*
> *of "tikkun olam" or the repair and healing of the world. This*
> *aptly expresses my core motivation in life, toward social jus-*
> *tice, toward creating a life that is meaningful and makes a dif-*
> *ference. I believe I get this from my Jewishness-Judaism,*
> *which for me is a blend of culture and spirituality.*

This blend of culture and spirituality embodied in the Jewish concept of *tikkun olam* not only motivates Penny's activism but also has
motivated the healing of her own world, the healing of her own
spirit, in confronting and dealing directly with her own internalized
oppression. It has been a process that has taken years; as for all of
us, becoming more authentically ourselves is an ongoing, lifelong
process that intersects with all aspects of our identity.

Spirituality and Mediating Among Multiple Identities

Identity is not monolithic. We are not only people with a race and
ethnic cultural history; we are also people who have a class background, a gender, and a sexual orientation. Given the extreme
homophobia that is part of the larger culture, it would be impossible to grow up and not have some internalized homophobia if one

were gay, lesbian, or bisexual. Of course, how one deals with this phenomenon of internalized oppression relates to other aspects of one's identity—one's race, class, culture, and so on. These multiple aspects of our lives interact as all aspects of our identity continue to develop. This is why (as noted toward the beginning of Chapter Six) Hays (2001) offers the ADDRESSING framework, which suggests a system for organizing the multiple cultural influences that affect development.

Unlike the Hays (2001) framework for dealing with cultural complexities, most models of identity development tend to foreground only one aspect of life experience at a time, such as race, culture, gender, class, or sexual orientation. It is important to look at how each thread, such as race or ethnicity, affects development overall, at the same time that one keeps in mind the whole. Thus, the race and ethnic identity models have focused primarily on culture, particularly on what it means to develop a positive identity when one is a member of a minority cultural group. Cass (1984) and Edwards and Brooks (1999) have discussed models of positive sexual identity development, focusing particularly on gay, lesbian, or bisexual identity. Again, these discussions have not included the component of spirituality in relation to positive cultural or sexual identity development. This is what makes Myers et al.'s conceptualization of identity development unique and appealing: it looks at the role of spirituality in transcending all bondages of oppression and developing a positive identity overall, whereas Hays (2001) tends to look at spiritual and religious orientation as one component that affects all aspects of development. But for some people, spirituality and claiming one's sacred face have an important role to play in mediating among multiple aspects of one's identity.

The story of Harriet Smith is a case in point. In her story, it is apparent how sexual orientation, culture, and class intersect with spirituality in dealing both with internalized oppression and with forming a positive view of self, grounded in spirituality and in aspects of her culture of origin.

Harriet is a forty-six-year-old nurse, an adult educator and a community activist, a white woman from a rural, Southern, working-class background who grew up in the Pentecostal Church. While growing up, she went to church four times per week. In considering the intersection of class, religious background, and culture, she reflected back, noting, "it [her religious upbringing] has to be understood in the context of being your culture. It's not your religion or spirituality, because it's everything you *are* and what you *do* and *how you live your life*. . . . It's your way of life!" Although she didn't have much class-consciousness growing up, in reflecting back she noted, "Pentecostal folks are pretty poor people." It was in this religious-cultural-class context where Harriet, who found meaning and identity in these intersections, began to wrestle with another important aspect of her identity: her sexual orientation.

After a marriage at sixteen and two children, she began dealing with her sexual orientation after an altercation and subsequent split from her husband: "He screamed at me that I was 'queer.' I had no idea what he was talking about. . . . He explained it to me and I thought, 'Wow! He's right.'" Harriet's religious tradition and her spirituality were extremely important to her, so at first she tried to find a way to reconcile her sexual orientation and her Pentecostal background. In her early twenties, she talked to many ministers and church people, who alternately made her feel guilty and hopeful, and one finally suggested, "leave it up to God." Harriet described a pivotal experience that happened about a year later:

> I got hurt playing softball and I tore my quadriceps so bad I passed out. I went to the best orthopedist in town, who put a splint on it. . . . I also believed in faith healing, and one night I went to the altar I felt this real coldness go into my leg, and then [it] got really hot, and I thought "wow" and [when] the minister told me—I took the splint off, and the big lump that was on my leg, it was gone! . . . Well that was a turning point for me, because I thought "why would God heal me, if

I was this person that was condemned to hell?" God wouldn't
do that for me, and I thought "OK, this is my sign that it's
OK for me to be a lesbian."

Although this particular experience was a significant turning
point for Harriet, in terms of her own acceptance of her lesbian sexual identity and dealing directly with her own internalized oppression, she knew she was not going to find public acceptance for it in
the Pentecostal Church. Yet in her heart, the authenticity of her
identity, confirmed through what she describes as this particularly
significant spiritual experience, gave her the courage to embrace
who she is and over time to ultimately develop a positive identity
as a lesbian.

Harriet eventually found spiritual community in a local Unitarian fellowship and through participating in monthly women's spirituality groups that supported both her spirituality and her activist
work with battered women and around lesbian and gay issues. As a
result of her own experiences in combination with a spiritual commitment to social justice work, she and her partner eventually co-
founded an adult education center based on the honoring of
"women's spirit" and the principles of adult popular education.
Their center offers programs and services that attempt to meet the
needs of some of the local poor and oppressed people, dealing
directly with the transformation of homophobia and other systems
of oppression, such as race and class. In their center's early days,
there had been much attempted violence directed at them, including death threats, the killing of their dog, and assaults on their
property. When the attorney who worked in defense of the violence
against them suggested that they consider leaving for their personal
safety, and asked "Don't you understand that this is the Bible Belt?"
Harriet replied: "Yes; that's why I'm here!" She reflected back on
these days not so very long ago, and went on to explain to me:

You see, I have had to turn and face my culture head on,
and say "No! You're not going to run me out of here like an

> *animal." Literally, I had rather be dead than for my kids or*
> *my family to see me having to flee because someone else has*
> *that power to make me leave!*

Harriet has stayed in the rural South because there is where her cultural roots are. She believes she must stay because of her felt responsibility to care for her family and to work for social change around transformation of systems of oppression of all kinds, including race, gender, class, and sexual orientation within this cultural context. In claiming her sacred face and her more authentic identity, she has found the courage to stand up and say no and challenge those things within her culture that are oppressive, and to say a resounding yes to those things that are life-giving. In so doing, as Abalos (1998) suggests, she has also engaged her political face. Grounded in her spirituality, she also takes great inspiration in the work and legacy of Harriet Tubman, who she noted, in spite of ill health,

> *managed to save about three hundred people from hell here*
> *on earth. Sometimes I think, "what can one person do?" One*
> *person can do a lot! That's my inspiration. I think of that*
> *every day. And when I get depressed, I look at [Harriet Tub-*
> *man] and just think about "if she could do it, I could do it!"*

It is clear how spirituality intersects with culture, class, and sexual identity in Harriet's story. Her spiritual experience, the meaning she associated with her healing experience at the altar in the Pentecostal Church in her early twenties, was a sign to her that her lesbian identity was a part of her authenticity and part of her spirituality. Indeed, hers is only one story, and clearly many other gay and lesbian identity stories come to the fore and are given spiritual meaning in ways different from Harriet's (Thompson, 1995). But it is also significant that this initial experience was mediated from within the familiarity of her childhood religious tradition inscribed in her rural Southern culture and working-class roots. Although she has long since moved away from the Pentecostal tradition, in reflecting back on her Christian Pentecostal roots that are still very much a part of who she is, she notes:

> I think your core beliefs, where do they come from? Mine came out of the Judeo–Christian church. I don't know if people can change what is in the core. . . First of all I believe in honesty. I believe in fairness, in justice.

Obviously, she takes this call to justice and honesty very seriously. In embracing her four faces, she has drawn on her spiritual or sacred face to become political, deal with her own internalized oppression, stand up against injustice within her own culture, and celebrate what leads to wholeness.

Harriet has also drawn on her spirituality to mediate among various aspects of her identity and to make a choice that leads to her greater wholeness. Although it might have been easier to leave and move to a community more accepting of her sexual identity, an equally strong component of her identity was her rural Southern cultural heritage. Thus her own spirituality helped her find the courage to accept all aspects of her identity and not choose among them. In thinking about her own history, culture, and spiritual development within this culture, she noted: "It was prophesied in my church that I would preach when I was fourteen years old!" She added that people now say to her ironically, "I guess you got your calling all right! You're just in a different place!" It seems that Harriet, in making a difference in her own community, has found her calling. Perhaps she has also found what Palmer (2000) suggests is "the seed of authentic vocation" (p. 9).

Summary and Brief Thoughts for Practice

This chapter has focused primarily on the role of spiritual experience in developing a positive cultural identity. It is grounded in the theoretical framework of David Abalos (1998), who discusses the importance of reclaiming four faces of one's being as part of the ongoing transformation process toward claiming a positive cultural identity: the personal face, the historical face, the political face, and the sacred face. Although Abalos writes more specifically about the Latino community in the United States, his insights are relevant to any group or individual who has been oppressed due to the history of slavery, colonization, or other systems of oppression. What is unique about Abalos's framework is that he calls attention to the importance of the sacred face, or the role of spirituality in dealing with the mechanisms of internalized oppression and reclaiming a positive identity. In this chapter, several of the cultural identity models were reviewed that capture the process of moving from a more oppressed identity to claiming a positive and pride-filled identity. Many of these models have not dealt directly with the role of spirituality in this process. An important focus of this chapter has been making the role of spirituality more visible by using the example of several people's stories and how they have claimed a more sacred face in relationship to multiple aspects of their identity.

This claiming of a more sacred face as related to dealing with culture is manifested in a variety of ways. In this chapter, the focus has been on dealing directly with and reclaiming oppressed parts of one's own identity as a spiritual process. This is important for those who have been marginalized because of their race, ethnicity, national origin, religion, social class, sexual orientation, disability, or gender. But part of the reclaiming process is challenging the ways the dominant culture has imposed such an oppressed identity through the hegemonic processes of education, media, family relations, or the government. To challenge is to take action, and as Abalos (1998) notes, to take action, or "to cast out demons in our personal lives and in society means that we have freed our sacred face" (p. 35).

What does this suggest for culturally relevant practice in adult and higher education contexts? As noted in the second chapter, according to Guy (1999) a purpose of culturally relevant education is "the reconstruction of learners' group-based identity from one that is negative to one that is positive" (p. 13). It appears that for many people spirituality has an important role in this process, and could be incorporated into classes that directly deal with cultural issues in a way that does not necessarily impose a spiritual or religious agenda. I often begin my own classes that focus on cultural issues with an assignment in which learners write aspects of their own cultural story, such as how their own awareness of their cultural identity developed. In particular, they describe their culture of origin in terms of their race, ethnicity, religion, and class background; the cultural mix of the communities in which they grew up; what messages they received about themselves and "others" through both the overt curriculum and the hidden curriculum in schools and in other institutions; and who were important cultural role models for them. In essence, in this initial assignment I attempt to pose questions that might help them think about how their cultural consciousness developed and the role of social structures in shaping their identity and their thinking. I also share my own process around these issues, particularly in understanding what it means to be white (a theme that will be taken up more in the next chapter) and to be a person of my gender, class, and so on, and the fact that I am still working to understand these aspects of my identity.

It would be easy to ask learners, in an assignment such as this, what role religion and spirituality had both in shaping their cultural identity and in helping them reclaim important aspects of their identity. It would also be appropriate to provide some readings and stories related to the role of spirituality in claiming a positive cultural or gender identity, and then for participants to reflect on its place in their own lives in light of the readings. Another assignment might focus on how they already have, or are currently in the process of, reclaiming their cultural identity by analyzing their life experience vis-à-vis some of the cultural identity models, or it might focus on reclaiming Abalos's four faces (the personal, political, historical, and sacred) relative to their own cultural lives. Indeed, engagement with such an analysis as an individual process could help learners develop a better understanding of their own cultural identity and spirituality. But if this analysis is carefully shared in a small group context, it could also help them have a better sense of how different the experience is of people of different race, culture, gender, religion, sexual orientation, and class groups depending on where they are situated relative to the dominant culture.

Dealing with issues based on culture, race, class, and gender can be controversial. So can dealing with spirituality as related to cultural identity. Although I offer some further thoughts on the connection of spirituality and culture to practice in far greater detail in Part Three, it is always important to remember that people are differently situated by virtue of their positionality (race, gender, class, and sexual orientation) relative to systems of power and privilege. As an instructor, I believe that adult learners need to share only what they are willing or want to share relative to these subjects. Further, I never ask my students to share what I am unwilling to share myself. So I will share the fact that I am still very much in process with reclaiming my own personal, political, historical, and sacred faces, and what this process has to do with various aspects of my own positionality; and that I still struggle to be centered in my own sense of spirituality in my own search for wholeness, which I believe is very much related to my attempts to stay grounded in my more authentic identity. As I am trying to stay grounded and live out of a more authentic place, I am trying to create an environment where they might do the same. Within the confines of higher education that includes reading, writing, and analysis, there also can be a certain level of freedom to consider the role of spirituality in relation to dealing with cultural issues and cultural identity. We all come to a greater sense of that authentic identity in different ways, and through a different sense of what spirituality is and its role (if any) in the process. As many theists and spiritual writers note, there may be one river but many wells (Fox, 2000). By digging deeper and finding new wells, we might understand the river better. And that river includes ourselves. It also includes each other.

8

Searching for Wholeness

Crossing Culture, White Identity, and Spiritual Development

Culture is never static. Just as identity is not one-dimensional, one's own cultural understanding changes with increased contact with people from other cultural groups and exposure to different ways that people organize their lives and social networks. Immigrants and those who have lived in countries not their own know this. But all of us, no matter what our cultural background, are far more likely to have closer contact and more intimate work or personal relationships with people of different race or ethnic identities, religious backgrounds, sexual orientations, or from different parts of the world now than even fifty years ago.

This increased contact is due to changes in both North American and global mobility, as well as the developments of technology that have made access to other parts of the world more easily available through air travel and the Internet. It is also due to the activism of those involved in various social movements that have worked for civil rights and rights for women, gays and lesbians, working-class and subsistence laborers, and people with disabilities, who have challenged oppressive norms in the dominant culture. As a result of these trends, developments, and activist movements, we are increasingly affected by different cultures and ways of being in the world, thus continually changing the cultural fabric of North America, as well as our understanding of our own culture. Further,

we are more likely to have contact with spiritual and religious traditions that are quite different from our own than was true at any
other time in human history.

Increased contact with those culturally, religiously, and spiritually different from ourselves means that we are likely to have more
opportunity to have cross-cultural learning experiences. Such experiences of "crossing culture" can come in a variety of forms that can
affect both our spirituality in the ways we "claim a sacred face" and
our cultural understanding. Some of these learning experiences
might happen as a result of having close personal relationships with
those of a different culture and spiritual orientation, through international travel or living in a country different than one's nation of
origin, or through formal education. This chapter focuses on the
connection of spirituality to crossing culture, as related to the spiritual search toward greater wholeness and toward claiming our more
sacred face.

Many who live in countries different from their nations of origin did not necessarily move to that country strictly out of personal
choice. Some move for survival for themselves or their families, due
to war or unrest in their countries of origin, or for other personal
survival needs. I begin this chapter with an examination of how
spirituality relates to shifting identities in a shifting geographical
context, primarily by drawing on the experience of one immigrant
woman. Next I examine the experience, predominantly of those
who are white and of Christian background, who cross spiritual and
cultural borders specifically to further their spiritual growth.

Spirituality and Shifting Identities in a Shifting Context

In the last chapter, I discussed the fact that people have multiple
identities, in that they have an identity based on their race or ethnicity, their gender, their sexual orientation, their social class, and
so on. We saw how Harriet Smith drew on her spirituality to medi-

ate among those multiple identities, including her identity as a lesbian, as a Southern woman from a rural area, and as one from a working class background. Harriet has lived in the same community her whole life. Although communities never remain static and are always changing incrementally, the cultural context in which she was negotiating various aspects of her identity remained relatively stable—at least much more so than if she had moved to a different geographical area. But those who are immigrants to North America (or elsewhere) generally negotiate various aspects of their identity and their spirituality against the backdrop of a very different cultural context than that of their home countries. Aiysha Ali, who was introduced in Chapter One, is one such example. Aiysha is a Muslim woman of East Indian descent who was born in East Africa, where her family had lived for several generations. Her immediate family left East Africa when she was six years old due to severe unrest in her country of origin and emigrated to England, where she lived for several years until her teens. She then moved to Canada for a few years and ultimately immigrated to the United States by her late adolescence.

Aiysha has been forced to cross culture, both literally and figuratively, many times throughout her life. Moving a number of times and having to negotiate being a member of a privileged group in some contexts but being a member of an oppressed or lower-status group in other contexts has made Aiysha have to negotiate her own shifting identity in a constantly shifting cultural context. These moves and identity shifts that are a part of her personal life experience, along with the fact that Aiysha is a professor with a subspecialty in multicultural issues, have forced her to think a lot about the development of her religious and cultural identity as an immigrant and a Muslim in the United States. In describing the connection between her ethnic identity and her religious identity, she noted:

> Being of East Indian origin AND a Muslim, not only here in
> the United States but everywhere I've lived, has served as a
> double reinforcement of my otherness. In some cases for me

it's a question of privilege. For example, in Africa where we were, there's no doubt that the Indian population was part of the business population, whereas in London, I was definitely NOT part of the privileged class. In terms of societal structures, I identified a lot more with the lower classes, and came to the U.S. with a thick cockney accent.

She discussed how for years living in the United States she was not able to separate being Muslim from her ethnic identity. "I never really saw my cultural identity as anything different from my religious identity because I'd been brought up to believe in Islam as a way of life, that everything you do is impacted by and impacts upon who you are as a religious person." Although she always remains both of East Indian ethnicity *and* Muslim, she has been able to separate analytically what this might mean.

If I were a Muslim but I was Caucasian, it would be very different because there would be elements of shared experience that would be points of stability. On the other hand, if I were East Indian and not a Muslim, depending on whether I were Christian or Hindu—again it would make a difference because if I were a Christian, it would be a lot easier, because I would feel despite my ethnic background that I was a part of society because it is a largely Christian milieu.

In being both an ethnic minority and a religious minority but as one who is educated with a doctoral degree and has both education and class privilege in the United States, Aiysha has developed the ability to cross cultural borders to be able to speak to many different groups and in many different contexts fairly comfortably at this point in her adult life. But developing this ability has been a process that has taken time, as there had always been pressure to blend in. She gave the example of how this had been manifested earlier in her life. In her Muslim community, occasions of joy are often marked with the application of henna. "In the past I would think very carefully of where I was going on the past two or three weeks, before putting on henna, I now do not hesitate to do it," she explained. At this point in her development, she does not try to blend in, but rather uses those occasions when people ask what she has on her hands as a point of education about Islam and about her East Indian ethnic heritage. She described how this shift has taken place over time and reflected on being both Muslim and East Indian:

> Before it was just a matter of fact for me. Now, it's still a matter of fact, but it's also a matter of pride. I've taken the attitude "This is WHO I AM. If you are going to know me and like me, you're going to know the whole of me, not just parts of me." So in a sense the dichotomization of my identity that I described at the beginning, I'm beginning to take that and create a whole from it in the way that I interact.

Aiysha attributes the shift that has taken place over time to formal education that has partly focused on the negotiation of cultural and religious difference, positive personal experiences in which she was deliberately in religious and culturally pluralistic situations that allowed her to experiment with being more overt with these aspects of her identity, and the experience of becoming a parent. Ironically, her exposure and close personal relationships with people of very different religious and cultural backgrounds has caused her to understand and reclaim her own culture and religious identity with pride and a sense of wholeness. But this sense of "the whole" is related to her spirituality, which is tremendously important to her.

> One of the things that I would say in terms of my spirituality, while it is definitely grounded in my cultural and religious identity, it's not exclusive to that. In other words, if I find resonance in other places, whether it's African, or Native American spirituality, or Hindu—other forms of spirituality, I'm

open to them. And not just religious traditions—but having my spirit moved in some way.

Aiysha's journey toward greater pride in who she is as an immigrant and a Muslim woman of East Indian descent who has had to negotiate her own shifting identity in many shifting contexts has been partly a spiritual journey. It is one that has led her to greater openness, understanding, and acceptance of many positions and ways of living not her own. Grounded more proudly and deeply in her own identity and spirituality has given her the courage to speak out with openness and with pride more publicly about her religious and cultural identity in this post–September 11, 2001 era. Finding the courage to do so for her is part of claiming her sacred face and living out her life purpose, while being grounded in her more authentic identity amid a shifting cultural and religious American landscape.

White Identity and Crossing Culture in the Ongoing Search for Wholeness

Like Aiysha Ali, many of those featured in the stories and examples in earlier chapters were not representative of the dominant culture in one way or another, either by virtue of their race, culture, sexual orientation, religion, or national origin. They were, however, familiar with the norms of cultural groups or religious traditions different from their own—that of the dominant culture. Although culture is never static and is always changing, the dominant culture with the greatest economic and public decision-making power in North America is still white, moneyed, male, heterosexual, of Christian background, and able bodied, to name some of the more obvious structural categories. These categories represent some of the invisible norms that people are often measured against, or even unconsciously measure themselves against, which can result in the phenomenon of internalized oppression. It is impossible to live in

North America without having a sense of these invisible norms. An important part of ongoing positive identity development for many who are not representative of these invisible norms is to reclaim the parts of themselves that are different or "other." As we saw earlier, for many, this reclaiming is partly a spiritual process. It is a search to become whole.

Perhaps it is easier to have a sense of how spirituality and becoming whole relate to reclaiming one's cultural or sexual identity when one is "other" than one of these invisible norms, such as a person of color, gay or lesbian, or Jewish or Muslim in primarily white Christian North America. Often people in North America who are white or who were socialized within the Christian tradition have little sense of their own culture. Perhaps when one is representative of the dominant culture, it is difficult to have sense of where that culture is. As many have recently discussed (Johnson-Bailey & Cervero, 2000; Shore, 2001; Sleeter, 1996) in considerations of race in adult education, whiteness is *the primary* invisible norm, the invisible standard that people are often measured against. To be fully conscious of what is so pervasive that it is almost invisible is difficult, just as fish probably have little or no consciousness of water. But if fish were not in water, they probably would very quickly have a sense of what water is.

How does spirituality intersect with culture and ongoing development for those who are more representative of the "water" of the dominant culture in North America: those who are white, heterosexual, and grew up in one of the Christian denominations? Of course whiteness is not a monolithic category, and there are some who have a strong sense of being of Irish, Italian, English, or other European descent. But many white people do not identify very strongly with their countries of origin or the cultures of their forebears, and in fact have little sense of their own culture at all. This lack of culture consciousness may be because their families have lived in North America for several generations, or because they are of mixed European ancestry from which it may be difficult to tease out what is German, what is English, and what is Irish. And although the amalgamation of white, heterosexual, and largely Christian culture in North America has different manifestations for different people, the ongoing spiritual development of white, heterosexual people of Christian background is related to their particular cultural background and tradition, as well as somewhat related to white Christian culture overall. To some degree, we often spiral back to our cultural roots, and move forward in an effort to become whole. There are a myriad of ways this spiritual development as connected to culture could be manifested. Since I interviewed people primarily about the connection of their spirituality to doing cultural and social justice, here I discuss two primary ways that it was manifested among those I interviewed who are white and of Christian background: (1) through developing a deeper understanding of white culture in general and one's own particular cultural identity within it, and (2) through making an active choice for crossing and examining spiritual traditions rooted in other cultures.

Spirituality and White Cultural Identity

The cultural, ethnic, and sexual identity models as discussed in the last chapter emphasize the identity development of those not representative of the dominant culture. Helms (1984), Chavez and Guido-DiBrito (1999), and Tatum (1997) have each discussed a model of cultural identity for white people who have begun to understand whiteness as a system of privilege. The model's basic tenet is that first one might experience a disorienting dilemma that makes white privilege visible. This usually happens in light of an experience in a personal relationship with a person of color, where one might witness or experience differential treatment that appears to be based on race. Over time, many who first become aware of the pervasiveness of white privilege may then begin to explore the assumptions they have unconsciously absorbed from their own culture of origin about what constitutes valid forms of knowledge or appropriate ways of being in the world. Further, many explore what it means to be an ally to people of color or other nondominant groups (such as the gay-lesbian-bisexual community, or people with disabilities) when one is a member of a dominant group. Such a process takes time, usually over a period of years, when there is more sustained involvement with nondominant groups. Although white identity theorists have not conceptualized this as a spiritual process per se, the spirituality of many who are white requires that they deal with social justice issues in general, including challenging racism and dealing with their own white privilege. Patricia Jones, a clinical psychologist and psychology professor in her early forties, describes her own journey to developing an understanding of cultural differences and what it means to be white or European American as integrated with her spirituality.

Patricia grew up Presbyterian and came from a long line of "preachers, teachers, and farmers," a culture that nurtured her spirituality and a concern for reaching out to others. She grew up both in the Midwest and Alaska. Since her adolescence, she interacted with many people from different cultural groups as a result of living in Alaska, traveling worldwide, and living overseas. While in college, she met and eventually married a Muslim man from North Africa. Her own European American cultural identity became visible to her because of her close personal relationships with her husband, her in-laws, and people of color in North America, Europe, and North Africa.

In many ways, Patricia's journey to understanding being white or European American parallels what Helms (1984) and Tatum (1997) discuss in their consideration of the white identity models. But because spirituality is also important to Patricia, it is not surprising that she would also consider how her spiritual journey relates to this process. In exploring her European American cultural heritage and how it connects to her Christian background and her current, more eclectic and individualistic spirituality, she noted:

Probably the strongest value-related influence in terms of my Christian heritage is individualism. I'm Euro-American and individualism was just a really powerful thing in my family. . . . And so my spirituality has taken a very individ- ualistic form. That's probably the Christian heritage piece, and then the social contributions—the preacher, teacher, mis- sionary heritage—not specifically linked to Christian beliefs, but it is a Christian thing: that you go out and do good in the world.

Patricia is making a distinction between white Christian culture and Christianity as an overt religious choice. The beliefs of her own family rooted in a Christian ethos and passed on to her through her "preacher, teacher, missionary heritage" were also rooted in the American emphasis on rugged individualism. Patricia is implicitly contrasting this more passive internalizing of individualism from Christian cultural values with what is an ongoing active religious choice for a specifically Christian path or spirituality.

Patricia's current spirituality is more eclectic and not exclusively Christian. However, her own values are rooted in the Christian tra- dition, and she explains that at earlier points in her life she would have defined herself as explicitly religiously Christian, in that she had directly studied and practiced it. But her exposure to many cul- tural and spiritual traditions through her close personal relation- ships with people of color expanded her own spirituality and put her in touch with what it means to have a European American cul- tural identity. In reflecting on her spiritual beliefs, using her under- standing of Islam as an example, she notes, "What my experience with Islam and Muslim people did for me in a very concrete way was to make me realize that I don't accept Christianity as the only way to spiritual fulfillment." However, in contrast to other individ- ualistic forms of spirituality that are prevalent in North America, hers requires that she attend to cultural issues:

As I have become more interested in the spiritual growth movement and Buddhism in particular, I've realized that there are people who are deeply spiritual but do not perceive culturally related forms of oppression. These individuals are all white. Before this, I had the idea that the spiritual transcends everything, and a deeply spiritual person would automatically have an understanding of such issues. It never occurred to me that a person could be deeply spiritual and not see cultural oppression and their own role in it. But apparently this is possible.

It is clear that Patricia's understanding of her own culture and what it means to be white or European American and her concern for cultural issues flow from her life experience and her own spiritual development. But it is also clear this understanding and concern developed in light of her relationships with people who were not white. Patricia is probably unusual in that she has directly explored what whiteness means and how it is melded with her Christian upbringing that also emphasized individualism. Her exposure to other cultures and religious traditions expanded her own spirituality to include a broader, more inclusive, and more multicultural perspective. But in so doing she has also spiraled back to embrace a broader understanding of her own cultural roots and identity, as she moves forward with a wider spiritual perspective in her own efforts to become more whole.

Spiritual Development Through Crossing Culture

A central element of Patricia Jones's story is that in crossing cultural borders, she was no longer wedded to her own religious tradition and no longer identified as exclusively Christian. As noted by many faith and spiritual development theorists (Fowler, 1981; Parks, 2000; Wuthnow, 1999), part of spiritual development appears to include exploring other spiritual traditions. But many do so by staying firmly grounded in their own faith traditions. As discussed in Chapter Five, Fowler found that those in his conjunctive faith stage of faith development were extremely committed to their own faith tradition, at the same time they were open to and interested in learning about other faith traditions.

Nadira Charaniya and Jane West Walsh (2001) conducted a study of adult Christian, Jewish, and Muslim participants involved in ongoing and sustained interreligious dialogue groups. Like the participants at the conjunctive faith stage of the Fowler (1981) study, all their participants were extremely committed to their own religious tradition. But their participants became involved in interreligious dialogue groups intentionally for a number of reasons. Many had significant life experiences with people of other cultures and spiritual traditions that provoked a desire for greater cross-cultural and cross-religious understanding. Most also had an intellectual curiosity coupled with a spiritual need to explore other traditions to have a greater sense of their own religious tradition, as well as that of the other. In addition, their own spirituality and interpretation of their own religious tradition required openness to other cultures and spiritual traditions.

Unlike Patricia Jones, the participants in this study remained committed to their own religious tradition and were strongly identified with a particular formal faith community, but like Patricia their need to further their own spiritual development in their ongoing search for wholeness meant exploring other religious traditions. And given that the participants in their study were white, African American, Jewish, and of Mid-Eastern and Indo-Pak descent, they were also engaged in cross-cultural as well as interreligious dialogue. They also began to understand more about themselves religiously and culturally in light of their engagement with "the other."

There are many people who remain totally or moderately committed to the religious tradition that they grew up in. But many others report that they are spiritual but not religious, and have developed a more individualist and eclectic spirituality similar to that of Patricia Jones, yet without Patricia's direct exploration of the connection of spirituality to culture. There are scores of thousands in North America, largely but not exclusively white, whose spirituality might incorporate some Eastern meditation practices from Buddhism, Hinduism, Yoga, or rituals common to Native American spiritual traditions, or insights from poets or philosophers from other cultures, such as the Sufi poet, Rumi. As an example, Lama Surya Das (1999), an American lama trained in the Tibetan tradition but raised Jewish, notes that most of those who attend his lectures were raised Christian or Jewish. Only some of these actually come to formally identify as Buddhist, or formally study Buddhism with a Buddhist teacher, or study the various Eastern cultures in which Buddhism is rooted.

It seems that many who have developed a more individualist spirituality, in their own search for wholeness, are drawn to spiritual traditions of other cultures because the insights from these traditions have not been easily available in their own. It may be that the messages received from the larger culture in North America, and largely affirmed by Judeo-Christian religious traditions as they have been practiced here, support a somewhat dualistic view of the world that has separated matter from spirit and the rational from the affective or symbolic. Further, in exploring the spiritual traditions rooted in other cultures, many are trying to reframe what was experienced as oppressive or guilt-inducing in their own religious tradition, and to find what is spiritually life-giving in other traditions. Because those who are white and European American often do not have a strong sense of culture, this quest to become whole by exploring spiritual traditions rooted in other cultures is viewed as a spiritual one, more or less devoid of direct attention to culture. For example, Nora, a woman in a recent class that dealt with spirituality and culture, explained that she did not relate at all as an adult to the spirituality inherent in her Italian-Catholic upbringing. In reflecting on what to bring for part of a class assignment that symbolized her spiritual and cultural heritage, she noted:

> *I couldn't find anything in my environment that spoke to my*
> *ancestral nationality, so I brought a book that has a special*
> *meaning to me, the Tao Te Ching. It connects my spirituality*
> *and a culture that I relate to, the culture of wholeness—feel-*
> *ing at one with all things.*

In order to nurture her own spirituality, she has found greater spiritual meaning as an adult in the *Tao Te Ching*, rooted in Chinese
culture, rather than what is rooted in her own. But Nora has not
become a committed Buddhist, or Taoist, nor has she explored the
connection of the *Tao Te Ching* to various Asian cultures. Rather
she has blended insights from another spiritual and cultural tradition with aspects of her own to create a more eclectic and individualist spirituality that facilitates for her a "culture of wholeness."

Although spiritual seekers in North America borrow elements
of spiritual traditions from other cultures in order to nurture their
own individualist spirituality, there are also those who cross spiritual traditions and seriously study and eventually identify with a different spiritual tradition and community than what they were raised
in. Maureen Abbott, a professor and social activist in her mid-fifties,
for example, was raised and heavily involved in the Methodist
Church through her later young adult years. Driven by the difficulties of a divorce and her resulting depression, she was introduced to
the practice of an Indian-based form of yogic meditation that is part
of the Siddha Yoga tradition. Over time, she has become extremely
committed to this tradition. She regularly makes pilgrimages to
India as part of her ongoing spiritual training, meditates and chants
regularly, and meets twice a week with a spiritual community. In reflecting back, she attributes her strong concern for social justice
issues and her activism to her Methodist background. But she also
notes that she was initially drawn to a sense of sacredness in the
Siddha Yoga tradition that she did not find available in the white
Methodist church communities in which she was raised:

They were a social gathering place, a source of social support
community when people were sick and dying, and they talked
about ethics, so it was kind of intellectual, but they had noth-
ing to offer in terms of helping people to have a deeper expe-
rience of God.

Maureen has great respect for her Methodist tradition. She values the
emphasis on social justice and an intellectual understanding of
the world. But at a significant point in her life, she needed something different from what she found available in her Methodist
background. In speaking more specifically about the spiritual draw
to Siddha Yoga and its view of the world, she adds: "It really is the
invoking of the spirit. . . . [It] both evokes that kind of spiritual
experience, but has an intellectual way of making sense out of it."
Thus, Maureen has found the experience of crossing culture to a
new spiritual tradition to which she is now committed to be one
that that has led to her greater wholeness.

The process of becoming committed to a different spiritual tradition, particularly one that is not related to one's culture of origin,
takes time. David Preston, also a professor in his late fifties, grew up
and was extremely active in the Catholic Church. He became dis-
illusioned with Catholicism as a result of a difficult divorce, and
eventually was introduced to and became committed to Vedanta, a
form of Hinduism also rooted in the culture of India. But the process
of becoming committed to it and taking the steps to initiation and
formalized study and direction with a swami took eight years. In
thinking about his spiritual journey, he describes the process of
breaking with Catholicism and then his introduction to Vedanta:

It took five years to break. And even then it wasn't a break
because I still felt a lot of comfort going back into the physi-
cal church, into the ritual church, into all those sacraments
that I still felt comfortable being a part of at the time. Until I

had something else to put in its place, it was still a comfort-
able place to go. But then when I met my wife, it was much
more immediate. Now I had someone who was talking about
different paths, multiple paths, all of which lead to the same
God.

This "having something to put in its place" was important for
David. Although he had found great meaning well into his adult
years in the Catholicism in which he was raised, after a point it no
longer met his spiritual needs. David was introduced to Vedanta
through a woman whom he later married. He found that his needs
were met by this spirituality rooted in Indian culture. Through his
study and initiation, he has given some serious thought to the connection between this spirituality and the culture of India in which
it is rooted.

The spirituality that I am trying to learn is not of my culture.
And it is deeply cultural. If anything, Indian culture is deeply
spiritual. But it is first philosophical. That which is spiritual
in India, before that is philosophical. Even the psychology out
of India is philosophical and spiritual; there is no separation.
So in a sense the cultural thing I'm trying to deal with is the
integration of that which is philosophical, psychological, social,
and spiritual. Because that's what the culture has always been
as [it is] represented in this particular spirituality. But in our
[North American] culture, those have been rather separate
domains.

It appears that David is drawn to what he perceives as being
more holistic in another culture as opposed to what he has experienced as being more separate or dualistic in his culture of origin.
Obviously, David has given this some consideration, as well as the
fact that Vedanta is rooted in the context of an Indian culture. But
it was more difficult for David to explain how his spiritual journey

relates to being specifically white or male. He does allude to the fact that North American culture seems to separate the domains of spirit and matter. But he does not relate this particularly to white culture, whereas people who are marginalized in North America tend to relate their spiritual journey more directly to reclaiming their cultural, ethnic, or sexual identity. Again, as Johnson-Bailey and Cervero (2000) note, because whiteness is the invisible norm, it tends to be invisible to those who are white.

It seems that a part of spiritual development for many people is to explore spiritualities rooted in cultural traditions other than their own. They might do so and remain committed to the religion of their culture of origin, as in the case of the participants in the Charaniya and West Walsh (2001) study. Or they might develop a more eclectic and individualist spirituality, such as that of Patricia Jones. And of course, in exploring other traditions, some seriously commit to and embrace a spirituality from another cultural tradition, as did David Preston. Indeed, this urge to explore other spiritual traditions may be evidence that no one spiritual tradition has a market on "the truth," and there are many paths. Perhaps in order to find one's own spiritual path and become whole one must explore what had been previously out of reach, due to the limitations of one's interpretation of one's own cultural and religious experience. By exploring other options and making one's own choices, perhaps one is laying claim to a deeper way to a more authentic spiritual and cultural identity.

Summary and Brief Thoughts for Practice

There are many ways that people go about claiming a sacred face in furthering their spiritual development as they search to become more whole. As discussed in Chapter Seven, one way is by drawing on one's spirituality to reclaim one's cultural and other oppressed aspects of identity. In this chapter, the focus is more on the experience of a search for wholeness specifically through the experience of crossing culture. First, I examined the shifting nature of identity in a constantly shifting geographical landscape through the experience of a Muslim woman who immigrated to the United States after living in three countries. Through her story, part of this chapter focuses on the role of spirituality in making sense of cross-cultural experiences from the perspective of one who was "other" to this culture based on her ethnicity, religion, and national origin. Her spirituality, along with her experiential learning opportunities and formal education, helped her claim greater wholeness and affirm her religious and cultural identity with increased pride.

The second part of this chapter focuses on two of the ways in which people who are white and who grew up in one of the Christian traditions have overtly chosen experiences crossing culture to further their own growth and search for wholeness. Patricia's way, for example, was by directly seeking out cross-cultural experiences through personal relationships with people who were different from herself based on race, ethnicity, or national origin. This cross-cultural seeking results, in many cases, in people understanding their own culture in new ways. In Patricia's case, this rethinking of her own culture, because of close relationships and experiences with those of other cultures, resulted in her thinking directly about what it means to be white in North America. As many writers note (Johnson-Bailey & Cervero, 2000; Sleeter, 1996; Shore, 2001), those of us who are white or European American have generally less of a sense of what it means to be white than those who are African American or Latino have of what it means to be people of color. As a result, most people who are white have given little thought to what it means to be a member of white culture or of whiteness as the invisible cultural standard against which nearly all are measured.

Although many white people in North America appear to have little sense of what it means to be white, many do, however, have a conscious understanding of what was available and what was missing for spiritual sustenance in their own religious traditions, whether or not these traditions were inscribed in white culture. In order to become more whole, there appears to be a tendency to seek out and nurture what has been missing in one's own tradition. Hence, another way people seek out greater wholeness is to directly seek out the spiritual wisdom rooted in other cultures. People do this in a variety of ways. Some seek out insights, ways of being, or honoring what is sacred, that are more embodied in other traditions in developing a more eclectic and individualist spirituality. Others might very seriously study and formally affiliate with a spiritual tradition very different religiously and culturally from their childhood traditions. Maureen and David are examples of those who have taken this path.

Understanding one's own culture in new ways or reclaiming one's cultural and religious identity as a result of cross-cultural experience is part of the ongoing search for wholeness. However, it is important to note that many people do not necessarily have cross-cultural experiences, either as a matter of circumstance related to their survival or as an overt choice through international travel, specifically so they can further their spiritual development or have a spiritual experience. Rather, many go about living their lives in search of growth opportunities. But when spirituality is important to them, the process of growth tends also to be viewed as a spiritual process and part of their development overall, including their spiritual development. Of course, when people specifically choose to cross spiritual traditions rooted in other cultures to find what is unavailable in the one in which they were raised, the motivation *is* their spiritual development, and they probably do come to some greater cross-cultural understanding. Although this experience probably causes them to think about aspects of their own religious and cultural tradition, it does not necessarily lead them to think about what it means to be white. In any case, these cross-cultural experiences are part of a search for wholeness that seems to call people to *move toward* being more authentically themselves, spiritually and culturally.

The implications for practice will be dealt with in detail in Part Three; nevertheless, a couple of brief remarks are in order here. In attempting to teach for cultural relevance, it is important to find ways for both people of color or those from different countries and cultures, and those who are white and of European ancestry to explore their cultural identity. This means providing readings and creating assignments that get at what it means to be white, as well as what it might mean to be of a specific European descent, such as Irish, or German, or Italian. You might find ways that all learners can explore how cross-cultural experiences have helped them understand various aspects of their own identity, and to interview each other and people outside the class about such experiences. Further, ask what role such experiences have played in their overall development and what, if anything, they have to do with their spiritual development. As we have seen in the four chapters that constitute Part Two on spiritual development and its connection to identity, there are many ways in which people continue their spiritual development, which is about the search for greater authenticity and greater wholeness. But spiritual development is connected to all aspects of our identity, including our culture, gender, and sexual orientation. It permeates all aspects of who we are. Indeed, understanding more about spiritual development is part of our search for wholeness.

Part III

Spirituality in a Culturally Relevant and Transformative Teaching Practice

In short, spirituality in education is about transformation. Not just hoping for transformation or wishing for transformation, or believing in transformation, or even talking about it, but actual transformation. Transformation is not necessarily hard; in fact it is quite easy. Things are changing all the time, even moment to moment. Can't we?

S. Glazer (1999, p. 248)

We hear a lot about education for transformation these days. Many new education books have "transformation" in the title, and there is much discussion of what teaching for transformation means at adult and higher education conferences. Some of these provocative discussions focus more on the transformation of the individual from a psychological perspective, others focus more on teaching for social transformation, and still others address the continuum between individual and social transformation (Cranton, 1994; Mezirow & Associates, 1990; 2000; Taylor, 1997). What all these discussions have in common is the transformative power of education for both learners and educators. Few considerations of "transformative education" deal specifically with issues related to culture, although in the 2000 edition of the *Handbook of Adult and Continuing Education* Ann Brooks has discussed particular cultures of transformation. But even fewer discussions about transformative learning have given consideration to the role of spirituality in teaching for social transformation, or its role in culturally relevant and critical multicultural approaches to adult and higher education.

From the stories featured in earlier chapters it is clear that spirituality has played an important role in the lives of many educators who try to teach for cultural relevance and social change. Their stories suggest that spirituality is an important part of claiming a more positive cultural identity and a more authentic identity overall for many people. It thus seems clear that spirituality can play a role in teaching for cultural relevance and social change. The chapters that constitute Part Three of this book are intended to look more specifically at how to develop a more spiritually grounded and culturally relevant pedagogy, and what it might look like in practice. Of course, as my colleague Ed Taylor and I have discussed elsewhere (Tisdell & Taylor, 2001), educational practice is always grounded in a philosophical or a "theory-in-practice" based on the educators' beliefs about the purposes of education, regardless of whether the educator can fully articulate that theory. Thus, Part III will also outline a theory-in-progress of a spiritually grounded culturally relevant pedagogy.

Educational theory needs to be relevant and grounded in practice. In order to tie both theory to practice and back, Chapter Nine will focus on a discussion of how one might consider approaching dealing with spirituality and culture in adult and higher educational contexts. Chapter Ten will provide a more in-depth exploration of the multiple influences on a spiritually grounded and culturally relevant pedagogy, and then will outline this theory-in-progress. Chapter Eleven applies the theory to real life practice in the sharing of stories of using the theory specifically in higher education settings. Chapter Twelve will explore the benefits and challenges of a spiritually grounded and culturally relevant teaching practice. Finally, the Epilogue to the book will provide some final reflections.

I hope these final chapters offer new insights about ways of incorporating spirituality and cultural relevance that provide not only new ways of thinking about transformative teaching but also ways of teaching that are congruent with each of our own individual growing, changing, more authentic identities and those of whom we work. As Glazer asks in the opening quote in talking about transformative teaching, "Things are changing all the time. . . . Can't we?"

9

Approaching Transformative Teaching
Grounded in Spirituality
and Cultural Relevance

Most educators probably hope that the work they do has a positive effect on learners' lives. Many educators, if they are teaching in areas that they care deeply about and that evoke their own passion, even hope that their educational work is transformative in some way. Some who try to teach for transformation are more concerned about personal transformation in learners' lives, whereas others are more interested in teaching for social transformation that creates greater societal equity. In speaking more specifically about education for social transformation and an educational vision for the twenty-first century that challenges power relations based on race, gender, class, and culture and attends to the environment, Edmund O'Sullivan (1999) writes, "I believe that any in-depth treatment of 'transformative education' must address the topic of spirituality and that educators must take on the concerns of the development of the spirit at a most fundamental level. Contemporary education suffers deeply by its eclipse of the spiritual dimension of our world and universe" (p. 259). Education, and all of life, probably suffers when we lose sight of the wholeness and interconnectedness of all things, lose our sense of passion, or refuse to acknowledge the multiple ways in which people construct knowledge.

Attending to spirituality in higher and adult education, particularly as it relates to emancipatory and transformative approaches to education, is about the engagement of passion, which involves the knowledge construction processes of the whole person. The engagement of people's passion is generally not only about critical reflection or "rational discourse," it is also about engaging people's hearts and souls, as well as their minds—or as Abalos (1998) suggests, the engagement of all four faces of their being: the personal, political, historical, and sacred faces. When new ideas and critical reflection are applied to and rooted in learners' culture, history, personal life experiences, and spirituality, education can be both passionate and transformative. Providing the space where learners can construct knowledge in their music, culture, art, and symbol-making in the engagement of the sacred face makes efforts at change very personal. Doing it in the community of a classroom or other communal educational activity also makes it political and has the potential to lead to social change. This indeed is transforming; it is also culturally relevant. Is it possible to engage these four faces, including the sacred face, in higher and adult education? If so what does it look like in practice, and how can one approach the work of education that is spiritually grounded and culturally relevant? This is the heart of Part Three of this book. This particular chapter begins by revisiting some background assumptions about the nature of spirituality and culture in the different contexts of higher and adult education.

Living Our Way into New Kinds of Thinking

Every educator needs to answer the question of what drawing on spirituality to teach for cultural relevance and social transformation might look like in practice, depending on the context in which he or she works. How any one person does this also depends on her or his cultural background and identity, cultural awareness, spirituality, and educational and life experiences around cultural issues. We are always in process with these issues, and as Parker Palmer (1980) suggests, we don't *think our way* into a new kind of living; we *live our way* into a new kind of thinking. While living our way into new kinds of thinking about spirituality and culture might play out differently in the contexts of higher and adult education, it is possible to consider what this suggests for education more generally.

Having Significant Cross-Cultural Relationships

Living our way into new kinds of thinking about spirituality and culture in education involves having relationships and new life experiences with people who are different than we. Such exposure and experience might be the result of living in a different country or culture all together for a significant period, having close personal relationships with members of different cultural groups, and being open to the spiritual insights of other cultural traditions. But it also involves dialogue and being with others who are also grappling with similar issues in education, and who attempt to ground their teaching for cultural relevance in their own spirituality, cultural identity, and experience. For example, the many educators that I have formally interviewed whose stories are featured thus far in this book have heavily influenced my own thinking about these issues and are helping me live my way into a new kind of thinking.

I want to highlight here the particularly important influence of two scholars and educator-activists, Derise Tolliver and Silvia Villa. Many of the ideas in this chapter were collaboratively developed with them; it's *our* thinking to a large degree, in that we've lived out, talked about, and written about some of these ideas in public forums elsewhere (see Tisdell, Tolliver, & Villa, 2001; Tisdell & Tolliver, 2000; Tolliver & Tisdell, 2001a, b). Further, as human beings we never develop ideas or ways of being in the world alone, and we certainly never live our way into new kinds of thinking about teaching for cultural relevance in isolation.

I cannot overestimate the importance of having significant relationships of crossing cultural borders with those who are of different cultural backgrounds here. I not only have more of an understanding of what it means to be African American or Chicana from my

relationships with Derise Tolliver and Silvia Villa and others who
are culturally different from me. I also understand more of who I
am, as a white woman of Irish-Catholic and Danish cultural heritage. And I am certainly *moving toward* being better able to teach
for cultural relevance from my work with members of different cultural groups and relationships with scholars and educators and the
many who have shared their lives and their stories with me. There
is a communal dimension to knowledge production rooted in spirituality as it connects to culture. As the African proverb says, "I am
because we are; we are because I am." Such a recognition brings to
the fore the wholeness that is part of spirituality (because *we are*),
and the importance of the individual (because *I am*). Further, the
proverb highlights the dialectical and paradoxical relationship of
the individual and the communal: within the individual is the communal, and within the community is the individual. The spiritual
is present perhaps in the tension of the dialectic and the paradox.

Creating an Environment Grounded in Authenticity

This emphasis on the wholeness and interconnectedness of all
things that is a hallmark of spiritual experience, the communal
nature of knowledge production, and the dialectical relationship
between the individual and the communal has important implications for what it means to create an emancipatory learning environment. According to Paulo Freire, there is a difference between
being an educator and a facilitator, and emancipatory educators (in
dialogue with learners) need to take active responsibility for creating the conditions in a learning environment that lend themselves
to education for social transformation (Freire & Macedo, 1995).
This suggests that as educators we need to be proactive in setting
up the environment if we want to draw on the transformative power
of participants' spirituality that connects with their cultural backgrounds. In considering how one might do this, it is helpful here to
review the seven assumptions about the nature of spirituality that
were highlighted in the first chapter. Spirituality is (1) about whole-

ness and connection through the mystery of a Life-force or divine presence, (2) about meaning-making, (3) about moving toward greater authenticity, (4) different from religion, though sometimes interrelated, (5) about symbolic and often unconscious processes often made more concrete in art forms such as music, visual art, image, symbol, and ritual that are manifested culturally, (6) always present (though often unacknowledged) in the learning environment, and (7) connected to significant peak experiences of a Life-force or divine presence that most often happen by surprise.

The implications of what *living* our way into new kinds of thinking suggests for teaching for cultural relevance in light of these components of spirituality are perhaps obvious in light of discussions in prior chapters. But some aspects of these assumptions are worth highlighting here in relation to teaching for cultural relevance. First, and most important, as noted in Chapter Six, spiritual development is at least partly about moving toward greater authenticity. Thus, in order to begin to consider what it means to develop a spiritually grounded approach to culturally relevant education, it is absolutely central for educators to try to be as grounded in their own spiritual and cultural authenticity as possible. Given that our identity is not static and is constantly changing with our deeper level of spiritual and cultural awareness, this is obviously not a perfect science, and takes some soul searching on the part of each educator about what this might mean. It does *not mean* imitating others' spirituality as grounded in their culture. It means being rooted and grounded in one's own. Perhaps an example will help clarify why.

In our work and presentations together, my colleague Dr. Derise Tolliver, an African American woman, often will begin our presentations related to spirituality and culture by the pouring of libations based on the spirituality of the Akan people of Ghana. In describing the purpose of this in a workshop that she and I conducted together, she writes, "The workshop began with the pouring of libations, a ritual of prayer, blessing, and remembrance, that has traditionally been practiced among Africans, as well as among members of other cultures. In our version, water was poured on the ground as the Creator (called by various names) and family, community and national Ancestors were invoked. This interactive activity introduced culture and spirituality as a foundation for the day's work" (in Tolliver & Tisdell, 2001a, p. 401).

The fact that Derise, not me, led the pouring of libations is central here. This simple ritual is very much rooted in her spirituality and cultural tradition as an African American woman who has also spent considerable time in Ghana and in studying the spiritual traditions of the Akan people and other African-centered spiritualities. She very effectively creates what feels like a sacred space in this opening activity because it is so very grounded in her own authenticity, and seems as natural to who she is as a fish swimming in water. In a sense, she shares how she has claimed her sacred face, grounding herself as she does in this simple one-minute act that is rooted in her cultural identity. It has the strong effect of inviting people into their authenticity, enabling them to reflect on who it is they are spiritually and culturally, and sets a tone for the rest of the workshop. But if Derise were not with me, I would not lead a ritual in pouring libations. For me to do so and imitate what I have seen Derise do so effectively would not only come off as fake, it would also be potentially culturally insulting to people of African descent, as it is not rooted in my own spiritual or cultural identity. Thus, it would not be authentic to who I am. In short, if we are trying to invite participants in a learning activity into their own authenticity, we need to be authentic in who we are, and not try to imitate who someone else is.

The insights of American Indian writers Vine Deloria (1992) and Ines Hernandez-Avila (1996) are helpful here. Both discuss the importance of spirituality as a holistic way of life among many American Indians rooted in their own cultures and traditions. All of us have something to learn from people and cultures whose spirituality seems to be rooted in a way of life. But Deloria and Hernandez-Avila also express concern about the misappropriation of meanings, rituals, and symbols in the current pop fascination with "Indian spirituality" as public consumption. They suggest that an authentic spirituality connotes ways of choosing to live and act, both on behalf of oneself and others, in a way of life that cannot simply be bought and sold in New Age spirituality stores. Further, they are wary of the use of cultural "artifacts" in public forums by those who are not members of the cultural groups, if and when not enough time or attention is given to its meaning to the cultural community in which it is grounded. Educators need to think not only about ways of being grounded in their own authenticity and how to bring that authenticity to the learning environment, but also about what is culturally respectful.

Fostering Cultural and Spiritual Respect

Cultural respect is foundational to teaching for cultural relevance. Although no culture or spiritual tradition has strict ownership on what is a way of making-meaning through symbol, music, image, ritual or celebration, there is a fine line between being influenced by another cultural tradition and stealing from or colonizing (or being colonized by) another cultural tradition. At the same time, neither spirituality nor culture remains static. Of course, when one spends time studying, meditating, and being with others in a different spiritual and cultural community, one's spirituality and cultural identity are going to be affected. Indeed, spiritual and cultural identity development is always ongoing. Further, if one is to be truly grounded in one's authenticity and draw on spirituality as a part of teaching for cultural relevance, one needs to be willing to take some risks in the adult learning environment. So often we come to our classrooms as educators or learners so absorbed with a task to be accomplished, a lesson to be taught, learned, or facilitated that we give little thought to what bringing our own authenticity (much less our spirituality!) that attends to teaching for cultural relevance might mean. After all, one could argue that learning is about the learners, and not particularly about the educator. Although this is true, communal educational activities such as classrooms are also relational activities. To attend to the spiritual is to attend to the interconnectedness of all things—to create a space for people to bring in new ways of discovering and sharing their authenticity. It is incumbent for educators to draw on and occasionally share their own authenticity *as people*, not so much simply as instructors fulfilling an educational role. Thus at times it might be appropriate to share the significance of one's own or others' creativity in the form of a poem, an art piece, a piece of music; and what about it touches one's soul, speaks to one's ongoing cultural understanding, or is a manifestation of authenticity. This authenticity invites learners into theirs.

Most spiritual experiences cannot be planned; indeed they happen by surprise. But it is possible to create educational conditions that are more likely to lead to transformative learning experiences that for some learners may touch on the spiritual. Creating such a space does not necessarily mean using the "s" word or overtly talking about spirituality. There may be times when it is appropriate to do so depending on the learning context, but often, direct discussion might seem far afield to the purpose of a learning activity. Attending to the spiritual does mean honoring the various dimensions of how people learn and construct knowledge by facilitating activities that include attention to the affective, the somatic, the spiritual, or symbolic, as well as the cognitive, and encouraging learners to do the same in their presentations. By doing so we set up environments that sometimes result in transformative learning experiences that are also experienced as spiritual by some people on occasion. Generally, these experiences seem to happen quite by surprise—in students' spontaneous creation of poetry in response to an exercise, in art, in music, in their dramatic presentations on a theme in the reading, or in movement. What is more often experienced as "spiritual" is when people's authenticity around culture and other aspects of their identity becomes visible in new ways and more connected to others (Tolliver & Tisdell, 2001b). Indeed, allowing

for these spontaneous moments and celebrating the wonder of it all
are part of living one's way into a new kind of thinking.

The Different Cultural Contexts
of Adult and Higher Education

How one attends to spirituality in the learning environment for cultural relevance is not only dependent on who the educator and the
participants are, it also depends on the particular context of the learning activity. Further, how one does this in adult or community-based
education contexts may be different than in for-credit higher education classrooms. Although all those I interviewed indicated that
spirituality informed their motivations and emancipatory educational practices, in general those working in community-based or
other kinds of adult education programs were less tentative than
those working in higher education in *how* they discussed or drew on
spirituality in their educational practices.

Community Adult Education

The community-based educators were less confined by the rational-
istic structures that have been the traditional hallmark of higher education. They felt freer to use different modalities to provide a different
kind of experience for people or simply to go with how communities
draw on the spirituality that is part of their lifeblood. Mariposa Yee,
a Chinese American community organizer who has worked with
community groups both in the United States and the Pacific Islands,
noted that she seldom brings up spirituality herself but that community groups often draw on various spiritual practices as part of their
own work. For example, the American Indian communities she
worked with in the Southwest would often begin community educational activities by acknowledging the Four Directions and the
Medicine Wheel; while in a Mexican American community, part of
their educational work was set in the context of a Catholic Mass.

Drawing on spirituality happens quite naturally in many community-based settings. Curry and Cunningham (2000) note that spirituality as a way of knowing is part of what they refer to as "co-learning" with the community on challenging gentrification and other social justice issues on Chicago's South Side. Aguilar and Woo (2000) also discuss it as an element of their work as a part of a national facilitation team that deals with diversity training issues with national service programs. In these instances spirituality is drawn in simply as a relevant part of the community or group's work. It is not the focus of their work; rather it is a way of opening and closing the space that facilitates, celebrates, or solidifies a community's social justice work together, or acknowledges the paradox of the unity and wholeness within the diversity and the diversity within the unity.

To be sure, some contexts lend themselves more easily than others to drawing in modes of being that seem to touch on the spiritual. This seems to be the case for those whose primary educational work involves music or art. The insights of musicians and artists, particularly as they relate to education for social transformation or in teaching for cultural relevance, are helpful to all of us who work in education more broadly. As noted in Chapter One, Lisa Riddle is a singer-songwriter and performer, a white woman who also does antiracism and environmental workshops, and whose music and concerts focus on social justice issues of all types. Lisa's spirituality strongly informs her work as both a performer and an educator in that she draws on it in setting an educational tone by providing what she refers to as a "container"—a kind of boundaried space where participants might have an experience together. She admits, however, that she is not fully conscious of how it works, and noted:

> I know how to do it. I don't know exactly how come I know
> how to do it; it has to do in part with the assumption that we
> are all in this together. I function very strongly when I come
> into a concert from a "we" perspective, and speak from that

place. So I've had people who in no way consider themselves
part of the "we" when they came in at the end will.

The fact that Lisa may not be able to explain exactly *how come*
she knows how to facilitate this sense of "we-ness" and the exact
ways she is drawing on spirituality, may be that when one is
grounded in one's own authenticity in a given space in time, there
is an un-self-conscious quality to that sort of authenticity—like, for
example, one is not usually conscious of breathing. There is also a
sense of wholeness or unity in such experiences of "we-ness." But
Lisa is clear that she is drawing on her spirituality, which is
grounded in her own cultural background that was very much
informed by the wilderness of Alaska where she grew up. In speaking to this point, in relationship to her work as a musician and as
an educator, she noted,

> *Music of course is evocative of the soul and of the emotions,*
> *so I'm modeling to a lot of people, that really it is not only*
> *safe, but IT'S GREAT to put this stuff out there. That's what*
> *I mean partly by tone. I have a great deal of confidence in my*
> *perspective drawing as it does from the larger wild commu-*
> *nity, and a lot of people have lost that confidence, particu-*
> *larly urban or raised urban—or just to have somebody who*
> *sort of looks like them, they can "phew," be there, be safe,*
> *be connected. I totally get that we should be and are grieving*
> *for what's happening on the planet. Of course we are! . . .*
> *When I'm structuring experience for people, I'm very aware*
> *of the effect of tone, so that the deeper the material, the lighter*
> *you have to have something else happening so that most peo-*
> *ple [don't] sink . . .; it allows people to stay with me.*

Now of course, most of us who are working in adult and higher
education are not concert performers, and might not have much
experience or musical ability to be able to work with tone and

music, which is indeed evocative of the soul, the way that Lisa Riddle can. But we can still create a boundaried space; we can also attend to the important dynamics of setting a tone, so that "people don't sink," and think about what will facilitate their ability to stay engaged, no matter what the educational setting is in which we work. Lisa and those working in community-based adult education settings or in student affairs in higher education did not need to be concerned about participants' analytical ability or clarity of written expression of readings and ideas with which those of us teaching higher education classes are concerned. Rather, Lisa and the community-based educators were concerned about creating an atmosphere that helps people be more present and open to new kinds of meaningful learning and experiences that included and drew on an affective component to think about and facilitate dealing with social change issues. Educators in these settings were not concerned that such learning experiences necessarily had to be explained in rational terms.

Higher Education and Spirituality

Many who work in student affairs and student services in higher education approach the topic of spirituality in ways similar to how the community educators noted above approach it. There is talk of transformational learning opportunities through extracurricular activities and an emphasis on the importance of spiritual development of students (Jablonski, 2001; Kazanjian & Laurence, 2000). These authors and practitioners appear to have less concern and less reticence about drawing directly on spirituality than those teaching for-credit classes in higher education.

In general, those teaching higher education classes were more hesitant than the community educators and student affairs colleagues about drawing on spirituality directly in their own teaching. They felt somewhat more confined by the structures of the higher education classroom that has traditionally emphasized rationality. None teaching higher education classes wanted to be seen as doing anything coercive, or as pushing a spiritual or religious agenda, or as otherwise being "unacademic." Yet many also talked about the importance of setting a tone. They spent time during the first class specifically setting a tone that would invite students to bring their whole selves into the learning environment, including their affective and other life experiences, particularly as related to the course content. Derise Tolliver, a psychologist by training, is quite direct about this in working in an undergraduate completion program with adult learners. She writes (in Tisdell & Tolliver, 2000):

> I use a variety of "spiritual" technologies in my work with adult learners. These are broadly described as spiritual because they, among other things, help raise conscious-ness, stimulate awareness, foster creativity and imagina-tion, connect us with grander issues of purpose and meaning, and facilitate connection with that which ani-mates us. For example, in the course that helps students plan their academic program, I always begin with a cel-ebration, complete with food and decorations. The class-room becomes festive, and is transformed into a special and sacred space for learning. Through this beginning, I communicate that I honor and value their presence, I honor who they are, and encourage them to acknowl-edge and celebrate themselves and their accomplish-ments at the beginning, just because they are, rather than waiting to the end to base it on some specific out-come. That occurs, also, but the ritual of celebration at the beginning invites the playful and passionate aspects to show up for the work. (p. 9)

She also begins almost all her class sessions with a very brief cen-tering exercise, though she doesn't use the term "spirituality" in facilitating this activity, and notes that learners interpret this exer-cise in different ways—some as a meditation, and others as a stress reduction and a way to transition from their busy work lives to their classroom educational space:

> I present this without reference to spirituality for those who may be offended or turned off by the concept. I always give folks the option of participating at whatever level they feel most comfortable. Thus, there is no coercion to participate in this activity if they choose not to. The weekly repetition of this activity becomes one of the course rituals.

The activities that Tolliver makes reference to are attentive to issues of setting a tone. She draws on the cultural piece, as noted earlier by acknowledging her connection spiritually and culturally to African spiritualities, particularly the Akan people of Ghana, but talks more about this connection in classes where it's relevant to the course content, such as her "Psychology from an African-Centered Perspective" class. Her courses always include readings related to cultural issues, and occasionally if relevant to the course, she will include readings that connect spirituality to culture. Although she is more direct than most professors in higher education in her attention to spirituality, the specific way she draws on it is somewhat dependent on the context.

Most of those teaching in higher education were somewhat less direct in their attention to spirituality as related to cultural issues than Derise Tolliver, but all that I interviewed were attentive to issues of setting a tone and tried to create a space for ways of knowing beyond the strictly rational. Most drew on it in more subtle ways, noting that spirituality would be acknowledged as it arose in the learning environment when learners brought it up, or that they would draw on it implicitly. For example, Nancy Epstein reported that in activities when students are bringing representations of themselves or their cultural backgrounds, she talks about her Japa ring (which she wears all the time), which, as noted in Chapter Five, is used in the repetition of the mantra *om namaha shivaya* that is part of the Yoga tradition of which she is a part. In instances such as these, those teaching in higher education settings shared some of themselves as people. Of course, virtually all professors within higher education settings talked about the importance of attending to the course content, in terms of discussing readings, students' writing, and presentation related to the course content. The aspects that are central to higher education were still present in their teaching; they just also created a space for the affective and symbolic dimensions of learning.

Chapter Summary and Conclusion

In this chapter, I have tried to set a context for how educators who want to draw on spirituality to create culturally relevant and transformative learning environments might approach attempting to do so. I emphasized that although one can make suggestions about how to think about such approaches, in reality, as Parker Palmer (1980) suggests, we do not think our way into a new kind of living; we actually live our way into a new kind of thinking. This *living our way into new kinds of thinking* plays out differently in the different contexts of adult, community, and higher education, and each educator needs to develop her or his own idea of what this might look like in practice.

Although the contexts of adult, community, and higher education are different, this chapter highlighted a few guidelines that might help educators in general approach dealing with spirituality and culture in their personal lives and their educational work. Some of these are an emphasis on the importance of developing significant personal relationships with people who are different based on race, culture, sexual orientation, or national origin; an environment grounded in the authenticity of the educator and the learner; and an emphasis on cultural and spiritual respect for all participants.

This chapter also looked at how the educators that I interviewed drew on spirituality in their more specific context of community adult education and in higher education. The context of an educational activity always informs educators how they might approach developing both their curriculum and pedagogy, and those teaching in higher education were more reticent about directly discussing spirituality in those terms than were community adult educators. Nevertheless, both groups of educators did draw on their own spirituality as connected to culture in different ways, and even those teaching in higher education would occasionally incorporate symbolic knowledge construction activities by incorporating the use of image, symbol, poetry, or music. In the following chapters, I will explore in far greater depth how one might consider new ways of living one's way to a new kind of thinking about these issues based on the stories and theories of other educators in light of one's own moving toward greater authenticity.

10

A Theory-in-Progress
of a Spiritually Grounded,
Culturally Relevant Pedagogy

*Philosophical Underpinnings
and New Directions*

E ducational theory must always be related to the world of practice; otherwise the theory is not very useful. Likewise, nearly all educators have an educational philosophy imbedded in what they do, in that they plan and conduct the educational activity based on beliefs specifically about the purpose of education in this context, and a belief in what educators and learners should be doing. Some practitioners have difficulty articulating what that underlying philosophy is and what their beliefs are; nevertheless they have them, and they are imbedded in their educational practices.

It is obvious that this book is based on a philosophy—a set of beliefs assuming that spirituality can play a significant role in culturally relevant education. This philosophy is based on multiple theoretical influences, some of which were briefly explained in Chapter Two. The purposes of this chapter are two-fold: first, to explore the existing theoretical influences on culturally relevant and transformative education and the role spirituality can play in it in adult and higher education; and second, to outline the elements of a theory-in-progress of a spiritually grounded, culturally relevant pedagogy specifically for higher education settings, and to consider how these elements can be used in general higher education practice.

Multiple Theoretical Influences

There are a variety of theoretical influences informing how to teach in a way that might lead to personal and social transformation around challenging power relations based on race, class, gender, culture, sexual orientation, and ableness. These theoretical influences have emerged in a context, and their insights offer practical direction to those working in both higher and adult education settings. As noted, there has been little inclusion of the role of spirituality in these discussions, and much of the literature that does exist I discussed earlier. Yet attending to spirituality can offer some possibility to both personal and social transformation.

Attending to the spiritual dimension of adult learning does *not* mean pushing a religious agenda. It *does* mean drawing in the affective domain through sharing the stories and feelings that put a flesh-and-blood face on the world of ideas. It also means drawing in the important ways people construct knowledge through image, symbol, art, music, ritual, gesture, and celebration that engages passion and that connects deeply with their cultural lives. This is specifically where spirituality connects to teaching for cultural relevance.

How one actually attends to spirituality in teaching for cultural relevance depends on the setting. In all situations, it does mean attending to the curriculum or the content of the activity, to the positionality and cultural identity of teachers and learners, and to finding ways in one's pedagogy to engage learners in activities that are culturally appropriate and asks them to be full participants in constructing new and meaningful knowledge about themselves and the world. A spiritually grounded educational philosophy for teaching for cultural relevance that attends to some of the issues that are a part of personal and social transformation easily builds on some existing theoretical influences and discussions within the fields of higher and adult education. These are reviewed below.

Transformative Learning

Probably the most often cited work in the field of adult and higher education that deals with transformation is rooted in Jack Mezirow's (1985, 1995) theory of transformative learning, which emphasizes critical reflection on assumptions and changing behaviors as a result of a disorienting dilemma. For Mezirow, and those who rely on his work, the unit of analysis has tended to be *the individual*, the apparent assumption being that social transformation is the sum of the parts, where the parts are transformed individuals. Many have critiqued Mezirow's work as being more a theory of individual rather than social transformation and as more driven by the role of rationality and critical reflection in challenging underlying beliefs (Taylor, 1997). Yet Mezirow's work, and that of those who rely on it, has made an enormous contribution to the myriad ways in which individuals may undergo a transformed perspective. More recently Mezirow and Associates (2000) have discussed learning as transformation as a theory in progress; several authors have talked about the importance of considering asymmetrical power relations (Belenky & Stanton, 2000), dealing with diversity issues (Kasl & Elias, 2000), and attending to some cross-cultural issues and understanding of "the other," which potentially results in social action (Daloz, 2000). In general, however, even these discussions of transformative learning based on the expansion of the work of Mezirow & Associates (2000) have given little to no attention to the role of spirituality in the transformative learning process.

There are other discussions of transformative learning in education, however, that do attend more to the role of spirituality. For example, Tobin Hart (2000) focuses on transformational learning from a transpersonal psychology and evolutionary consciousness perspective that includes attention to the spiritual. But Hart does not deal with the relationship of spirituality to cultural identity or teaching for cultural relevance. Clearly, Parker Palmer's (1998,

2000) work on the connection of spirituality and education, attention to graced moments in teaching and learning, brief considerations of social action, and mention of culture slightly touch on the
connection of spirituality to culture. Kazanjian and Laurence's
(2000) consideration of spiritual and religious pluralism specifically
in higher education suggests implications for working across difference that more directly relate to teaching for cultural relevance.
And as we have seen, both Abalos (1998) and O'Sullivan (1999)
highlight the important role of spirituality in education for social
transformation around cultural and environmental issues.

Critical and Feminist Pedagogy

Because many discussions of transformative learning focus more on
the transformation of the individual, those who are interested in
social transformation tend to draw on different theoretical traditions
that deal more directly with how to teach to challenge *power relations* based on race, gender, class, sexual orientation, and ableness.
Much of this literature is informed by Brazilian activist and educator Paulo Freire (1971), whose work initially focuses on education
for challenging class relations in literacy settings in Brazil and eventually gave rise to the critical pedagogy literature (Brookfield, 1995;
Sleeter & McClaren, 1995; Shor, 1996). These discourses on challenging power relations now include critical and feminist pedagogy,
the critical multicultural and resistance postmodernism literature,
and antiracist and Africentric perspectives on education. At this
point all these discourses have begun to influence each other to
some extent, but there are distinct threads among them.

Feminist pedagogy initially developed out of two distinct bodies of literature: the literature that focused on women's propensity
to connected ways of being and knowing following the work of
Carol Gilligan (1982) and Belenky et al. (1986); and the critical
pedagogy literature with an emphasis on challenging patriarchy and
racism that arose out of women's studies and thinkers such as bell

hooks (1989), as well as influences in critical pedagogy. As a body of literature, feminist pedagogy calls attention to the important ways women (and some men) construct knowledge through connection and relationship and to the role of the affective dimension in learning. This has important implications for attending to spirituality, as the spiritual dimension of learning is about the connection and interrelationship of all things. Many feminist and womanist writers also discuss the role of gender as it intersects with race, class, culture, and sexual orientation (Cannon, 1996; Johnson-Bailey, 2001; hooks, 1994; Hart, 1992; 2001; Maher & Tetreault, 1994; Sheared, 1999). Discussions of feminist pedagogy tend to foreground the five following issues in teaching and learning: (1) the construction of knowledge, (2) voice, (3) authority, (4) how positionality (of both teachers and learners) shapes teaching and learning, and (5) identity as constantly shifting and developing (Maher & Tetreault, 1994; Tisdell, 1998; 2000b). The factors of positionality and identity as constantly shifting or developing connect directly to spirituality and cultural relevance in that spiritual development emphasizes the movement toward greater authenticity and the ongoing development of authentic identity. Further, the issue of positionality connects directly to cultural identity.

Multicultural Education and Critical Multiculturalism

Teaching for cultural relevance is strongly connected to the wide body of literature on multicultural education. Some versions of it simply focus on cultural differences without attention to power differentials based on race, ethnicity, or culture; other approaches focus very specifically on challenging power relations. Building on their earlier work, Sleeter (1996) and Grant and Sleeter (1999) identify five approaches to multicultural education that are in use by educators that have somewhat different epistemological assumptions and different implicit definitions of what *multicultural* means. These approaches include (1) teaching the culturally different,

(2) the human relations approach, (3) single-group studies, (4) the "multicultural education" approach, and (5) education that is multicultural and social reconstructionist.

As noted elsewhere (Tisdell, 1995), some of the differences in underlying assumptions are that the first two approaches tend to be more individual and psychological, and more or less accept the epistemological grounding that has traditionally been operative in education based on the belief that knowledge is neutral. There is no real attention to who is represented in the curriculum, who determines what counts as knowledge, or the power relations that may have shaped the knowledge production process. More particularly, the educational emphasis of the "teaching the culturally different" approach is on how to educate culturally different "others" to assimilate and be more successful in the dominant culture, rather than on challenging or changing the system. The human relations approach has similar underlying assumptions but focuses more on helping people of different cultural groups learn to live together harmoniously, particularly as individuals, from a psychological perspective. The emphasis is the development of interpersonal communication skills to reduce prejudice and create understanding among human beings by promoting positive feelings and attitudes that students have about themselves and others as members of various racial, ethnic, gender, or cultural groups—but again, there is no real direct attention to how unequal structural power relations have shaped society or direct discussion of racism. An assumption underlying this approach is that students learn better in an environment that promotes individual and psychological safety among its members.

Grant and Sleeter's (1999) last three approaches—single group studies approach, what they refer to as "the multicultural education" approach, and the social reconstructionist approach—focus more on social structures and emphasize the significance of power relations in shaping the knowledge production and dissemination process. These approaches are broadly termed "critical multicultural approaches" because their focus on power relations is based on the assumption, as hooks (1994) observes, that "no education is politically neutral" (p. 37). The single group studies approach, rather than focusing on several groups at a time, focuses more on the detailed historical, social, and cultural experience of one particular group to promote an in-depth understanding of the educational needs of that group, such as African Americans, American Indians, gays and lesbians, or people with disabilities. The curriculum is based on the work of members of the particular group and the way knowledge is defined in their own communities. By contrast, the multicultural education approach examines power relations of multiple groups from a comparative perspective, whereas the social reconstructionist approach blends a comparative perspective with direct strategies for social change. The reconstructionist approach not only sees knowledge as political, but it also emphasizes that participants themselves can and should take control in challenging the way knowledge has been defined, constructed, and disseminated.

Strongly related to some of the discourses of critical multiculturalism are the resistance postmodernist discourses in education that focus on how power relations shape our understanding of our identity (Pagenhart, 1994; Sleeter, 1996). The emphasis of postmodernism in general is deconstruction, which is in part what makes these discourses so complicated. But the emphasis on the importance of deconstructing and understanding how race, gender, and class relations have shaped or constructed our understanding of identity is key to understanding how one can reclaim that identity anew. Unlike ludic versions of postmodernism, which simply emphasize deconstruction for its own sake, resistance postmodernists would see deconstruction *and reclaiming* of one's cultural identity as an important part of challenging power relations (Lather, 1991; Sleeter, 1996). A hard-core postmodernist might have trouble with the notion of an "authentic" identity, since postmodernists tend to emphasize the notion of identity as socially constructed and would problemetize any notion of an "essential" or "authentic" self. Yet resistance postmodernists would see the value of challenging power relations and reclaiming one's identity anew as being part of working for individual and social change. Some might also recognize that spirituality can be a part of that reclaiming process.

Spirituality and Culturally Relevant Approaches to Education

Many authors have discussed the current debates, the confluences and differences, among various approaches to critical and feminist pedagogy, multicultural education, critical multiculturalism, and resistance postmodernist approaches to education (Banks, 1997; Gay, 1995; Giroux, 1992; Sleeter & McLaren; 1995; Sleeter, 1996; Ross-Gordon, 1994). Indeed there is confusion about what one means by the term *multicultural education*, since some versions do not deal with challenging the power relations of the dominant culture and some do. Thus some authors rarely use the term, and might speak more specifically about the focus of their work, and use a more specific descriptor such as "antiracist education" (Bonnett, 2000). Further, the broad focus on education that challenges power relations based on multiple social structures, and multiple groups of adults in culturally pluralistic or comparative approaches, means that the educational needs of individuals or specific groups can easily become obscured. This has resulted in the more particular emphasis on strategies of antiracist education and dealing with whiteness as a system of privilege (Kincheloe et al., 2000; Johnson-Bailey & Cervero, 2000), on educational models from an Africentric perspective (Colin, 1994; Colin & Guy, 1998; Smith & Colin, 2001; Peterson, 1996), or on specific cultural groups. In this respect, these discussions would be similar to what Grant and Sleeter (1999) have referred to as "single group studies" in their discussion of approaches to multicultural education. This has resulted in the consideration of what is more specifically relevant to different cultural groups in discussions of culturally relevant education, and that does challenge power relations and affirms the cultures, identities, and ways of knowing from specific cultural groups (Guy, 1999).

Clearly, there is a place for spirituality in teaching for cultural relevance. Although the multiple bodies of literature dealing with culture cited above, for the most part, do not deal with the role of spirituality in education around cultural issues, developing a spiritually grounded theory of teaching for social relevance and cultural transformation clearly draws on and places this work in a spiritual context. In particular, such a theory would highlight the importance of trying to draw on transformative moments in learners' lives, the importance of connection and relationship, the ongoing development of identity, and the culture and positionality of both learners and educators that are foregrounded in the educational approaches and theoretical influences cited above. But it adds to these modes by also drawing on other ways learners construct knowledge through the unconscious and symbolic processes that are grounded in their cultural identities and that encourage the claiming of the sacred face. Some brave souls such as David Abalos (1998), Derise Tolliver, and Dillard, Abdur-Rashid, & Tyson (2000), along with many others, are drawing on spirituality as it connects to culture in their higher education classroom. Based on their insights it is possible to identify central elements of what a spiritually grounded theory-in-progress of teaching for cultural relevance might be and what guidelines it offers for practice. I take this up next.

A Spirituality Grounded and Cultural Relevant Theory-in-Progress for Higher Education

Because higher education presents some special concerns relative to creating a place for the spiritual dimension of adult learning in general, and more specifically in teaching for cultural relevance, it is useful to give some further consideration to teaching in these contexts. A spiritually grounded approach to teaching for cultural relevance in higher education is neither about pushing a religious agenda nor about giving up in any way the critical analysis aspects of what the higher education classroom has traditionally been about. Learners would obviously still read books and articles, write papers, do projects, and create presentations based on readings and the intellectual content of the course. Whether one actually discusses spirituality directly or creates a space more implicitly depends on the content and context of the course. Since a fundamental assumption of this book is that spiritual experiences happen by surprise and cannot be planned, it might seem contradictory to try to create a space for acknowledging the spiritual dimension. Nevertheless, it is possible to design a curriculum and a learning environment that attends to the symbolic domains of learning that are part of spirituality. Therefore, I will outline some central elements of a spiritually grounded theory-in-progress of a culturally relevant pedagogy for higher education. Many elements of this theory are applicable to other adult education settings as well, but some of these elements are more specific to for-credit higher education settings.

Elements of a Spiritually Grounded and Culturally Relevant Pedagogy

Based on the prior discussion, there are seven principles or elements of a spiritually grounded and culturally relevant pedagogy for higher education classrooms that is potentially transformational:

1. An emphasis on authenticity (both spiritual and cultural)
2. An environment that allows for the exploration of:
   - The cognitive (through readings and discussion of ideas)
   - The affective and relational (through connection with other people and connection of ideas to life experience)
   - The symbolic (through art forms such as poetry, visual art, music, drama)
3. Readings that reflect the cultures of the members of the class, and the cultural pluralism of the geographical area relevant to the course content

4. Exploration of individual and communal dimensions of cultural and other dimensions of identity

5. Collaborative work that envisions and presents manifestations of multiple dimensions of learning and strategies for change

6. Celebration of learning and provision for closure to the course

7. Recognition of the limitations of the higher education classroom, and that transformation is an ongoing process that takes time

As noted earlier, authenticity begins with instructors' bringing their more authentic self to the classroom in light of their spiritual and cultural identity. Further, it means also being true to what one is comfortable doing and not doing, leading and not leading in the learning environment. Team-teaching enhances some possibilities. But creating a space that draws on spirituality and attends to cultural issues does not mean that instructors have to be the expert in all matters. Rather, one can and should draw on students' and others' expertise and authenticity by having them lead and facilitate activities and discussions in which they have talent and expertise. This is what emancipatory education is: having participants take some responsibility for their own learning, use their particular talents and expertise, and discover their own increased capacity for making change happen as they connect with others.

Curriculum and Pedagogy

Creating an environment that allows for multiple dimensions of learning includes attending to the cognitive, affective and relational, and symbolic dimensions of learning. Courses in higher education will almost always include readings that deal with some ideas and theoretical issues relevant to the course content. It is the instructor's responsibility to provide a forum whereby learners can develop an understanding of the material. This probably includes

but is not limited to writing papers and having class discussions related to the readings. But the affective and connective dimensions
can be incorporated in papers and class discussions as well by exploring how the theory relates to their life experience or their relational
or emotional lives. Or learners might conduct interviews with those
in their cultural communities with some expertise related to the
topic and analyze how responses relate to the theories discussed.
There are a variety of ways that the symbolic domain could be incorporated. For example, during specific activities or relevant points
in the course, participants might bring a symbol or create or share
an art piece, a poem, a drama, or music that encapsulates their
learning. Or the symbolic domain could be incorporated as part of a
closure activity. Such activities tie the theoretical and cognitive
world to learners' affective and experiential world, and further
anchors their learning in the symbolic world. These multiple components create a more holistic approach to learning, which is more
likely to be transformational. Further, as we have seen, spiritual
experiences are those that get at the wholeness and interconnectedness of all things. Thus, creating learning experiences that are
more holistic might be experienced as, or at least touch on, the spiritual for some.

Obviously, in teaching for cultural relevance, it is important to
create a culturally inclusive curriculum. Such a curriculum includes
providing readings from a culturally pluralistic perspective, as well
as readings by or about members of cultural groups represented in the
class, if possible. One can also draw on learners' cultural experience
by encouraging them to reflect on how the themes of the readings
or course content relate positively or negatively to their own or other
cultural communities. Further, one could encourage them to write a
paper drawing on the ideas in assigned or other readings and through
other ways of collecting information that would be beneficial to their
own or other cultural communities. In classes that focus on culture,
gender, psychology, or sociology, it is easy to see how learners might
explore the individual and communal dimensions of cultural iden-

tity, perhaps through exploring Abalos's (1998) four faces. But it is also possible to do this in some way in all courses, from business to medicine.

Too often in higher education students engage in learning in strict isolation. But significant learning is often not solitary. Furthermore, activities that facilitate social transformation are almost never solitary; after all, social transformation is, by definition, communal. Although it is important to read and absorb course material, it is also important to encourage learners to work collaboratively on some projects. These projects could include written book reviews and accompanying creative presentations that highlight a particular theme of the book and incorporates cognitive, affective, and symbolic dimensions; or projects that envision and model how the course content can be used with real communities in a way that is culturally relevant to them. Such collaborative work serves three purposes: (1) it connects learners with each other and with real communities, (2) it relates theory to real-life practice, and (3) it encourages learners' embodiment and modeling of ideas in cognitive, affective, and symbolic ways to the entire class. These collaborative activities can also serve as a springboard to the closure to the class. Creating a space for the spiritual dimension of learning means paying as much attention to closing the course as one did in setting up the environment at the beginning. It is important to at least briefly honor and celebrate the learning that has taken place. Students' closing presentations that incorporate multiple dimensions of ways of constructing knowledge often set the tone for a celebration and closure to a course, which may be as simple as a one-minute ritual or closing statement or as elaborate as a party or event students plan together.

Finally, it is important to acknowledge the limitations of higher education as a transformational educational space. As Jennifer Gore (1993) notes in her discussion of "institutionalized pedagogy as regulation," there are limitations on the emancipatory potential of the higher education classroom, such as instructors' need to give grades, monitor the limits of time, and fulfill other roles that might be somewhat contradictory to a completely emancipatory learning situation. Further, much education for social transformation that draws on spirituality and culture happens outside classrooms in community-based groups, religious institutions, student affairs offices, and campus and community cultural groups. Those teaching higher education classes might draw on the expertise of these activities on campus and in the community to further enhance culturally relevant education.

Chapter Summary and Conclusion

In this chapter I presented an emerging theory of a spiritually grounded and culturally relevant pedagogy and some general thoughts on what it looks like in practice. I began by presenting some of the multiple theoretical underpinnings that inform this theory-building. These underpinnings include educational theories that highlight learning as transformation; that foreground the significant role of how the positionality (the race, gender, class, or sexual orientation) and cultural identity of both teachers and learners affect how classroom dynamics unfold; and that deal directly with culture, race, class, and gender issues in education. In particular, these theoretical strands include transformative learning, critical and feminist pedagogy, multicultural education and critical multiculturalism–resistance postmodernism, and Africentric perspectives, along with other culturally specific educational models that make up the literature on culturally relevant education. Given that these approaches tend not to discuss the role of spirituality in education, this review took place specifically in light of what a spiritually grounded approach might offer in relation to these strands.

The central elements and principles of a spiritually grounded and culturally relevant pedagogy specifically in higher education were then highlighted. These include but are not limited to the seven elements of (1) an emphasis on authenticity, (2) an environment that allows for the exploration of the cognitive, affective, and symbolic dimensions of learning, (3) culturally relevant readings, (4) exploration of cultural identity, (5) collaborative work and presentations that deal with strategies of change and multiple dimensions of learning, (6) celebration, and (7) a recognition of the possibilities and limitations of emancipatory learning potential in higher education environments. Some general thoughts about how to apply these principles to practice were also discussed. More specific examples will be provided in the next chapter.

11

Stories from the Field

Spirituality and Culture in Adult Higher Education Classrooms

Educators must determine for themselves how they might incorporate spirituality and culture in a way that is true to who they are and is relevant to the educational context in which they work. How different educators have done this in their own practices was discussed to some degree in Chapter Nine in considering ways of approaching a spiritually grounded, culturally relevant pedagogy. Chapter Ten then laid out the elements of a spiritually grounded and culturally relevant theory-in-practice specifically for higher education.

In the examples in Chapter Nine, educators drew on their own spirituality in the educational context in ways that were consonant with who they are. Although there was an element of vulnerability in drawing on it, as there always is when one opts to bring one's whole self to the learning environment, in most cases the educators did not necessarily use the word "spirituality." As has been said many times throughout this book, drawing on spirituality is not about pushing a religious or even a spiritual agenda. It is about providing experiences whereby individuals have the potential to construct knowledge through image, symbol, music, art, and more intuitive ways of knowing. But whether or not such experiences are experienced is "spiritual" varies from person to person.

Over the years in discussions of spirituality and education, many have asked what the difference is between spiritual and emotional experience. Indeed, when someone does experience something as "spiritual" there is often strong emotion attached to it. But emotional experiences and spiritual experiences are not the same necessarily. People can have significantly positive emotional experiences that are not necessarily experienced as spiritual. Further, people can have spiritual experiences, such as experiences of synchronicity as discussed in Chapter Four, that are not overly emotional. Of course, there is some emotion that is attached to everything we do. But whether something is experienced as "spiritual" is entirely determined by the one experiencing it and may or may not be attached to strong emotion. It seems, however, that especially significant spiritual experiences do have strong emotion attached to them. But most important experiences in our lives have strong emotion attached to them, even if they are not experienced as "spiritual." This is probably why important experiences, spiritual or otherwise, are remembered as such: precisely because they do have strong emotion attached to them.

The purpose of this chapter is to provide a few stories and examples of how some educators have drawn on spirituality in their practices. The most detailed examples are from my own educational practice. These are offered only as examples; it is up to you to determine what would be most appropriate to do in your settings in light of your own context, your own positionality, and who your learners are. I begin the chapter by considering how educators have drawn on spirituality in culturally diverse higher education classrooms. I then discuss the less likely situation of the more culturally similar higher education classroom.

Spirituality and Culture in Diverse Classrooms

Most classrooms contain a diverse group of learners. Although they might be primarily of one cultural group (in higher education this is usually white and European American), there are usually members of other cultural, class, or marginalized groups among learners. Generally speaking, the classroom is a vulnerable space for people who are marginalized. It is an even more vulnerable space for those who represent but one or two members of a particular group in a sea of people more representative of the dominant norm (Johnson-Bailey, 2001).

If one is trying to create what bell hooks (1994) refers to as a teaching community, it is important for all learners to feel that they have allies in the group or classroom, especially if the course content is about cultural issues. Even when the content is not particularly about cultural issues, students (or faculty) who are different from the dominant norm of a given situation, because of their culture, religion, sexual orientation, social class, or gender, often are more vulnerable. Thus if one is teaching a course in a way that draws on one's own spirituality and attempts to take into account cultural issues, it is helpful to attend to ways participants can be allies for each other. This creates the possibility also of creating what Sharon Daloz Parks (2000) refers to as a mentoring community.

Chris Larson, the music professor who was introduced in Chapter Five, spoke to this point of working to be an ally and helping students to be allies for each other. He notes that although he almost never talks about religion in his classes, particularly his own, in a broader sense he draws on spirituality in his way of approaching music and in his commitment to diversity. Although his task is often to teach music theory, or certain music skills, he does try to draw on music from different cultures in order to teach for cultural relevance and also to be mindful of those who might feel marginalized or vulnerable in the classroom. He talked specifically about dealing with this immediately following the September 11, 2001 terrorist attacks on the World Trade Center, the Pentagon, and that resulted in the plane crash in Pennsylvania. He wondered what he could possibly do in his music appreciation class the next day. "Everything seemed so trivial," he said in the wake of the world events, and wondered, "What am I going to say that's going to have any relevance? Should we have a moment of silence, should we listen to something kind of spiritual, like the Bach Mass in B minor?"

Chris assumed that the two Muslim women students in his class were probably feeling vulnerable in general (along with other members of Muslim communities) in the face of potential anti-Muslim sentiment. He also recognized that the terrorists themselves were not in any way representative of Islam. Thus, he decided it would be more appropriate and educational to listen to something that arose more out of the tradition of Islam. "I thought maybe it would give us a different sense. . . . And so I did some research the night before on Islamic chant, and found some great things on the improvisatory character of the chant." He described being nervous about doing this the next day, but opted to have a discussion, play the chants, explain some aspects of the chant, and draw connections to other cultures and traditions. He described having quite a good discussion in which many participated, including the two Muslim women students, who also felt very supported by the activity. Perhaps this is a particularly obvious example of when and why students who are "other" might feel vulnerable in a classroom, but it is also a good example of how to help participants be allies for each other. Chris explained that a very strong sense of community has developed in this particular class. Although he doesn't attribute it to this discussion in particular, he does attribute it to a plethora of activities and discussions, including the discussion that day, which have been a part of the class.

A Critical Incident

The focus of Chris Larson's classes is music; yet he brings in cultural elements to his classes. Others teach higher education classes in which the specific focus of the class is culture and diversity, and issues such as race, culture, gender, sexual orientation, and ableness are the primary course content. The single most transformative moment I have ever had in a classroom took place in one such class, a master's level education class that I team-taught with an African American colleague several years ago. We planned the class from a critical multicultural perspective, and more or less followed the list of principles of a spiritually grounded, culturally relevant pedagogy outlined in the Chapter Ten. I have talked in explicit detail about this incident elsewhere (Tisdell, 2001) from the standpoint of how positionality issues play out in higher education classrooms. However, I did not discuss it in relation to spirituality, and given that it was the single most important spiritual experience that I've had in a classroom, I briefly summarize the incident again here.

The incident took place during the afternoon session of the last day of a class that was taught in a day-long format of four full days. It was the last small group's presentation based on learners' experience of working through a book of their own choosing that dealt with cultural issues—in this case bell hooks' (1994) *Teaching to Transgress: Education as the Practice of Freedom*. There were sixteen students in this class—five men, eleven women; four students of color, and the remainder white. One student was hearing impaired, so all classes were signed; another openly acknowledged being bisexual. The remainder of the class was more or less representative of the white, dominant culture. As is typical in these classes, there had been some conflict in the class, but it was fairly limited.

This particular activity on *Teaching to Transgress* was facilitated by three very articulate students—Mary, an African American woman with considerable experience as a full-time adult educator in a post-secondary setting; Sam, a white hearing-impaired man who taught in a community college; and Nora, a white woman, a foreign language part-time teacher. They began their presentation by each taking a turn in setting the context. They discussed some of the conflict among them in planning the presentation, somewhat based on race and class differences, as well as how they worked through it (largely between Mary and Nora). They explained that bell hooks (1994) talks about "engaged pedagogy" and that we were not going to *talk* about engaged pedagogy; rather, we were going to *do it.* Our task was to go around the room and pass a "talking stick" and comment on what this class meant in changing our consciousness. Participants had the option of speaking or passing. The three facilitators began and modeled the process. In going around the circle the first round, all the students of color spoke. Many of the white students passed, but some also spoke. Most of those who did speak quite emotionally about their experience of developing understanding of how systems of privilege and oppression work. Many cried. I passed (thinking that I did not want to do anything to affect the process). My teaching partner spoke.

The stick was then passed to Susan, a white high school teacher, who was very well liked and highly respected by her peers. She explained what the class brought up for her: her father had been murdered a few years before by two African American men who had broken into the house during the night. Susan was there when it happened. She heard the door break down. She heard her father run downstairs. She heard the shots. She heard the quiet. She went downstairs, finding her father's body in a pool of blood. She explained her response to this death—that the murderers were the victims of a racist society, a racist educational system. While she didn't condone or accept their murderous behavior, this was why she was doing her antiracist work as a teacher. She cried—the painful reality of the whole experience of her father's death was present with her, and now present within the circle of this group. There was silence in the room. You could hear a pin drop. Many were wiping their eyes.

The stick passed, and finally arrived back at Mary. She commented on Susan's remarks, saying she was sorry that someone "who looks like me has caused you so much pain." She went on to say something to the effect:

> *I just want to point something out here. I have been through many classes and in-services dealing with diversity issues. I am often one of the few people of color in the room. Often*

I feel like my pain is supposed to be on display, and that white folks often have the privilege of sitting in silence, and sometimes watch me bleed. Today, in going around this circle, I want to point out all the people of color and differently-abled people have spoken, and all the white folks that spoke cried. And I am struck with how willing those of you who spoke are to share your pain with me. And when you share you pain with me, I am much more willing to share mine with you.

She turned to Susan, who by this time had stopped crying, and thanked her for her courage and willingness to share her pain. The stick went around the circle one more time. Some people spoke, making some closing remarks (myself included). The three student facilitators closed the exercise. We took a break. After the break, my teaching partner and I facilitated a brief closure activity to the whole course—a short reading from Audre Lorde's (1984) essay "The Transformation of Silence into Language and Action," with parts for each participant, and a short one-line sung antiphon that everyone sang together at various points in the reading. Then we all left, many of us forever changed by this experience.

The Spiritual in the Transformational

This was the single most transformational moment I have ever had in a class. Many participants also indicated as such in their final paper in which they had to apply the theory and intellectual material of the course to an analysis of their experiences dealing with diversity and equity issues in and outside of the class. I do not know exactly what made the event transformational to other people in the room. It is safe to say that for everyone present this certainly was an experience that was packed with emotion. I do not know whether it was a spiritual experience for others, but it was for me. What was spiritual about it for me was that it brought together rationality and affect, theory and practice, passion and possibility, pain and transformation, symbol and ritual, and a level of authenticity and vulnerability that I have never experienced before in a higher education setting. The experience resulted in healing, new insight, greater understanding, and a shared sense of community among most in the class. It was this combination of elements that made it feel spiritual to me.

I think what made it feel most spiritual to me was that in this open exchange of vulnerability, and in the participants in the class being as real as they could be in that moment, seemed to offer healing and hope. Susan did not go down the road of racial hatred in the aftermath of her father's murder. She had been doing antiracist work for a long time in her own teaching long before she arrived in this class. Although she never spoke of her dad's death to the whole class prior to this experience, she had spoken rather passionately about antiracist education in earlier class sessions. Our knowing this offered hope. Mary responded to Susan's pain with empathy, insight, and her own vulnerability. Sharing this with the group offered hope. In their own vulnerability, particularly the students who spoke in the first round, the engaged presence of all the students offered hope. I think nearly all the students shared this sense of hope. In one of the closing papers reflecting on the readings and educational practice, a student wrote that she wondered what bell hooks' engaged pedagogy might look like in practice. She commented that this experience made her understand engaged pedagogy, and "It works!"

What was also both spiritual and transformational for me was the new insight and understanding I developed as a result of this experience, both about myself as a teacher-learner and about students as teachers-learners. I discovered something new about how power relations work in the classroom, particularly in those designed to challenge society's power relations. Up until that time, I had generally thought of speaking and "coming to voice" as a sign of power, and over the years, I have observed that those who benefit by more systems of privilege by virtue of their positionality are more likely to dominate the classroom speaking space, and often have more power in the classroom. I had not thought of silence necessarily as a way of maintaining power and privilege in a classroom. Further, I had not initially noticed that the most marginalized (namely the people of color and the person with a disability) and the white participants most willing to be vulnerable who were the ones to speak in the first round of the circle. Mary's very important insight in this regard was transformative for me at that moment.

Silence can have multiple meanings; it can be an unwillingness to be open or vulnerable, which can be a way of maintaining power and control. On a conscious level, I thought my own initial silence was about not wanting to disrupt the process that the students had very effectively created. But my African American teaching partner spoke. Perhaps on a less conscious level I, too, along with the other white participants who said nothing during the first round, did not want to be vulnerable. Perhaps this was an unconscious way of maintaining my own white privilege. The incident not only made me think about the way positionality shapes dynamics in classes focusing on systems of privilege and oppression. It also made me think more about the multiple meanings of silence and voice, as well as how to create a space where people might be authentic. Mary's outstanding facilitation, in particular, taught me something about that. She seemed so spiritually grounded in her own cultural wisdom and experience and own authenticity that it moved the group into theirs; perhaps that was why she was so effective in her facilitation of a very emotionally laden situation. Overall, the experience helped me understand more of what it might mean for me to be more authentic and the role of spirituality and its connection to culture. It also taught me something of what it means to educate the white teacher as ally (Titone, 2000). In that regard, several of the participants in this class, and many others, have been the real teachers. But through them and with them, all together we have created mentoring communities when we didn't even know it was happening. Spiritual experiences do indeed happen by surprise!

Although this was a significant spiritual moment in my own teaching practice, a couple of general comments are in order here about drawing on spirituality in the classroom. First, this was an experience facilitated by the students in the class; it was not facilitated by my teaching partner or by me. I would probably not have facilitated such an experience myself, because I would be concerned that by virtue of the power of my own position, students would feel that I was requiring them to be more vulnerable than they wanted to be in signing up for the class. But for them to facilitate such an experience for each other places the power of the instructors in a different place.

Even though my teaching partner and I were nothing more than full participants in the situation, we did plan and set up the course overall so that students would be in teaching roles. We included all elements of the spiritually grounded theory-in-progress discussed in the last chapter. We tried to attend to issues of authenticity by telling aspects of our own stories related to our cultural background and positionality during the first class. We set up the environment to include cognitive, affective, and symbolic knowledge construction elements and included readings that reflected the cultures of people in the room. Students wrote cultural stories and papers analyzing readings related to their own practice, and conducted collaborative presentations. Thus we did set up the environment in the hopes that students could explore these multiple dimensions of learning. Still, they needed to activate their own power from within in order to conduct and participate in the activity. Indeed they did, and it was a transformative experience for most people in the room, and a spiritual experience at least for one!

Spirituality and Cultural Relevance in Culturally Similar Communities

Most higher education classrooms are composed of students of culturally diverse backgrounds, but sometimes in higher education efforts are made to deal with the educational needs of specific cultural communities. One such program is the Latino-focused Master of Adult Education program at National-Louis University (NLU), a cohort model based on the usual master's cohort program. In this case, however, courses were redesigned in cooperation with members of the Latino community in order to ensure their cultural relevance to those communities. Students take two classes per term of integrated course content, which include many readings by Latino authors and educators. All classes are team-taught by an NLU faculty member and a bilingual member of the Latino community. I had the privilege of team-teaching with this cohort on a number of occasions. Although all the students in this cohort are Latino, being "Latino" is certainly not a monolith. Two of the participants were Colombian or Colombian-Argentinean. The rest were Puerto Rican, but even being Puerto Rican is not a monolith, as there are those who were born on the Island, those born in Chicago, and those whose lives have been characterized by a fairly constant migration between the Island and the mainland. Identity is never monolithic.

The subject of spirituality was rarely a topic of direct discussion in this group, but the subject of culture and identity was part of every course, from research methods to adult development to program planning. There were occasions when connections were made to spirituality, because the work of David Abalos (1998) served as a theoretical backdrop to the two team-taught courses during one term—Instructional Communications, and Qualitative Research Methods in Education—which Silvia Villa and I team-taught together. Given that Abalos's (1998) theoretical framework suggests that the way toward social transformation for the Latino community is by reclaiming cultural identity through examining each of the four faces of one's being—the personal, historical, political, and sacred faces—there was a connection to the spiritual in relationship to the sacred face. There were many spiritual moments (at least for me) that were directly related to spirituality and culture over the course of this cohort together. I attribute this to the emphasis on reclaiming of the four faces, which clearly called all of us, including me, the only Anglo in the group, to be more authentic.

Just as in the diversity class discussed above, what I experienced in this class as a spiritual moment was the result of a presentation given by two of the students, and it happened by surprise. Part of the assignment of the research methods class was to conduct a mini-pilot qualitative or action research project. Students needed to present the findings of their project during the last class of the term. Two of the students did a pilot project in a writing class that one of them was teaching at a local community college primarily to students whose first language was Spanish. They developed a series of activities on how to teach writing in a way that was culturally relevant to Latino students. In addition to presenting some of the research results, as part of their class presentation they demonstrated one of the writing activities by conducting it with our group. The assignment involved writing a six-line poem in which each line began with *Yo soy* (or "I am") and then was filled in with memories from childhood in relation to what foods reminded them of home, what places were special in their barrio or community, what events were significant, what special "sayings" they remembered, what their heritage was, and who their people were. We were encouraged to write in Spanish or in English. Some wrote primarily in Spanish, and I wrote entirely in English; but most wrote in Spanglish to represent the bicultural and bilingual nature of their identity. We had less than ten minutes to complete the exercise.

The two facilitator-presenters then asked us to present our poems, and nearly all did. By the time we were finished, there was hardly a dry eye in the room. One poem was as profound as the next, highlighting pride and pain, culture and tradition, love and loss, passion and politics. With only ten minutes to write, people wrote the first thing that came to their minds in response to each of the questions. There had not been time for a lot of editing; thus what we shared was the depth of authenticity. This included much of what was tremendously important and foundational to who each of us is and what is special to our own identity—partly in Spanish, partly in English, definitely real, shared in this community that had become an important mentoring community for all of us.

The exercise touched the unconscious of our imaginations. It was not imagination in the sense of fantasy, but rather imagination that is very real but that often lies in the depth of our unconscious or semiconscious (Parks, 2000). Brought forth and shared in this community, the work of our imaginations became part of the reclaiming of the sacred face. It also became part of the political face, as featured in the newsletter that the students created, *Voces Y Caras* ("Voices and Faces"), which documented part of their education as a transformation journey and featured some of their poems and their experience of what it means to do culturally relevant education in their own communities. In addition, they presented some of their work at the 2000 Midwest Research to Practice Conference in Adult, Continuing, and Community Education (see Tisdell, Sanabria, et al., 2000) and at the national 2001 Adult Education Research Conference (Heaney et al., 2001). But they also developed a deeper appreciation of the power of their imagination rooted in the reality of their own cultures and identities as they work with their own communities.

In writing and presenting their work these students are trying to transform the fields of adult and higher education to be more inclusive of the plurality of the Latino experience. This effort, along with the work in their own communities, is social transformation that is deeply rooted in their cultural identity. It is not fueled only by this one poetry writing exercise in this class; rather it is fueled by their whole lives and work in their own communities, but was enhanced by this culturally relevant education experience that connected culture and spirituality. This poetry writing exercise was one among many transformational and spiritual moments for me (and for many others) in the group. Who would have thought it would happen in a research methods class! Again, it happened by surprise.

Chapter Summary and Conclusion

This chapter presented some stories from real life practice in which educators and students have implicitly drawn on spirituality in creating a culturally relevant learning environment in higher education. It began with a discussion of the difference between spirituality and emotion in the learning environment, and noted that although spiritual experiences often have strong emotion attached to them, they don't always. Furthermore, not all emotional learning experiences are necessarily spiritual.

Most spiritual experiences that people refer to that relate to the higher education learning environment not only take place by surprise, they also take place not so much because of what the instructor does but because of what the learners do with the learning that has occurred. Whether or not a learning experience is experienced as "spiritual" depends on the learner. But conditions can be created, even in higher education, that seem to increase the likelihood that learning will be transformational and have a spiritual component to it. This happens most often when learners connect with each other, take risks with their own facilitation and presentations in the learning environment, particularly when they unite cognitive and intellectual material with their affective response, and demonstrate how it is manifested symbolically and creatively in a way that is a learning experience for all or most in the classroom. Although this happens generally as a result of what students do with the learning, the instructor has some responsibility for setting up an environment that allows for such learning and expression of it to happen and that encourages students to embrace their cultural identity and be creative in their demonstration of learning.

It is the community of learners who are simultaneously teachers and learners together in the culturally relevant learning environment that makes learning transformational and that occasionally results in spiritual experiences for some. Such learning needs to be celebrated. As O'Sullivan (1999) suggests in his discussion of the role of spirituality in transformative education that deals with environmental and justice issues, educational models are needed that include ways of honoring a sense of awe and mystery, sanctuary and silence, and celebration: "Celebration must be accomplished at all levels of our conscious awareness. From time immemorial the celebratory experience is consistently associated with the sense of the sacred. This sense of the numinous quality of all existence is seen in all cultural expressions of the sacred. . . . For creatures of the millennium, we must remind ourselves that we are about a great work. It is a joy to be part of this grandeur" (pp. 280–281).

It is indeed a joy to be a part of the grandeur of great work. Trying to develop educational models that are culturally relevant, that are part of transforming systems for greater equity and justice, and that honor the earth and all the creatures in it is a great work that is worthy of celebrating. People often need spiritual and human support to continue that great work, as it is often very difficult work. This is what spiritually grounded practice offers to culturally relevant education.

12

The Possibilities and Challenges of Spiritually Grounded, Culturally Relevant Teaching

Los zapatitos me aprietan
Las medias me dan calor
Y cuando miro al cielo
Me dan los rayos del sol.

Author Unknown

This is the first poem that educator, activist, and musician-dancer Tito Rodriguez[1] remembers learning in Spanish when his family moved back to Puerto Rico from Chicago when he was five years old. He didn't really know what the poem meant, for up until that time, Tito primarily spoke English, though both his parents were Puerto Rican. A recurrent migration process between Chicago and Puerto Rico characterized his childhood, in light of which he was also constantly learning, relearning, and switching languages between English and Spanish for years at a time. Tito explained the special meaning of the poem for him—an explanation, which to me, gets at the heart of what spirituality and culture and culturally relevant education are all about.

The poem roughly translated means: "My little shoes are too tight on me; My socks make my feet sweat: And when I look at the sky, I am bathed by the rays of the sun." Tito described when he first

1. This is Tito's real name; it is not a pseudonym.

became aware of just how significant this poem is in his life. He was trying to memorize a poem in a college Spanish class, when he suddenly found himself reciting this first childhood poem that he had ever learned in Spanish.

> It was like falling into a trance. I was transported back in time to my childhood years. I felt the tropical heat of Puerto Rico. I smelled the grass and herbal plants of my backyard, and found myself sitting down in our imaginary school reciting the poem. In my dream state the world mixed with images of my childhood, and for the first time in my life, I understood the meaning of the poem. . . . I woke up from my trance in tears. Then, I understood that this experience and this poem have always been a parallel in my life. Such a simple poem made me understood that life was ever changing and, at times, it will hurt you (tight), that it's OK to suffer (sweat), but that one must overcome adversity and have faith (look into the sky), and after hard work one will enjoy the fruits of that work (sunshine, warmth and light). This revelation forced me to reflect on the work I had done in high school and my community in previous years. It gave me insight on the work I needed to continue.

Tito's further explanation, and how his life story continued to unfold, gives additional insight about why the poem has such important meaning. Tito moved back to Chicago, more or less permanently when he was fourteen, and attended high school and college here. He actually knew little English when he returned because he had been primarily speaking Spanish since the time he was five. As noted in Chapter Seven, where other aspects of his story are highlighted, under the guidance of an important teacher and mentor during his high school years who introduced him to Puerto Rican history, art, and dance, Tito began the process of reclaiming his cultural identity. Tito has continued the tradition of mentoring as his own mentor, Orlando, had mentored him. He works with youth and adults, introducing them to a deeper understanding of the world of his culture and theirs through the arts, dance, and music in formal education and community education settings. He has founded a dance and music troupe whose purpose is to do culturally relevant education. Now at forty, Tito sees this as an important part of his life's purpose; it is the work of his very soul and is deeply connected to his spirituality and his culture.

I highlight Tito's flashback experience of the poem and its importance to him for a number of reasons that help summarize the connection between spirituality and culture, and what this connection implies for teaching for transformation and cultural relevance. First, the experience of getting in touch with the significance of the poem was a spiritual experience for Tito. As discussed in Chapter Three, like the many spiritual experiences reported elsewhere in this book it was triggered by imagination, as well as symbol in the art and language of the poem itself, deeply connected to his culture. This is obvious in his reference to the sound of the Spanish language, the feel of the tropical heat of Puerto Rico, and the smell of the grass and herbal plants in the backyard. In addition, as is typical of many spiritual experiences, this one was characterized by a strong affective component, as Tito described coming out of his "trance" in tears.

Second, this spiritual experience triggered by the poem and Tito's imagination caused him to spiral back to a significant memory in time and place. As we saw in Chapter Five, a hallmark of spiritual development is this process of moving forward and spiraling back. And in this spiraling process, Tito also got more in touch with what he sees as his life purpose: to continue moving forward and to do his educational work through music, arts, and dance as a way to teach people about culture, cultural pride, and how to make change happen through drama, art, dance, and creative presentational knowing. This not only puts people in touch with their cultural roots; it puts them in touch with their own embodied spirituality. Third, as noted in Chapter Seven, the experience was also fundamentally about Tito's cultural and more authentic identity. Indeed, the process of spiritual development is an ongoing spiral process of claiming and reclaiming one's more authentic identity, which includes one's cultural identity. The experience again brings to light the role that spirituality can play in ongoing cultural identity development. Fourth, Tito's spiritual experience brings to light as another example the important way he has constructed knowledge through what Fowler (1981) refers to as unconscious and symbolic processes, what Parks (2000) refers to as imagination, and what Heron (1996) refers to as imaginal or presentational knowing. To be sure, this has been little discussed in higher and adult education in general, much less how these processes connect to teaching for cultural relevance. But given that these realms connect to how people construct knowing and meaning on a fundamental level, these forms of knowing are an important area in the transformational learning process and important to teaching for cultural relevance.

In summarizing and making sense of what has been discussed in earlier chapters, I'd like to conclude the book in these last two chapters by briefly reflecting on what the themes highlighted in this book suggest for the connection between spirituality and teaching for cultural relevance in higher and adult education in light of the three lines of the poem above. This chapter will include reflections on the first two lines, and will be in two parts: (1) the relationship among adult development, spirituality, and teaching for cultural relevance; (2) the perils and possibilities of a spiritually grounded approach to culturally relevant higher education at this time; some final reflections on spirituality in teaching for cultural relevance and social transformation.

Los Zapatitos Me Aprietan! Spirituality, Adult Development, and Teaching for Cultural Relevance

Sometimes *los zapatitos nos aprietan*—our shoes *are* too tight, literally and metaphorically. When the way we have defined our identities becomes too tight, too stifling, we either settle, stagnate, or become rigid as we try to fit into those roles and identities too small for us; or we grow and change. I'd like to think that most of us change and grow. What is the role of education in that process and what does it have to do with a spiritually grounded approach of teaching for cultural relevance and social transformation?

The Interrelationship of Adult Development and Adult Learning

Many have discussed the role that education plays in facilitating adult development, from discussions on the importance of mentoring (Daloz, 1999) to the role that formal higher education plays in the development of adult learners (Pratt, 1998; Taylor, Marienau, & Fiddler, 2000) to the connection between adult development and adult learning more generally (Clark & Caffarella, 1999; Merriam & Caffarella, 1999). This topic is also a focus of many of the contributors in the recent discussion of Mezirow and Associates (2000) on transformational learning as a theory in progress. To be sure, these are very important and excellent discussions for how educators might teach in a way that not only facilitates adult learning but also facilitates adult development. A limitation of the discussions, however, is that with some exceptions (Chavez & Guido-DiBrito, 1999; Tatum, 1997), of the many who note in passing the important dimension of culture, few really *deal* with it as a significant part of adult development that affects learning. In a similar way, authors who specifically talk about culturally relevant education tend not to focus on what Kathleen Taylor (2000b) refers to as "teaching with developmental intention" (p. 151), although they generally refer in passing to how culturally relevant education affects learners' development (Guy, 1999; Sheared & Sissel, 2001). This of course is partly due to the difference and emphases of the two groups of authors.

Attending to cultural issues in teaching with developmental intention is important for a couple of reasons. First, there is often an assumption in much of the education literature that education facilitates development. Ideally, this is true. But for people of color in North America, formal education has often been more about what Freire (1974) refers to as "education as domestication"—about education to fit into social roles in a system that was created by those with the most power to determine what should count as knowledge, what and who should be represented in what kinds of ways in the readings and school curriculum, and ultimately who should fit what kinds of career roles. This, of course, is more true of the K-12 schooling system than adult education, for as Heaney (1996, 2000) has discussed, adult education grew out of a different set of traditions—those of social movements trying to make change in society. But many adult educators are working in formal higher education settings. If those of us working in higher education settings are not more direct in our attention to how culture affects development and learning, we potentially risk being an extension of "education as domestication."

Second, not specifically dealing with culture or gender in discussions of teaching to facilitate adult development can inadvertently propagate the idea that attending to culture is something that only cultural "experts" or those with particular expertise in multicultural or culturally relevant education need to be concerned about. As was obvious in the many stories in this book, the cultural dimension was absolutely central to understanding these adults' spiritual and overall adult development. Further, to understand anything about their spiritual development, it was important to understand some of their cultural background, because spirituality is often mediated and manifested through the ritual, imagery, art, and music that is a part of cultural experience. For example, to understand why the poem featured at this chapter's opening was important to Tito and a symbolic manifestation of the spiritual dimension of his life, one needs to know not only what the Spanish words mean but also understand the cultural context of his life.

A spiritually grounded approach to culturally relevant education in higher education is partly about teaching with developmental intention around facilitating learners' greater authenticity, and that affirms and attends to their cultural identity and spirituality, and that attends to their critical thinking about the subject matter of the course. This does not mean neglecting the content of the course, whether it is leadership, mathematics education, or sociology. One would hope that a greater understanding of how culture, and one's cultural self, connects to the content of the course would facilitate a greater sense of being able to move to action and apply the work of the course. If knowledge engages one's passion, it activates more energy to create change in one's personal and professional life, in one's community, and in the world. How can we cultivate this engagement of passion and understanding of culture in ourselves as well as our students? Perhaps one way is by understanding how our own culture and spirituality has affected our own life choices and those of educators and other people who are very different from us. Such understanding might help us draw on our passion more effectively in our practices.

Understanding Educators' Cultural and Spiritual Development

This book is not only about teaching for cultural relevance; it is also about the related issue of understanding how spirituality interfaces with culture in the lives of a very multicultural group of adult educators and how their spirituality develops. Some of their stories are probably similar to some of our own; many are probably very different. The hope is that understanding both those who are like us and those who are very unlike us helps us facilitate (1) moving toward greater authenticity in our lives and in our work as educators; (2) working more effectively with those who are of a different culture, gender, class, or sexual orientation; and (3) drawing on symbolic and imaginal forms of knowing in new ways that touch into people's cultural lives to some degree and in some cases their spiritual lives as well.

But I want to highlight here a few insights that have not yet been considered thus far that can add further insight about spirituality, religion, and culture in relationship to spiritual development and teaching for cultural relevance. First, it is important to remember that the educators chosen for this book represent a particular group of educators. They were chosen specifically because they were teaching higher education classes dealing with race, gender, class, or sexual orientation or were otherwise trying to bring some cultural or spiritual perspective to their teaching about education; or they were doing community work around cultural or social justice issues. In addition, they were chosen because they indicated that spirituality was a strong influence in their educational work, either implicitly or explicitly. Thus this is not just *any* group of educators, it is a *particular* group of educators, who are going to have a more heightened awareness of both spirituality and cultural issues in relationship to education than others might. (See the methodology discussion in the Appendix.) That being said, a few additional insights about this particular group of educators are in order.

The Place of Religion in Educators' Spirituality

With only a couple of exceptions, the educators I interviewed grew up and were socialized in a particular religious tradition. Virtually all of them made a distinction between religion and spirituality and nurtured and valued a spiritual perspective on life. Only a few of them were actively involved in the religious traditions in which they were raised. Further, most (not all) were somewhat ambivalent about organized religion. On the one hand, they valued the important ways religion helps people make meaning of their lives through significant ritual, symbols, and ways of honoring life's important events; on the other, they were disturbed by how religious traditions have been used and distorted throughout the ages as a way to control people physically or psychologically, to maim, colonize, or kill in the name of "God," from the time of the distortion of Christianity in the Christian crusades to the distortion of Islam in the recent September 11, 2001 terrorist attacks. Of the more than thirty people who participated in this study, only four have been steadfastly committed to the religions of their childhood throughout their lives. In all four of these cases, the participants were members of a marginalized group. Aiysha Ali is both of East Indian descent and a Muslim; Raul Guerrero, a practicing Roman Catholic, is Filipino; Chris Larson is Mormon; and Sue Kim is Korean American involved with the Korean Presbyterian Church. In light of their marginalized status in society due to their ethnicity, culture, national origin, or religion, they probably found a particular support in their faith communities for their ethnic and spiritual identity that was not as available in other places in society. Thus although they had questioned their religious traditions and had some difficulties with various aspects of them, they have remained committed to their religious traditions and communities throughout their lives and have found a strong sense of support in those communities.

The rest of those I interviewed had spent time away from the religious traditions of their childhood; but all spiraled back to reclaim aspects of those traditions that continued to be important. Only a few, however, became actively committed and involved in their childhood religious traditions or similar communities. A few others had converted to other religious or spiritual traditions and had gone through formal study both in their initial conversion process and throughout their lives. The vast majority—more than two-thirds— had developed more of an eclectic spirituality and considered themselves spiritual but not religious. Given that the participants valued and placed strong emphasis on the importance of community and that spirituality strongly informed their cultural and social justice work, the fact that less than a third were involved in religious communities was initially somewhat surprising.

On further reflection this made some sense. Given that most of them teach classes or work in programs where they are problematizing and trying to change *structural* power relations based on culture, race, class, gender, sexual orientation, or ableness, it is perhaps not surprising that many of them would also have trouble with similar structural oppression in aspects of organized religion. Most did respect, however, the wonderful aspects of religion that provide a sense of community and expressions of ritual and cultural meaning-making that relate strongly to the spiritual. And they might occasionally attend religious rituals or activities for various occasions. Raul Guerrero, who has always been involved with a Catholic worshiping community both in the Philippines and in the United States, noted that in spite of his problems with many of the "isms" within Catholicism, he needs to be involved with a spiritual community on a regular basis. He spoke about his Catholicism rather poignantly:

> I move in and out. . . . The truth is I'm uncomfortable being in, and I'm uncomfortable being out, and the truth is I think my wholeness is somewhere in between. . . . My identity is somewhere in between, and I guess I refuse the modernist tendency to pin me down, categorize me, and if it's postmodern to be able to dance between, to play in between, to float in between, then I am postmodern.

On an intellectual level, Raul is referring to the emphasis in postmodernism on challenging the notion of categories. But on a spiritual level, he emphasizes that wholeness is found *somewhere in between*. Perhaps it is in the tension of the dialectic and in our lived experience of "in-between-ness"—of both being in, and not being in—that we are ultimately pulled open to the spirit.

The Enduring Power of Spiritual and Cultural Symbol

From a spiritual and cultural perspective, some of this lived experience of "in-between-ness" might be manifested in the enduring (but often unconscious) attachment to the symbols, music, and some of the rituals from childhood religious traditions and the conceptual meanings attached to them that many still held as important. The positive endurance of these aspects of their childhood religious traditions was of value to all of them, even those who had serious issue with structural systems of oppression in their religions of origin. For example, although Greta Schmidt has long since moved away from Catholicism, the symbolic meaning of Resurrection—the promise of new life after a dark night of the soul—continues to be an important metaphor for her. Similarly, even though many had moved away from their childhood religious tradition, they did often spiral back and "re-member" those aspects of it that were life-giving, at the same time that they integrated and were exposed to new ideas, new spiritual traditions, and had further spiritual experiences as adults. This aspect of the study is similar to what Wuthnow (1999) found in his study of people who grew up religious, and was especially evident in his more recent study of spirituality among artists (Wuthnow, 2001).

It is important also to note that aspects of their childhood tradition that they were particularly attached to are also deeply rooted in a cultural identity. For example, we see evidence of this in the cultural and spiritual significance of La Virgen de Guadalupe as Chicana for Julia Gutierrez, in the music of Aretha Franklin as representational of the African American experience for Anna Adams, in the significance of wilderness for Lisa Riddle who grew up in Alaska, and in particular music for everyone. Furthermore, in nearly all cases the women who specifically mentioned spiritual symbols or those in whom they found inspiration, specifically mentioned feminine symbols embodied as reminiscent of their culture. Some of the spiritual figures mentioned were Aretha Franklin, La Virgen de Guadalupe, Harriet Tubman, the feminine Buddhist wisdom figure Kuan Yin, female ancestors, and Sojourner Truth (to name a few). Further, three now identify largely with one of the Yoga traditions, which is led by a woman. Although only a few noted that feminine figures were important spiritual figures for them specifically because they were women, it may be that on an unconscious level these spiritual figures are important in affirming their gender identity and their spirituality as women. There was less of an identifiable pattern here among the men. But whether there is an identifiable gender pattern would need to be the subject of a further research.

As a general rule, the white or European American participants had less of an overt sense of their cultural identity development than the people of color or those marginalized because of their sexual orientation, religion, or national origin. This less overt sense of identity probably stems from the fact of dominance itself: those of us who are white "float" more in the "water" of the dominant culture, so the culture might be so omnipresent as to be less visible. As the saying goes, "It's hard to see the forest through the trees." For the most part the people of color developed their spirituality by embracing and reclaiming their cultural identity very directly and discovering their spirituality more deeply in that process. Those who were European American tended to develop their spirituality further by crossing culture and spiritual traditions. Sometimes crossing culture and spiritual traditions led them to study their own religious and cultural traditions with new eyes and embrace them more deeply; but in many cases this experience was part of developing either a more eclectic spirituality or a sense of a larger view of spirituality that helped them explore new parts of themselves. It may be that in all cases participants embraced a new dimension of spirituality that was different from what is traditionally represented or obviously available in the churches of the dominant culture. This also needs to be the subject of further study.

The Dialectic of Inner Reflection and Outer Action

Most of those whose stories are featured here talked about the fact that the spiritual was found in creating a balance between inner reflection and outer action. For the most part, being able to sustain doing social justice and cultural work that was grounded in their spirituality involved living an integrated way of life that included a way of thinking about and being in the world. Such an integrated view of their work as a way of life was reminiscent of Matthew Fox's

(1996) discussion of the reinvention of work as related to what he refers to as the interconnection of "inner work" (through centering, meditation, and experience of the realm of mystery) and "outer work" (working for greater balance in the world). Furthermore, these integrated modes of work both in the paid and not-for-pay workforce were seen as part of their life's purpose, and were integrated with their personal and cultural history and in many cases an ancestral connection as well. There was a strong desire both to give back to their own communities and to create a more equitable society. This notion of creating community in a larger, more global sense was significant to most of them. In this respect, their stories are similar to some of the participants in the Daloz et al. (1996) study on community and commitment. Further, their emphasis on community was something that they very much tried to bring to their classrooms.

Understanding more about the connection between spirituality and culture in the lives of these educators offers some implicit suggestions for ways of teaching for cultural relevance in higher and adult education. Like the many educators featured in this book, many of those in our higher and adult education classrooms and learning activities are there partly because their metaphorical shoes have gotten too tight. Many are in search of a meaningful education that will connect their spiritual and cultural selves with doing meaningful work in the world. In that respect they probably are not very different from this group of educators, who have tried to be honest with themselves and are in search of new shoes that will expand to fit who they are becoming.

Las Medias Me Dan Calor! The Perils and Possibilities of a Spiritually Grounded Approach to Culturally Relevant Education in Higher Education Classrooms

Sometimes *las medias nos dan calor*—our socks make our feet hot and sweaty. Sometimes there is too much literal heat; other times it is the heat of our own nervousness. The prospect of trying to develop and live out a more spiritually grounded approach to adult and higher education that is culturally relevant and transformative offers many possibilities but can also be nerve-wracking, and it poses some questions. Robert Kegan (2000) asks one such question at the end of his chapter on a constructivist-developmental approach to transformative learning: "'The spirit,' Hegel wrote in *The Phenomenology of Mind*, 'is never at rest but always engaged in ever progressive motion, in giving itself a new form.' How might we understand transformational learning differently—and our opportunities as educators—were we better to understand the restless, creative processes of development itself, in which all our students partake before, during, and after their participation in our classrooms?" (p. 69).

I think the answer to Kegan's question is clear; and it is found right inside the Hegel quote that precedes the question. It has to do with trying to better understand and attend to matters of the spirit that Hegel referred to when he noted that the spirit is always engaged in giving itself new form—in growing out of its once comfortable old shoes. Attending to the spirit is part of the work of transformation. Since attending to the spirit often takes us to the heart of our cultural selves, it is connected to culturally relevant education. Teaching in such a way offers many possibilities, but elements of it make some parts of us nervous.

Teaching is an art. Part of what is potentially nerve-wracking about attending to spirituality and culture in a way that truly involves learners in the engagement and ongoing unfolding of the course is that it is always full of surprises. It is not as predictable as giving a lecture. If one simply disseminates information, and is the "sage on the stage" and doesn't really allow for discussion save for questions and answers from "the sage," it is easy to keep control of the process. This might be an effective way to transmit a lot of information, or as Freire (1974) would say, to provide "banking education," but this is certainly not transformative education.

The Discomforts of Dealing with Culture and Spirit

If one really deals with course content in a way that is transformative and culturally relevant and also grounded in spirit, one needs
to involve and engage learners. But dealing with cultural issues
always has the potential to be uncomfortable. After all, even if it is
never spoken, it is hard to ignore the history of racism in North
America; or that of the colonization of American Indians, First
Nations people, or Mexicans; or the Japanese internment of World
War II that not only affected Japanese Americans but anyone of
Asian descent. These realities are a shameful part of the history
of this continent and should not be ignored, since the effects are
far reaching and still influence the lives of those in our classes and
educational spaces. Dealing with cultural issues can make people
uncomfortable to some degree for a whole host of reasons. It is
potentially that much more uncomfortable when one is teaching
classes that are specifically about race, culture, class, sexual orientation, disability, national origin, or religion.

But it is also very rewarding, often transforming and engaging
and important work. It is never dull. And there are ways of doing
this more effectively than others—by team-teaching when possible
and by incorporating an affective dimension of learning that allows
for a place to deal with the emotional aspects of the course. It is also
helpful to allow a space to draw in spirit—a place for imaginal or
symbolic forms of knowing through art, music, or movement. This
is not a panacea and will not do away with the discomfort of dealing
with the reality of racism, sexism, classism, heterosexism, ableism,
or religious bigotry and of working to challenge those systems in the
classroom and in society. But drawing in spirit can create some sense
of a way to move from cognitive to affective to symbolic and to
other forms of knowing that can sometimes create a different way
of moving a discussion or educational experience forward. It is not
easy, however, and perhaps more difficult when one doesn't have a

teammate or teaching partner. It is perhaps somewhat easier in situations with groups that have an ongoing relationship that has
developed over time, such as in cohort programs. There is often
greater trust in such groups, which makes dealing with issues at a
deeper level over time easier.

Finding a way to draw in the imaginal dimension that is based
on music or art or poetry helps people put some of their learning,
including their feelings, emotions, sense of passion, and spirit, in a
different kind of form that potentially touches on the spiritual.
Sharing it in some kind of community also can be quite unifying.
So can singing or dancing or finding some way to celebrate, which
as O'Sullivan (1999) notes, is an important part of the transformative learning process.

Spirituality and Religious Pluralism in the Higher Education Classroom

One of the concerns that many have about drawing on spirituality,
especially in the higher education classroom, is of its connection
and confusion with religion. As we have seen, there is in fact a connection between spirituality and religion for many people, since
often, spiritual experiences are given new meaning and dimensional
understanding in light of one's religious background and beliefs. But
at the same time most spiritual experiences do not actually happen
in the context of one's religion; they happen in the context of living
one's life. Nevertheless, many educators have expressed concern
about drawing on spirituality in the higher education classroom for
two primary reasons: they don't want to be seen as pushing a religious or even a spiritual agenda; they are nervous about uninten-
tionally setting up a situation that could provide a forum for a
religious fundamentalist agenda by one or more members of the
class. On the one hand, creating an environment that can attend
to the spiritual dimension needs to be handled with care to avoid
these pitfalls; on the other hand, these pitfalls are more often a fear

than a reality, though it is important not to underestimate the fact that these things can and do happen. Yet when one is providing a space for spirit in imaginal knowing processes through tapping into the symbolic domain of music, movement, art, and so forth, one is not all that likely to get into heated discussions related to religious fundamentalism. Again, I emphasize that creating a space for the spiritual dimension doesn't necessarily mean directly using the "s" word or talking directly about spirituality.

However, one need not completely avoid talking about spirituality or religion either. If one is dealing with cultural issues, it would be difficult to avoid the potential anti-Arab sentiment that is out there, along with the general lack of understanding about Islam and confusion of Islam with terrorist activity. Diana Eck's (2001) work on a new religious America is extremely timely here, as is Charaniya and West Walsh's (2001) consideration of interreligious dialogue as an important area of border-crossing work around religious pluralism. Kazanjian and Laurence's (2000) recent work on dealing with spiritual and religious pluralism on college campuses is also an excellent resource. If we are teaching for transformation and for cultural relevance, we have an obligation to try to make the learning environment as safe as possible for Muslim or Arab students, as well as those who are African American, Latino, American Indian, Asian, lesbian, or gay. As hooks (1994) notes, the idea of a "safe" learning environment may be more of a construction of white privilege, since North American classrooms are generally far safer for the dominant culture majority, a point that has been discussed at length elsewhere. Nevertheless, there are some environments that are safer than others, and it is important to try to create as safe a place as possible for transformation to happen. This does not mean that there will not be discomfort. Transformation is always uncomfortable; it is hard to be open to new ideas, to do the preparation work of reading new and difficult material, to think about different ideas, and to really listen to classmates and colleagues with open ears. Indeed, nothing of value is ever easy. But many can live with the discomfort if it feels relatively safe in the space to do so, and if they are confident that new learning is happening in spite of the discomfort.

There is, of course, a chance of having to deal with religious fundamentalism in the classroom or of religious positions (not necessarily exactly fundamentalist) that seem to make some groups more vulnerable than others. For example, many who are involved in conservative religious traditions may at times not be very open on gay, lesbian, or bisexual issues. Of course everyone has a right to their religious beliefs, but they do not have the right to impose them on others or to make others feel put down or "less than" because of differing religious positions. Indeed this is a tricky balance, and perhaps can be handled by pointing out that there are multiple ways of viewing the world on many issues, and that there is no one right answer. But of course those coming from a fundamentalist perspective may believe that there is only one right answer (theirs). But remember from the discussion of Fowler's stages of faith development in Chapter Five: many adults are at conventional faith stages where it is difficult to accept anything that deviates from the interpretation of their religious authorities, whereas those at the individuative-reflective and conjunctive faith stages and beyond are more likely to be open to positions other than those of their own religious authorities. Having some sense of this might suggest ideas for dealing with learners representative of these different stages more effectively.

Aiysha Ali described her relatively recent experience of dealing with some of this in her own class entitled "Race, Religion, and Education," which began within a couple of weeks after the September 11 terrorist attacks. As noted earlier, Aiysha is Muslim of East Indian descent. In this class, given the course content and what was happening in the world, she decided that she would directly discuss her own Muslim identity in a class primarily made up of Latino and African American undergraduates, many of whom were from conservative Christian, and in some cases fundamentalist, backgrounds. She invited questions from them, at the same time that she assured them that the terrorists were not representative of Islam. She said that she never felt attacked by the students but did feel the strong urgency in their questions. She tries to make it a point in such conversations not to become defensive, but to recognize that many who seem to ask questions in a quasi-accusatory or agitated tone of voice are doing so more out of a lack of understanding and a request for information. She can therefore usually respond in a way that is disarming and in a way that they feel heard. Although she noted that she never felt personally attacked, she sensed that some students may have been concerned that she did, as two of the women hung around afterwards to help her negotiate car trouble. Aiysha took this as a sign of their care-taking of her and wanting to make sure she was OK, as well of their support. Aiysha is actually quite comfortable having such conversations; she has had many of late, and further has a fair amount of expertise in dealing with these issues. She is also quite comfortable in her own identity and has a way of inviting people into theirs, so she can handle such issues in classes more smoothly than many of us.

Vulnerability in the Classroom

Probably the biggest fear about drawing on spirituality in the classroom in doing culturally relevant education is the fear of the vulnerability of both ourselves and our students. To draw on spirituality is to be authentic in the classroom. Perhaps we wonder what the university might think, or our colleagues and students, if we were to be more overt in the way we draw on spirit. But a deeper concern might be trying to figure out just what it means to be authentic. To be authentic is scary and makes one feel vulnerable. But being authentic does not necessarily mean being more self-disclosing than seems "appropriate" in the situation. ("Appropriate" is in quotes here, because I'm not sure exactly what "appropriate" means in this context, since many would say that creating a space for the spiritual at all is "inappropriate" in a higher education class.) To me, it feels "appropriate" to be self-disclosing and to share something personal, important, and transforming if it is related to the topic of the course; it feels "inappropriate" when it seems more of the instructor's need to talk about her or himself irrespective of the course content.

Unfortunately, these are very gray areas that are dependent on the context of the class, who the instructor is, and who the learners are. One area that is not gray is that learning in the classroom needs to be primarily about the learners and not about the teacher. Nevertheless, we learn in the context of relationships, and some of the most important learning I have engaged in was when people have shared their significant and transformative moments related to a topic, or when they clarify the mysterious theoretical world under study by giving me a practical example from their own lives I can relate to. It is easier and perhaps far less threatening to simply come into classrooms wearing our "teacher" hat as content expert, and either intentionally or inadvertently leave our "person" hat at the door. This happens all the time in higher education, and it is perfectly appropriate. But it is not transforming. And although this is not inauthentic, it is not authentic in the sense of bringing our whole selves with us into the learning environment. If we are hoping that our students in our classes will bring their whole selves to the classroom, we also need to be willing to do so to some degree ourselves. Deciding the degree to which it feels appropriate to do this is everyone's individual decision, based on a host of factors including one's race, gender, class, sexual orientation, tenure status, and relationship with a group. As Johnson-Bailey and Cervero (2000) note, faculty members who are not representative of the dominant culture by virtue of their race, national origin, or sexual orientation are far more vulnerable to begin with than their white, heterosexual, native born North American colleagues. Indeed, this needs to be kept in mind in determining how to deal with spirit, culture, and one's authenticity and vulnerability in the higher education classroom.

Another concern that we might have about drawing on spirituality in the classroom is not so much our own vulnerability but that of our students. When one touches into the imaginal domain, one not only potentially touches into the spiritual, but often one touches into lots of emotion and affect. As was discussed in the last chapter, drawing on the spiritual is not necessarily the same as drawing on the affective and relational domain. Yet often spiritual experiences do have lots of emotion attached to them, but they don't always, and there are, of course, varying degrees of emotion attached to any experience. In any case, students generally feel more comfortable when they have an option of *not* participating in a particular activity and of substituting something else. This does not mean that students get out of doing required assignments, although it could mean that some aspects of required assignments might need to be renegotiated.

It's also very important *not* to abuse the power of our position in the classroom to put people in a vulnerable position that they might not have bargained for in signing up for a course. For example, as an instructor, I probably would not have facilitated the engaged pedagogy exercise that the three students facilitated in my diversity class several years ago that was discussed in the last chapter. Although it was the single most transformative moment I have ever had in a classroom, I would have been afraid that because as an instructor I have some power over students in the sense that I have to give grades, I would be putting them in more of a vulnerable position than was appropriate in my position. But students facilitated this experience for each other so that power imbalance was not an issue. Further, everyone was given the option of either passing or speaking in the activity itself. Mary, the student who facilitated this very emotional experience so brilliantly, has excellent facilitation skills, much better than mine would have been if I were in the same position, or if I had needed to intervene in light of the emotionally laden nature of the situation. It was the result of her skills and her authenticity, along with how she and the rest of the group handled themselves, that made it a transformational learning experience that touched on the spiritual for several members of the class. I am very grateful for what was the most powerful moment I've ever had in a classroom, at the hands, hearts, and authenticity of the participants in that class. I think of them in many ways as a mentoring community.

The Creation of Cultural Mentoring Communities

Trying to teach for cultural relevance and social transformation that is grounded in one's spirituality is hard work. No one can do it alone. Finding or creating mentoring communities that support this work is crucial. Sharon Daloz Parks (2000) talks about the importance of mentoring communities in facilitating the development and the "worthy dreams" of young adults. She specifically discusses the mentoring communities of higher education, professional education, the workplace, travel, the natural environment, families, and religious communities.

The need for mentoring doesn't stop with young adulthood (Daloz, 1999). Further, those who are trying to develop an approach to teaching for cultural relevance grounded in their spirituality that is potentially transformative also need cultural mentors and cultural mentoring communities. We might find some of them in the same places that Parks (2000) mentions. We need multiple mentors and multiple communities. They can be found in organizations that are a part of the life-blood of ethnic communities. Cultural mentors can be found among faculty colleagues of different cultural groups who come together to discuss what it means to do culturally relevant education. They can be found among a small group of colleagues who study what it means to be white and to have white privilege, not only from the perspective of white people but also from people of color. Cultural mentoring communities can be found in our own diverse classrooms where there is a critical mass of people from a particular cultural group that will tell you (if you ask) what it means for them to do culturally relevant education.

We need cultural mentors both from within our own culture and from different cultures. Many of my colleagues and friends from different cultural groups have been important cultural mentors for me. So have the students from my classes. Some of the people mentioned in this book have become very important cultural mentors to me: Derise Tolliver, Silvia Villa, and Tito Rodriguez in particular. None of them is a member of my own cultural group, but they let me know more of what it means to be culturally relevant to their respective African American, Mexican, and Puerto Rican communities. They also let me know sometimes when I've been culturally inappropriate, or more often "culturally irrelevant." I make mistakes, and they help me in my learning. I like to think I help them in their learning, too—certainly not about their own culture, but about some aspects of my own and about aspects of navigating within the dominant culture of which I am a part.

We also need to find cultural mentoring within our own communities. I need to try to understand better what it means to be white and of Irish-Catholic descent. This is a life-long process. I understand more about this partly from members of my own cultural group when we specifically talk about it. Further, no one enjoys or understands singing the songs from my childhood and cultural and religious tradition the same way as those I grew up with or who sat in classrooms so much like Sister's in *Late Nite Catechism*. And there's no one who quite understands the meaning of certain rituals, ways of being, or particular sayings my mother and her family and friends used than members of my own cultural community. There is a way that I understand and am understood, and feel at home with all its comforts and discomforts, in going back to revisit some of those traditions with family and friends from a similar background. This is partly what makes me who I am. There is also a way that I feel utterly not at home and not understood in those situations, too, because that is not at all entirely who I am anymore. As much as there are comforts in my own cultural group, there are also discomforts, ways I no longer fit, because I don't live only inside that community anymore. In that sense I live partly in the "in-between-ness" that Raul Guerrero spoke of. But the mentoring I receive from my own cultural community is incredibly important; it helps me take pride in who I am and in many (not all) of the cultures and traditions of my own ancestors. Mentoring from other cultural communities helps me understand that all the world is not like me. It helps me move beyond myself and understand a bigger world, and helps me in the process of *moving toward* being able to teach for cultural relevance. This is why we need multiple cultural mentoring communities.

Just like the metaphorical socks that make our feet hot and sweaty, the process of trying to teach for cultural relevance makes us nervous, hot, and sweaty because it offers both challenge and nurturance, both perils and possibilities. But with the help of cultural mentoring communities, we can face the challenge of living in the "in-between-ness" that occasionally pulls us open to the spirit.

Epilogue

Final Reflections
Moving Forward to the Future

"*Ycuando miro al cielo, me dan los rayos del sol!*" As the final lines of the poem cited at the beginning of the last chapter say, "when I look into the sky, I am bathed in the rays of the sun!" Just as Tito Rodriguez notes, sometimes the process of growth means that we grow out of once comfortable shoes that are now too tight; we suffer through the growth process in the challenges offered by the metaphorical socks that make us sweat in the hard work of the labor of transformation. Yet there are occasions when we look into the sky, and catch a glimpse and live in the bliss of the rays of the sun, the rays of inspiration. Occasionally, we live in the shimmering moments of our spiritual experiences and catch a glimpse of the wholeness and interconnectedness of all creation that helps our lives make sense.

Trying to teach for cultural relevance and social transformation is not easy. Just because we try to do it does not mean we are successful. In fact sometimes it seems that we are absolutely unsuccessful. The debates in the field of adult education between what constitutes individual and social transformation are age-old. But it seems to me that part of the answer is not in one over the other. Part of the answer is found in the experience of the "in-between-ness" that Raul Guerrero spoke of. We cannot teach for cultural relevance and social transformation without dealing with the individual. It is only when individuals are transformed and find bigger shoes that are a better fit for who they are becoming that social transformation can happen, since society is made up of individuals. Hardly a new thought! Clearly many have made this argument from Mezirow (1995) to the many who rely on his work.

But at the same time it is not enough to focus *only* on the individual and their various individual psychological and spiritual transformations. That would not constitute teaching for social transformation. Individuals always develop in a sociocultural context and have life experiences that are mediated by and manifested in a sociocultural context that is informed in part by power relations based on race, culture, gender, sexual orientation, national origin, and ableness. Therefore, in thinking about teaching for social transformation we need to think about, tap into, and provide a forum where individuals can examine how those systems have informed who they are in order to reclaim their cultural, gender, and sexual identities anew. Indeed this is a life-long process, but one that is part of teaching for cultural relevance and social transformation.

The metaphor of "in-between-ness" is significant to our discussion on a number of levels. Elsewhere, I noted the unit of analysis in poststructural feminist pedagogies as being the "connections between" the individual and the structural, and how social structures inform the ongoing, constantly shifting identities of the individual (Tisdell, 1998). Similarly, if one wants to teach for cultural relevance, one needs to provide an experience not only in which individuals can explore the *connection between* their own identities and the sociocultural forces that shape them. They also need to make meaning and draw on the knowledge base and ways of expressing it that inspire their passion, that honor who they are, and that continue to be a source of hope, agency, and celebration of the way they make meaning and work for social transformation in the application of what they are learning.

The metaphor of "in-between-ness" is an important spiritual metaphor as well. It seems that many of the spiritual experiences, as discussed in Chapter Four, were experiences of having a sense, not only of catching a glimpse of the wholeness and interconnectedness of all things, but also of being for a moment in the "in-between" that seems to pull us open to the spirit. I experienced this most profoundly personally in being with my mother in the five days of her dying process, which literally felt as though she was between the worlds. In being inside of that experience with her, I caught a glimpse of being between the worlds, too. I'll never forget the gentle squeeze of her hand in the moment when she crossed over and moved beyond the in-between. But many who reported spiritual experiences had this experience for a moment of living "in-between." As Raul Guerrero says, "to dance between, and to play between" might perhaps be postmodern. But perhaps it is also to be open to the spirit that is manifested through cultural expression, in the music that we make, in the poetry that we create, that comes out of some unknown in-between place in the depth of our souls, in the art piece that seemed to create itself out of nowhere in these in-between worlds that are at the juncture of our spiritual and cultural experiences. Indeed, these out-of-nowhere and in-between-ness experiences happen by surprise. To be sure, they are a part of culturally relevant education.

Appendix

Research Methodology: Constructing Knowledge on Spirituality and Culture in Adult and Higher Education

As explained in the first chapter, the stories and ideas in this book are based primarily on the interviews I conducted with a multicultural group of educators who work in adult, community, and higher education. These interviews were a part of a qualitative research study based on my own strong belief in the importance of bringing a spiritual perspective to teaching to challenge power relations based on race, gender, class, religion, sexual orientation, and national origin in adult and higher education, but being unsure how to do it. In essence, I conducted these interviews initially to learn how to be a better teacher and learn how others who were teaching the kinds of classes I was teaching drew on their spirituality.

The research for this book initially began in 1998. The purpose of that initial study was to find out how spirituality influenced the motivations and practices of a multicultural group of women adult educators who teach for social change, were strongly informed by a specific religious tradition as a child, and have renegotiated a more relevant adult spirituality. I was also interested in the spiritual development of these women, how it changed over time, and how it influenced and motivated their practices around teaching for cultural relevance and social change. In this initial study, "women teaching for social change" included two groups of women: (1) women working in higher education either teaching classes that were specifically about culture, gender, race, class, sexual orientation, or disability issues, or teaching in programs aimed at meeting the education needs of specific marginalized groups; and (2) women working as educators (in the broad sense) as community activists. There were sixteen women participants in this initial study, the results of which I have summarized elsewhere (Tisdell, 2000a).

The results and the process of the initial study fascinated me. It became clear to me that the spiritual development of these educators was intimately connected with their cultural identity development, which clearly affected their ability to teach for greater cultural relevance. I wanted to continue the study with both men and women, focusing on participants' spiritual development, its connection to their cultural backgrounds, and how they felt it related to their educational practices development.

The Participants

A total of thirty-one educators (twenty-two women and nine men) participated in the study, whose stories are featured in some way in this book. All participants were chosen based on the following criteria:

1. They were educators who were working in higher and adult education settings and attempting to deal directly with cultural issues in one way or another in their learning activities.

2. They indicated that spirituality was a strong influence on their work.

Most were trying to teach for social transformation, based on a critical multicultural perspective, by directly attempting to challenge power relations and discussing systems of power and privilege in their classes and educational activities. Three participants, however, did not appear to fit this profile; these participants seemed to deal with cultural issues more from a psychological perspective.

Of the twenty-two women participants, nine are white, four are African American, four are Latina, three are Asian American, one is American Indian, and one is of East Indian descent. Of the nine who are white, two grew up Catholic, three are Jewish, three are Protestant, and one was not socialized in a religious tradition. All four Latinas grew up Catholic; all four of the African American women grew up Protestant (although two were strongly influenced by Catholicism in their educational backgrounds). All three of the Asian American women grew up Protestant (although two had some Buddhist influence). The American Indian participant grew up Catholic; and the woman of East Indian descent is Muslim.

Of the nine male participants, four are white, two are African American, one is Filipino, one is American Indian, and one is Puerto Rican. Of the white men, three grew up Catholic and one is Mormon. Both the Filipino and the Puerto Rican men grew up Catholic, the American Indian grew up in the Assembly of God tradition, and the two African American men grew up Protestant but one converted to Islam early in his young adulthood.

Theoretical Framework

In general qualitative research attempts to find out how people make meaning or interpret a phenomenon (Merriam, 1998). Some forms are strictly interpretive and only want to know how participants make meaning of their life experience. Other forms with critical, feminist, or cultural theoretical underpinnings are concerned with giving voice to those who have been silenced or marginalized (McLauglin & Tierney, 1993; Vaz, 1997) and with the emancipatory possibility for those participating in the research (Lather, 1991; Kincheloe & McLaren, 1999). This study was informed by a critical poststructural feminist theoretical frame, which is concerned with giving voice to participants whose perspectives have been marginalized or ignored. But such a framework suggests that the positionality (race, gender, class, and so forth) of researchers, teachers, participants, and students affects how one gathers and accesses data, how one constructs and views knowledge, and how one deals with "crossing borders" in research and teaching (Fine, 1998; Denzin & Lincoln, 1998; Tisdell, 1998). Thus, my own positionality as a white, middle-class woman who grew up Catholic and has tried to negotiate a more relevant adult spirituality, and who also teaches classes specifically about race, class, and gender issues, were factors that affected the data collection and analysis processes. I approached the interviews as a shared conversation and looked at the process as an ongoing one whereby we constructed knowledge together. So if participants asked me a question in the interview, I briefly answered it. This is what makes it a shared conversation.

This study was about a *multicultural group* of adult educators, in which more than half the participants were people of color (nineteen out of thirty-one). My primary purpose was to find out how these educators interpret how their spirituality influences their work in their attempts to teach for social change and cultural relevance, and how their spirituality has changed over time since their childhood. I was attempting not only to provide some data-based information about how their spirituality informs their work, I was also trying to examine the cultural aspects of spirituality. In essence, I was interested in looking at the often ignored sociocultural dimensions of spirituality and in explicitly making visible the spiritual experience of people of color, as well as the experience of white European Americans, which is the group that the spirituality literature in North America tends to be primarily about.

Data Collection and Analysis

The primary means of data collection were audiotaped (and transcribed) semistructured interviews that lasted from an hour and a half to three hours, and in some cases, written documents outlining significant aspects of their personal cultural or spiritual histories. Given the theoretical framework, I did share with all of the participants some of my own background (in roughly five to ten minutes) prior to the data collection process to explain why I was interested in the topic. In essence I gave participants a snippet of my own attempts as a white woman at antiracist and gender-inclusive adult education, and of the general way in which my background and current spirituality inform my work. Due to time constraints this was kept to a minimum, though I did tell participants that I would be happy to share more about that at a later time, and also asked participants if they had questions prior to the interview. I believe this provided a context for why I was doing this work, helped create a rapport with participants, and made the interviews a shared conversation wherein specific topics were pursued as they arose naturally. Furthermore, I was attempting to avoid what Michelle Fine (1998) and others refer to as "othering" the participants—to avoid gathering very personal data from participants while giving none about myself. Thus I gave participants the opportunity to ask me questions as they so desired. Interviews focused on participants' definitions of spirituality; the sharing of three significant spiritual experiences; and how their spirituality has changed over the years, how it motivates and informs their adult education practice, and how it relates to their own race-ethnicity and cultural background. Many participants also provided written documents (of their own writing) that addressed some of their involvement in social action pursuits or issues directly related to their spirituality, or they sent e-mails offering further clarification on issues we had discussed. Hence, the multiple sources of data collection methods of interviews and documents were a means of triangulation.

Data were analyzed throughout the study. At the suggestion of Merriam (1998), a preliminary analysis was done after each interview. Data were coded and recoded according to the constant comparative method until themes began to emerge. At this point, member checks were conducted with several of the participants to increase dependability of findings. Those whose stories are featured heavily in this book have read and commented on the accuracy of their portrayal. These member checks were extremely important, particularly because many of the participants' stories are very different from my own. This element contributed to enhancing the dependability and validity of the findings of the study.

Knowledge Construction as a Communal and Collaborative Process

As noted, the study was informed by a critical feminist poststructural theoretical frame. Typically, the term *critical* has two meanings in research: (1) dealing with and challenging power relations (as in "critical theory" or "critical pedagogy"), and (2) facilitating some sort of action among participants while the study is going on. This study was critical in the sense that to some extent it dealt with power relations. In its initial stages, it was not a participatory or critical action research study, in that for the most part I did not do anything to try to make anything happen while the research was going on. Yet part of the larger purpose of the study was that I was hoping to make something happen *as a result of* the study. Most obviously, I was trying to open up the discussion about the place of spirituality in emancipatory education.

In the process of conducting the study, I met many interesting people who were involved in similar work. I met some incredible people who have enriched my own spiritual development and have helped me understand the interplay between spirituality and culture in my own life in new ways, which not only affected my own educational practice but also affected how I wrote this book. As noted in Chapter Nine, Derise Tolliver has been extremely influential in that regard. In the later stages of data collection for this book, she and I began collaborating on some further work together around this topic. We have made presentations at conferences, conducted workshops, and developed and taught a course together: "Spirituality and Culture in Adult Education." As women of different race and cultural backgrounds informed by different spiritual traditions, our collaboration as educators is enriched by the other's involvement and creates the possibility of far greater explorations of spirituality and culture in the adult learning environment than either of us could do alone. I owe much of the thinking that went into this book to my collaboration with her, and to one of my teaching partners, Silvia Villa, and to the many who have been my cultural teachers and mentors throughout the years, and certainly to all the participants in this study. Creating knowledge is always a collaborative process. I am only the scribe.

References

Abalos, D. (1998). *La Communidad Latina in the United States*. Westport, CT: Praeger.

Aguilar, V., & Woo, G. (2000). Team teaching and learning in diversity training for national service programs. In M. J. Eisen & E. Tisdell (Eds.), *Team teaching and learning in adult education* (pp. 73–72). New Directions for Adult and Continuing Education, no. 87. San Francisco: Jossey-Bass.

Anzaldua, G. (1987). *Borderlands/La frontera: The new Mestiza*. San Francisco, CA: Aunt Lute.

Banks, J. A. (1993). Approaches to multicultural curriculum reform. In J. A. Banks and C.A.M. Banks (Eds.), *Multicultural education: Issues and perspectives* (pp. 195–214). Needham Heights, MA: Allyn and Bacon.

Banks, J. A. (1997). Multicultural education: Characteristics and goals. In J. A. Banks & C.A.M. Banks (Eds.), *Multicultural education: Issues and perspectives* (3rd edition). Boston: Allyn and Bacon.

Bateson, M. C. (1995). *Peripheral visions: Learning along the way*. San Francisco: Harper Perennial.

Baumgartner, L., & Merriam S. (Eds.). (1999). *Adult learning and development: Multicultural Stories*. Malabar, FL: Krieger.

Beck, D., & Cowan, C. (1996). *Spiral dynamics: Mastering values, leadership, and change*. Malden, MA: Blackwell.

Belenky, M., Clinchy, B., Goldberger, N., & Tarule, J. (Eds.). (1986). *Women's ways of knowing*. New York: Basic Books.

Belenky, M., & Stanton, A. (2000). Inequality, development, and connected knowing. In J. Mezirow and Associates (Eds.), *Learning as transformation: Critical perspectives on a theory in progress* (pp. 71–102). San Francisco: Jossey-Bass.

Berry, T. (1999). *The great work: Our way to the future*. New York: Bell Tower.

Bolen, J. (1994). *Crossing to Avalon: A women's midlife pilgrimage*. San Francisco: Harper San Francisco.

Bolen, J. S. (1979). *The Tao of psychology: Synchronicity and the self*. New York: Harper and Row.

Bonnett, A. (2000). *Antiracism*. New York: Routledge.

Borysenko, J. (1996). *A woman's book of life: The biology, psychology, and spirituality of the feminine life cycle*. New York: Riverhead Books.

Borysenko, J. (1999). *A women's journey to God*. New York: Riverhead Books.

Brookfield, S. (1995). *Becoming a critically reflective teacher*. San Francisco: Jossey-Bass.

Brooks, A. (2000). Cultures of transformation. In A. Wilson & E. Hayes (Eds.), *The handbook of adult and continuing education* (pp. 132–146). San Francisco: Jossey-Bass.

Cannon, K. (1996). *Katie's canon: Womanism and the soul of the black community*. New York: Continuum.

Cass, V.C. (1984). Homosexual identity formation: Testing a theoretical model. *Journal of Sex Research, 20*, 143–167.

Castillo, A. (1996). *Massacre of the dreamers: Essays on xicanisma*. Albuquerque, NM: University of New Mexico Press.

Charaniya, N., & West Walsh, J. (2001). Interpreting the experience of Christians, Muslims, and Jews engaged in interreligious dialogue: A collaborative research study. *Religious Education, 16*(3), 351–368.

Chavez, A. (2001). Spirit and nature in everyday life: Reflections of a *Mestiza* in higher education. In M. Jablonski (Ed.), *The implications of student spirituality for student affairs practice* (pp. 69–80). New Directions for Student Services, no. 95. San Francisco: Jossey-Bass.

Chavez, A., & Guido-DiBrito, F. (1999). Racial and ethnic identity development. In M. C. Clark & R. Caffarella (Eds.), *An update on adult development theory* (pp. 39–48). New Directions for Adult and Continuing Education, no. 84. San Francisco: Jossey-Bass.

Christ, C., & Plaskow, J. (Eds.). (1992). *Womenspirit rising*. San Francisco: Harper.

Cimino, R. (2001). *Trusting the sprit: Renewal and reform in American religion*. San Francisco: Jossey-Bass.

Clark, M. C. (2001). Off the beaten path: Some creative approaches to adult learning. In S. Merriam (Ed.), *The new update on adult learning theory* (pp. 83–92). New Directions for Adult and Continuing Education, no. 89. San Francisco: Jossey-Bass.

Clark, M. C., & Caffarella, R. (Eds.) (1999). *An update on adult development theory*. New Directions for Adult and Continuing Education, no. 84. San Francisco: Jossey-Bass.

Colin, III, S.A.J. (1994). Adult and continuing education graduate programs: Prescription for the future. In E. Hayes & S.A.J. Colin, III (Eds.), *Confronting racism and sexism*. New Directions for Adult and Continuing Education, no. 61. San Francisco: Jossey-Bass.

Colin, III, S.A.J. & Guy, T. (1998). An Africentric interpretive model of curricular orientations for course development in graduate programs in adult education. *PAACE Journal of Lifelong Learning, 7*, 43–55.

Cone, J. (Ed.) (1990). *A Black theology of liberation*. (20th Anniversary Edition). Maryknoll, New York: Orbis.

Courtenay, B. (1994). Are psychological models of adult development still important for the practice of adult education? *Adult Education Quarterly, 44*(3), 145–153

Cranton, P. (1994). *Understanding and promoting transformative learning*. San Francisco: Jossey-Bass.

Cross, W. (1971). Toward a psychology of black liberation. The Negro-to-Black convergence experience. *Black World, 20*(9), 13–27.

Curry, R., & Cunningham, P. (2000). Co-learning in the community. In M. J. Eisen & E. Tisdell (Eds.), *Team teaching and learning in adult education* (pp. 73–82). New Directions for Adult and Continuing Education, no. 87. San Francisco: Jossey-Bass.

D'Souza, D. (1992). The visigoths in tweed. In P. Aufderheide (Ed.), *Beyond PC: Toward a politics of understanding*. New York: Graywolf.

Daloz, L. (1999). *Mentor: Guiding the journey of adult learners*. San Francisco: Jossey-Bass.

Daloz, L. (2000). Transformative learning for the common good. In J. Mezirow and Associates (Eds.), *Learning as transformation: Critical perspectives on a theory in progress* (pp. 103–124). San Francisco: Jossey-Bass.

Daloz, L., Keene, C., Keene, J., & Parks, S. (1996). *Common fire: Lives of commitment in a complex world*. Boston: Beacon.

Darder, A., Torres, R., & Gutierrez, H. (Eds.) (1997). *Latinos and education*. New York: Routledge.

Deloria, V. (1992). *God is red*. Golden, CO: North American Press.

Denzin, N., & Lincoln, Y. (Eds.) (1998). *The landscape of qualitative research*. Newbury Park, CA: Sage

Dillard, C., Abdur-Rashid, D., & Tyson, C. (2000). My soul is a witness: Affirming pedagogies of the spirit. *International Journal of Qualitative Studies in Education, 13*(5), 447–462.

Dirkx, J. (Ed.). (1997). *Nurturing soul in adult learning.* New Directions for Adult and Continuing Education. San Francisco: Jossey-Bass.

Dirkx, J. (2001). The power of feelings: Emotion, imagination, and the construction of meaning in adult learning. In S. Merriam (Ed.), *The new update on adult learning theory* (pp. 63–72). New Directions for Adult and Continuing Education, no. 89. San Francisco: Jossey-Bass.

Eck, D. (2001). *A new religious America.* San Francisco: Harper.

Edwards, K., & Brooks, A. (1999). The development of sexual identity. In M. C. Clark & R. Caffarella (Eds.), *An update on adult development theory* (pp. 49–58). New Directions for Adult and Continuing Education, no. 84. San Francisco: Jossey-Bass.

English, L., & Gillen, M. (Eds.) (2000). *Addressing the spiritual dimensions of adult learning: What educators can do.* New Directions for Adult and Continuing Education, no. 85. San Francisco: Jossey-Bass.

Erikson, E. (1980). *Identity and the life cycle: A reissue.* New York: Norton.

Etter-Lewis, G. (1993) *My soul is my own: Oral narratives of black women in the professions.* New York: Routledge.

Fenwick, T. J., & Lange, E. (1998). Spirituality in the workplace: The new frontier of HRD. *Canadian Journal for the Study of Adult Education, 12*(1), 63–87.

Fine, M. (1998). Working the hyphens. In N. Denzin & Y. Lincoln (Eds.), *The landscape of qualitative research* (pp. 130–155). Newbury Park, CA: Sage.

Flannery, D. (2000). Identity and self esteem. In E. Hayes & D. Flannery (Eds.), *Women as learners* (pp. 53–78). San Francisco: Jossey-Bass.

Fowler, J. (1981). *Stages of faith: The psychology of human development and the quest for meaning.* San Francisco: Harper and Row.

Fowler, J. (2000). *Becoming adult, becoming Christian: Adult development and Christian faith.* San Francisco: Jossey-Bass.

Fox, M. (1996). *The reinvention of work.* San Francisco: HarperCollins.

Fox, M. (2000). *One river, many wells.* New York: Putnam.

Freire, P. (1971). *Pedagogy of the oppressed.* New York: Herder & Herder.

Freire, P. (1974). *Education for critical consciousness.* New York: Continuum.

Freire, P. (1996). *Letters to Christina.* New York: Routledge.

Freire, P., & Macedo, D. (1995). A dialogue: Culture, language and race. *Harvard Educational Review, 63*(3), 377–402.

Gardner, H. (1993). *Multiple intelligences: The theory in practice.* New York: Basic Books.

Gay, G. (1995). Critical pedagogy and multicultural education. In C. Sleeter and P. McLaren (Eds.), *Multicultural education, critical pedagogy, and the politics of difference*. Albany, NY: SUNY Press.

Gilligan, C. (1982). *In a different voice*. Cambridge, MA: Harvard University Press.

Giroux, H. (1992). *Border crossings*. New York: Routledge.

Giroux, H., & McLaren, P. (Eds.). (1994). *Between borders: Pedagogy and the politics of cultural studies*. New York: Routledge.

Glazer, S. (Ed.). (1999). *The heart of learning: Spirituality in education*. New York: Putnam.

Gore, J. (1993). *The struggle for pedagogies*. New York: Routledge.

Grace, A. (2001). Using queer cultural studies to transgress adult education space. In V. Sheared & P. Sissel (Eds.), *Making space: Merging theory and practice in adult education* (pp. 257–270). Westport, CT: Bergin & Garvey.

Grant, C., & Sleeter, C. (1999). *Turning on learning: Five approaches to multicultural teaching plans* (2nd Ed.). San Francisco: Jossey-Bass.

Groome, T. (1999). *Christian religious education*. San Francisco: Jossey-Bass.

Gunn Allen, P. (1992). *The sacred hoop*. Boston: Beacon Press.

Guy, T. (Ed.). (1999). *Providing culturally relevant adult education: A challenge for the twenty-first century*. New Directions for Adult and Continuing Education, no. 82. San Francisco: Jossey-Bass.

Hamilton, D., & Jackson, M. (1998). Spiritual development: Paths and processes. *Journal of Instructional Psychology. 25*(4), 262–270.

Hart, M. (1992). *Working and educating for life: Feminist and international perspectives on adult education*. New York: Routledge.

Hart, M. (2001). Transforming boundaries of power in the classroom: Learning from La Mestiza. In R. Cervero & A. Wilson (Eds.), *Power in practice: The struggle for knowledge and power in society* (pp. 164–184). San Francisco: Jossey-Bass.

Hart, M., & Holton, D. (1993). Beyond God the father and mother: Adult education and spirituality. In P. Jarvis & N. Walters, *Adult education and theological interpretations* (pp. 237–258). Malabar, FL: Krieger.

Hart, T. (2000). *From information to transformation: Education for the evolution of consciousness*. New York: Peter Lang.

Hayes, E., & Colin, S. (Eds). (1994). *Confronting racism and sexism in adult education*. New Directions in Adult and Continuing Education, no. 61. San Francisco: Jossey-Bass.

Hayes, E., & Flannery, D., with Brooks, A., Tisdell, E., & Hugo, J. (2000). *Women as learners*. San Francisco: Jossey-Bass.

Hays, P. (2001). *Addressing cultural complexities in practice: A framework for clinicians and counselors*. Washington, DC: American Psychological Association Press.

Heaney, T. (1996). *Adult education for social change: From center stage to the wings and back again* (Information Series No. 365. ERIC Clearinghouse on Adult, Career, and Vocational education). Ohio State University.

Heaney, T. (2000). Adult education and society. In A. Wilson & E. Hayes (Eds.), *Handbook of adult and continuing education* (pp. 559–572). San Francisco: Jossey-Bass.

Heaney, T., Sanabria, R., Tisdell, E., & Latino Cohort Members Martinez Franceschi, G., Figueroa, W., Garcia, D., Garcia, M., Lugo, L., Rivera, S., & Rodriguez, T. (June, 2001). Reinventing the adult education curriculum within an urban Latino community. *Proceedings of the 42nd Annual Adult Education Research Conference* (pp. 173–178). East Lansing: Michigan State University.

Helms, J. (1984). Toward a theoretical explanation of the effects of race on counseling: A black and white model. *The Counseling Psychologist, 12*, 153–165.

Hernandez-Avila, I. (1996). Meditations of the spirit: Native American religious traditions and the ethics of representation. *American Indian Quarterly, 20*(3–4), 329–352.

Heron, J. (1996). *Co-operative inquiry: Research into the human condition*. Thousand Oaks, CA: Sage.

Hill Collins, P. (1998). *Fighting words: Black women and the search for justice*. Minneapolis: University of Minnesota Press.

Hill Collins, P. (2000). *Black feminist thought* (2nd ed.). New York: Routledge.

Hill, R. (1995). Gay discourse in adult education: A critical review. *Adult Education Quarterly, 45*(3):142–158.

Hirsch, E. D. (1988). *Cultural literacy: What every American needs to know*. New York: Vintage Books.

hooks, b. (1989). *Talking back: Thinking feminist, thinking black*. Boston: South End Press.

hooks, b. (1994). *Teaching to transgress: Education as the practice of freedom*. New York: Routledge.

hooks, b. (1999). Embracing freedom: Spirituality and liberation. In S. Glazer (Ed.), *The heart of learning: Spirituality in education*. New York: Putnam.

hooks, b. (2000). *All about love*. New York: William Morrow.

Horton, M., & Freire, P. (1990). *We make the road by walking: Conversations on education and social change*. Philadelphia: Temple University Press.

Hunt, C. (2001). *Turtleback rider. Metaphor as a vehicle for reflective practice*. Proceedings of the 31st Annual Conference of SCUTREA (Standing Conference on University Teaching and Research in the Education of Adults) 2001 (pp. 202–206). London, England: University of East London.

Isasi-Diaz, A. (1993). *En la lucha/In the struggle: Elaborating a mujerista theology*. Minneapolis: Fortress Press.

Jablonski, M. (Ed.). (2001). *The implications of students' spirituality for student affairs practice*. New Directions for Student Services, no. 95. San Francisco: Jossey-Bass.

James, W. (1902/1982). *The varieties of religious experience*. New York: Penguin Books.

Johnson-Bailey, J. (2001). *Sistahs in college: Making a way out of no way*. Malabar, FL: Krieger.

Johnson-Bailey, J., & Cervero, R. (2000). The invisible politics of race in adult education. In A. Wilson & E. Hayes (Eds.), *Handbook of adult and continuing education* (pp. 147–160). San Francisco: Jossey-Bass.

Jung, C. G. (1961). *Memories, dreams, and reflections*. New York: Vintage Books.

Kahf, M. (1999). Around the Ka'Ba and over the creek. In K. Kurs (Ed.), *Searching for your soul*. New York: Shoken Books.

Kasl, E., & Elias, D. (2000). Creating new habits of mind in small groups. In J. Mezirow and Associates (Eds.), *Learning as transformation: Critical perspectives on a theory in progress* (pp. 229–252). San Francisco: Jossey-Bass.

Kazanjian, V. H., & Laurence, P. L. (Eds.). (2000). *Education as transformation: Religious pluralism, spirituality, and a new vision for higher education in America*. New York: Peter Lang.

Kegan, R. (1982) *The evolving self: Problem and process in human development*. Cambridge, MA: Harvard University Press.

Kegan, R. (1994). *In over our heads: The mental demands of modern life*. Cambridge, MA: Harvard University Press.

Kegan, R. (2000). What "form" transforms? A constructive-developmental approach to transformative learning. In J. Mezirow and Associates (Eds.), *Learning as transformation: Critical perspectives on a theory in progress* (pp. 35–70). San Francisco: Jossey-Bass.

Kincheloe, J., & McLaren, P. (1999). Rethinking critical theory and qualitative research. In N. Denzin & Y. Lincoln (Eds.), *The landscape of qualitative research* (pp. 1260–399). Newbury Park, CA: Sage.

Kincheloe, J., Steinberg, S., Rodriguez, N., & Chennault, R. (Eds.). (1998). *White reign: Deploying whiteness in America*. New York: St. Martin's Press.

Koenig, H., McCollough, M., & Larson, D. (2001). *Handbook of religion and health*. New York: Oxford University Press.

Ladson-Billings, G. (1995). *The dreamkeepers: Successful teachers of African American children*. San Francisco: Jossey-Bass.

Lama Surya Das. (1999). *Awakening to the sacred: Creating a spiritual life from scratch*. New York: Broadway Books.

Lather, P. (1991). *Getting smart*. Routledge: New York.

Lerner, M. (2000). *Spirit matters*. Charlottesville, VA: Hampton Roads.

Loder, J. (1998). *The logic of the spirit: Human development in theological perspective*. San Francisco: Jossey-Bass.

Lorde, A. (1984). *Sister outsider*. Freedom, CA: Crossing Press.

Maher, F., & Tetreault, M. (1994). *The feminist classroom*. New York: Basic Books.

Mandelker, A., & Powers, E. (Eds.). (1999). *Pilgrim souls: A collection of spiritual autobiographies*. New York: Simon & Schuster/Touchstone.

Mankiller, W., & Wallis, M. (1993). *Mankiller: A chief and her people*. New York: St. Martin's Press.

Marty, M. M. (2000). *Education, religion, and the common good*. San Francisco: Jossey-Bass.

McIntosh, P. (1988). White privilege: Unpacking the invisible knapsack. *Peace and Freedom* (July/August), 10–12.

McLaren, P. (1994). Multiculturalism and the postmodern critique: Toward a pedagogy of resistance and transformation. In H. A. Giroux & P. McLaren (Eds.), *Between borders: Pedagogy and the politics of cultural studies* (pp. 192–222). New York: Routledge.

McLaughlin, D., & Tierney, W. (Eds.). (1993). *Naming silenced lives*. New York: Routledge.

Merriam, S. B. (1998). *Qualitative research and case study applications in education*. San Francisco: Jossey-Bass.

Merriam, S. B., & Caffarella, R. (1999). *Learning in adulthood*. San Francisco: Jossey-Bass.

Mezirow, J. (1985). Concept and action in adult education. *Adult Education Quarterly, 35*(3), 142–151.

Mezirow, J. (1995). Transformation theory of adult learning. In M. Welton (Ed.), *In defense of the lifeworld: Critical perspectives on adult learning* (pp. 39–70). Albany, NY: State University of New York Press.

Mezirow, J. & Associates. (1990). *Fostering critical reflection in adulthood*. San Francisco: Jossey-Bass.

Mezirow, J., & Associates (Ed.) (2000). *Learning as transformation: Critical perspectives on a theory in progress*. San Francisco: Jossey-Bass.

Moody, L. (1996). *Women encounter God: Theology across the boundaries of difference*. Maryknoll, NY: Orbis.

Morrison, M. (1995). *The grace of coming home: Spirituality, sexuality, and the struggle for justice*. Cleveland, OH: Pilgrim Press.

Morton, P. (2000). A faculty perspective on magic, meaning, and desire in the educational process. In V. Kazanjian & P. Laurence (Eds.), *Education as transformation: Religious pluralism, spirituality, and a new vision for higher education in America*. New York: Peter Lang.

Myers, L., Speight, S., et al. (1991). Identity development and worldview. *Journal of Counseling & Development 70*, 54–63.

Nakashima Brock, R. (1989). On mirrors, mists, and murmurs In J. Plaskow & C. Christ (Eds.), *Weaving the visions* (pp. 235–243). Harper: San Francisco

Nieto, S. (1995). From brown heroes and holidays to assimilationist agendas: Reconsidering the critiques of multicultural education. In C. Sleeter & P. McLaren (Eds.), *Multicultural education, critical pedagogy, and the politics of difference* (pp. 192–220). Albany, NY: SUNY Press.

O'Sullivan, E. (1999). *Transformative learning; Educational vision of the 21st century*. Toronto, CA: Zed Books.

Pagenhart, P. (1994). "The very house of difference": Toward a more queerly defined multiculturalism. In L. Garber (Ed.), *Tilting the tower* (pp. 177–185). New York: Routledge.

Palmer, P. (1980). *The promise of paradox*. Notre Dame, Indiana: Ave Maria Press.

Palmer, P. (1998). *The courage to teach*. San Francisco: Jossey-Bass.

Palmer, P. (2000). *Let your life speak*. San Francisco: Jossey-Bass.

Parham, T. (1989). Cycles of psychological nigrescence. *The Counseling Psychologist, 17*(2), 187–226.

Parks, S. D. (2000). *Big questions, worthy dreams*. San Francisco: Jossey-Bass.

Perry, W. (1970). *Forms of intellectual and ethical development in the college years*. Austin, TX: Holt, Rinehart & Winston.

Peterson, E. (Ed.). (1996). *Freedom road: Adult education of African Americans*. Malabar, FL: Kreiger.

Phinney, J. S. (1990). Ethnic identity in adolescents and adults: Review of the research. Psychological Bulletin, 108, 499–514.

Plaskow, J., & Christ, C. (Eds.) (1989). *Weaving the visions*. San Francisco: Harper.

Pratt, D. (1998). *Five perspectives on teaching in adult and higher education*. Malabar, FL: Krieger.

Rodriguez, J. (1994) *Our lady of Guadalupe: Faith and empowerment among Mexican-American women*. Austin, TX: University of Texas Press.

Root, M. (1996). The multiracial experience: Racial borders as a significant frontier in race relations. In M. Root (Ed.), *The multiracial experience: Racial borders as the new frontier* (pp. xiii –xxviii). Thousand Oaks, CA: Sage.

Ross-Gordon, J. (1994). Toward a critical multicultural pedagogy for adult education. *Proceedings of the 35th Annual Adult Education Research Conference* (pp. 312–317), Knoxville: University of Tennessee.

Ross-Gordon, J. (1999) Gender development and gendered adult development. In M. C. Clark & R. Caffarella (Eds.), *An update on adult development theory* (pp. 29–38). New Directions for Adult and Continuing Education, no. 84. San Francisco: Jossey-Bass.

Rossiter, M. (1999). Understanding adult development as narrative. In M. C. Clark & R. Caffarella (Eds.), *An update on adult development theory* (pp. 77–85). New Directions for Adult and Continuing Education, no. 84. San Francisco: Jossey-Bass.

Ruether, R. (Ed.) (1996). *Women healing earth.* Maryknoll, NY: Orbis.

Sanford, J. (1977). *Healing and wholeness.* New York: Paulist Press.

Sheared, V. (1994). Giving voice: An inclusive model of instruction—A womanist perspective. In E. Hayes & S. Colin (Eds.), *Confronting racism and sexism* (pp. 63–76). New Directions for Adult and Continuing Education, no. 61. San Francisco: Jossey-Bass.

Sheared, V. (1999). Giving voice: Inclusion of African American students' polyrhythmic realities in adult basic education. In T. Guy (Ed.) *Providing culturally relevant adult education: A challenge for the twenty-first century.* New Directions for Adult and Continuing Education, no. 82. San Francisco: Jossey-Bass.

Sheared, V., & Sissel, P. (Eds.) (2001). *Making space. Merging theory and practice in adult education.* Westport, CT: Bergin & Garvey.

Shor, I. (1996). *When students have power.* Chicago: University of Chicago Press.

Shore, S. (2001). Talking about whiteness: "Adult learning principles" and the invisible norm. In S. Sheared and P. Sissel (Eds.), *Making space: Merging theory and practice in adult education* (pp. 42–56). Westport, CT: Bergin & Garvey.

Simmer-Brown, J. (1999). Commitment and openness: A contemplative approach to pluralism. In S. Glazer (Ed.), *The heart of learning: Spirituality in education* (pp. 97–112). New York: Putnam.

Sleeter, C. (1996). *Multicultural education as social action.* Albany, NY: SUNY Press.

Sleeter, C., & McLaren, P. (Eds.) (1995). *Multicultural education, critical pedagogy, and the politics of difference.* Albany: SUNY Press.

Sloan, R. P., Bagiella, E., Powell, T. (1999). Religion, spirituality, and medicine. *Lancet, 353*(9153), 664–667.

Smith, S., & Colin, III, S.A.J. (2001). An invisible presence, silenced voices: African Americans in the adult education professoriate. In S. Sheared & P. Sissel, *Making space: Merging theory and practice in adult education* (pp. 42–56). Westport, CT: Bergin & Garvey.

Southard, N. (1996). Recovery and rediscovered images: Spiritual resources for Asian American women. In U. King (Ed.), *Feminist theology from the third world*. Maryknoll, NY: Orbis.

Sumrall, A., & Vecchione, P. (Eds.). (1997). *Storming heaven's gate: An anthology of spiritual writings by women*. New York: Penguin.

Tatum, B. (1997). *"Why are all the Black kids sitting together in the cafeteria?"* New York: Basic Books.

Taylor, E. (1997). Building upon the theoretical debate: A critical review of the empirical studies of Mezirow's transformative learning theory. *Adult Education Quarterly, 48*(1), 34–59.

Taylor, E. (2000a). Analyzing research on transformative learning theory. In J. Mezirow (Ed.), *Learning as transformation* (pp. 285–328). San Francisco: Jossey-Bass.

Taylor, K. (2000b). Teaching with developmental intention. In J. Mezirow (Ed.), *Learning as transformation* (pp. 151–180). San Francisco: Jossey-Bass.

Taylor, K., Marienau, C., & Fiddler, M. (2000). *Developing adult learners: Strategies for teachers and trainers*. San Francisco: Jossey-Bass.

Terkel, S. (2001). *Will the circle be unbroken?* New York: The New Press.

Thompson, M. (1995). *Gay soul: Finding the heart of gay spirit and nature*. San Francisco: Harper.

Tisdell, E. J. (1995). *Creating inclusive adult learning environments: Insights from multicultural education and feminist pedagogy*, Information Series No. 361. Columbus, OH: ERIC Clearinghouse on Adult, Career, and Vocational Education.

Tisdell, E. (1998). Poststructural feminist pedagogies: The possibilities and limitations of a feminist emancipatory adult learning theory and practice. *Adult Education Quarterly, 48*(3), 139–156.

Tisdell, E. (1999). The spiritual dimension of adult development. In M. C. Clark & R. Caffarella (Eds.), *An update on adult development theory* (pp. 87–96). New Directions for Adult and Continuing Education, no. 84. San Francisco: Jossey-Bass.

Tisdell, E. (2000a). Spirituality and emancipatory adult education in women adult educators for social change. *Adult Education Quarterly, 50*(4), 308–335.

Tisdell, E. (2000b). Feminist pedagogies. In E. Hayes & D. Flannery with A. Brooks, E. Tisdell, & J. Hugo (Eds.), *Women as learners* (pp. 155–184) . San Francisco: Jossey-Bass.

Tisdell, E. (2001). The politics of positionality: Teaching for social change in higher education. In R. Cervero & A. Wilson (Eds.), *Power in practice: Adult education and the struggle for knowledge and power in society*. San Francisco: Jossey-Bass.

Tisdell, E, Sanabria, R., & Cohort Members Martinez Franceschi, G., Figueroa, W., Garcia, D., Garcia, M., Lugo, L., Rivera, S., & Rodriguez, T. (September, 2000). Addressing the adult education needs of the Latino community: Critical pedagogy in action in a Latino focused master's level cohort. *Proceedings of the 19th Annual Midwest Research to Practice eConference in Adult, Continuing and Community Education*. Madison, WI: University of Wisconsin.

Tisdell, E., & Taylor, E. (2001). Adult education philosophy informs practice. *Adult Learning, 11*, 6–10.

Tisdell, E., and Tolliver, D. (2000). The role of culture and spirituality in teaching for social change in adult higher education classes. *Proceedings of the 19th Annual Midwest Research to Practice Conference*. Madison, WI: University of Wisconsin.

Tisdell, E., Tolliver, D., & Villa, S. (2001). Toward a culturally relevant and spiritually grounded theory of teaching for social transformation and transformational learning. *Proceedings of the 42nd Annual Adult Education Research Conference* (405–411). East Lansing, MI: Michigan State University..

Titone, C. (2000). Educating the white teacher as ally. In J. Kincheloe, S. Steinberg, N. Rodriguez, & R. Chennault (Eds.), *White reign: Deploying whiteness in America* (pp. 159–176). New York: St. Martin's.

Tolliver, D., & Tisdell, E. (2001a). Travelers' tales of trying to teach for transformation: The spiritual dimension of culturally relevant adult education. *Proceedings of the 31st Annual Conference of SCUTREA* (Standing Conference on University Teaching and Research in the Education of Adults) 2001 (pp. 399–403). London, England: University of East London.

Tolliver, D., & Tisdell, E. (2001b). Going deeper: The role of spirituality, cultural identity, and sociopolitical development in teaching for transformation. *Proceedings of the 20th Annual Midwest Research to Practice Conference* (127–132). Charleston, IL: Eastern Illinois University.

Vaz, K. (Ed.). (1997). *Oral narrative research with black women*. Newbury Park, CA: Sage.

Vella, J. (2000). A spirited epistemology: Honoring the adult learner as subject. In L. English & M. Gillen (Eds.), *Addressing the spiritual dimensions of adult learning: What educators can do* (pp. 7–16). San Francisco: Jossey-Bass.

Wade-Gales, G. (Ed.). (1995). *My soul is a witness. African American women's spirituality*. Boston: Beacon Press.

Walker, A. (1984). *In search of our mothers' gardens*. Fort Washington, PA: Harvest Books.

Walters, S., & Manicom, L. (Eds.). (1996). *Gender in popular education*. London: Zed Press.

Watts, R., Griffith, D., & Abdul-Adil, J. (1999). Sociopolitical development as an antidote for oppression—theory and action. *American Journal of Community Psychology, 27*(2), 255–271.

Welch, S. (1999). *Sweet dreams in America: Making ethics and spirituality work*. New York: Routledge.

Wilber, K. (2000a). *A theory of everything: An integral vision of business, politics, science, and spirituality*. Boston: Shambhala.

Wilber, K. (2000b). *Integral psychology: Consciousness, spirit, psychology, therapy*. Boston: Shambhala.

Williams, D. (1993). *Sisters in the wilderness: The challenge of womanist God-talk*. Maryknoll, New York: Orbis.

Winter, M., Lummis, A., Stokes, A. (1995). *Defecting in place: Women claiming responsibility for their own spirituality*. New York: Crossroads.

Wuthnow, R. (1998). *After heaven: Spirituality in America since the 1950s*. Berkeley: University of California Press.

Wuthnow, R. (1999). *Growing up religious*. Boston: Beacon Press.

Wuthnow, R. (2001). *Creative spirituality: The way of the artist*. Berkeley: University of California Press.

Ziegler, J. (1998). Spirituality returns to the fold in medical practice. *Journal of the National Cancer Institute 90*(17), 1255–1257.

Zukov, G. (2000). *Soul stories*. New York: Fireside.

Index